A Music for the Millions

Antebellum Democratic Attitudes and the Birth of American Popular Music

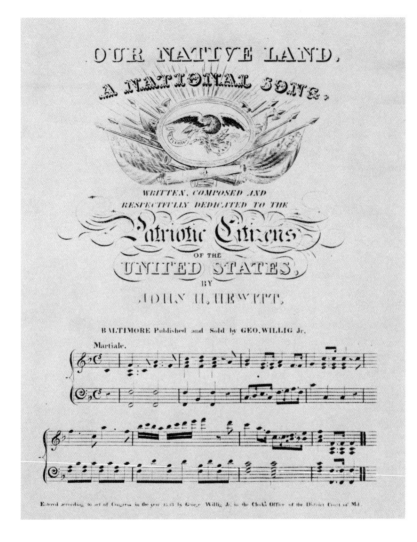

Plate 1. *Our Native Land.* The eagle that "sits enthroned" is the emblem of militant nationhood, in defense of "freedom," "liberty," and "the Union."

A Music for the Millions

Antebellum Democratic Attitudes and the Birth of American Popular Music

by
NICHOLAS TAWA

THE SOCIOLOGY OF MUSIC No. 3

PENDRAGON PRESS   NEW YORK

MT

THE SOCIOLOGY OF MUSIC SERIES

No. 1   *The Social Status of the Professional Musician from the Middle Ages to the 19th Century*, Walter Salmen, General Editor (1983) ISBN 0-918728-16-9

No. 2   *Big Sounds from Small Peoples: The music industry in small countries* by Roger Wallis and Krister Malm (1984) ISBN 0-918728-39-8

Library of Congress Cataloging in Publication Data

Tawa, Nicholas E.
  A music for the millions.

  (The Sociology of music ; 2)
  Bibliography: p.
  1. Music, Popular (Songs, etc.)--United States--19th century--History and criticism. I. Title. II. Series.
ML3477.T38 1984   784.5'00973   83-26222
ISBN 0-918728-38-X

Table of Contents

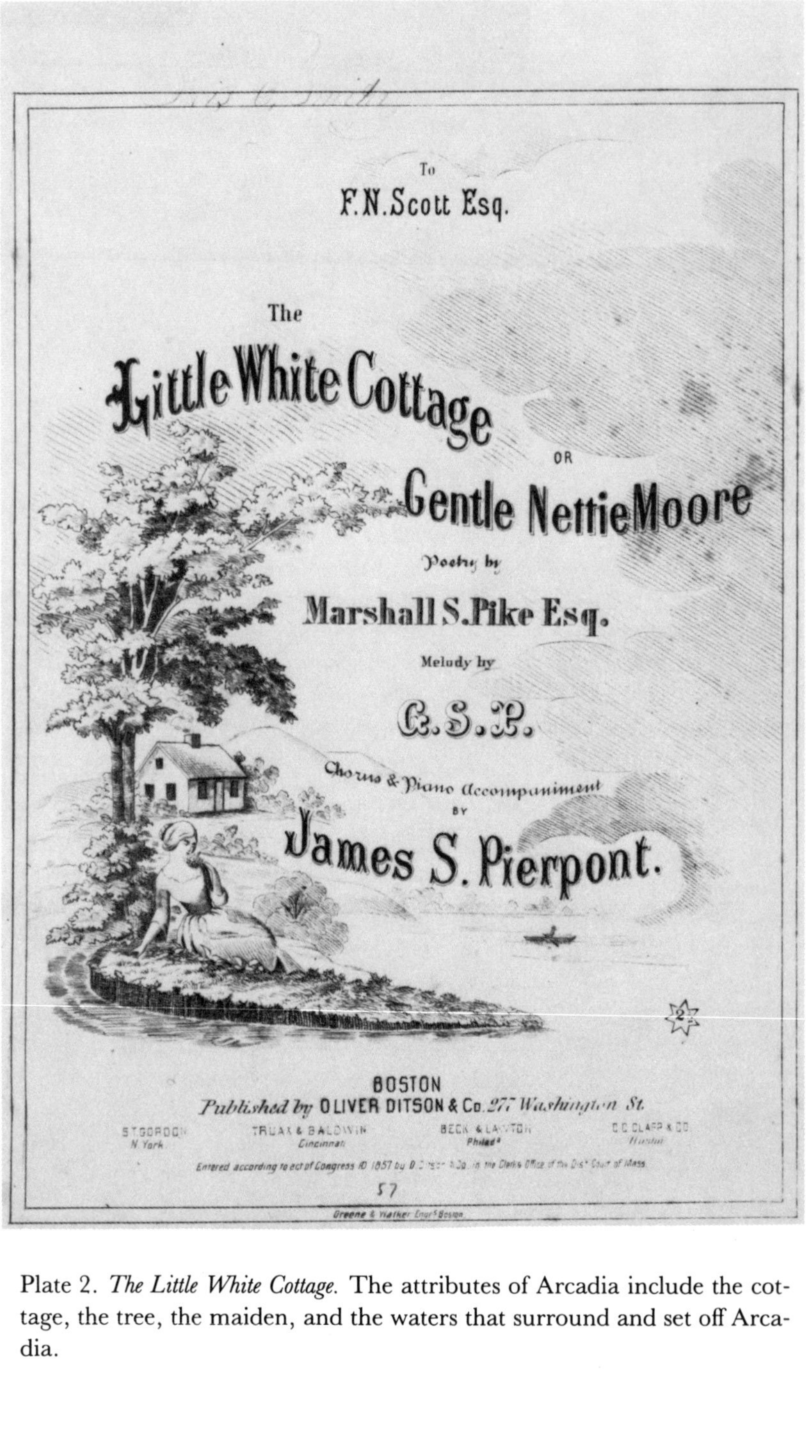

Plate 2. *The Little White Cottage.* The attributes of Arcadia include the cottage, the tree, the maiden, and the waters that surround and set off Arcadia.

Preface

In this book, I put forward the claim that the American popular song that emerged in the three decades before the Civil War was in at least one significant respect a novel cultural expression. Yes, it did comprise simple and tuneful music adapted to the understanding of the masses—"a music for the millions," as it came to be described in the 1850s. Yes, it did often display the weaknesses inherent in nostalgia and sentimentality. And yes, it did contain the prejudices of early Americans. It also, however, supplied a great majority of these Americans with a structure for living and answers to the riddles of their existence, even as it recreated them.

The years that followed Andrew Jackson's election to the Presidency of the United States were filled with conflict and contradiction—social, economic, political, and psychological. Large numbers of Americans were leaving behind their assured identities in the rural farms and hamlets that they had called home and were journeying to the many urban centers sprouting throughout the country. Through relocation, they hoped to find opportunity to better themselves financially. At the same time, other Americans were traveling westward after gold, silver, or free land.

What many of these wayfarers soon had in common was a sense of rootlessness, of having no sympathetic connection with their new environments. They dwelt in a strange dog-eat-dog world, where nobody seemed to care about anybody else, and where nature and man-made institutions played fast and loose with their right to survive and with their concepts of right and wrong.

Even those men and women who continued to live in the old homesteads began to develop a melancholic view of life. Every family had a loved one whose existence had been cut short by disease or sudden catastrophe. Here and there were parents who had lost contact with a departed son and prayed he still survived. Horrible stories reached them about the depraved living in the cities, about Indians massacring Western settlers, and about starvation in the California mining camps.

In addition, men and women worried over the larger problems of nationhood that remained to be solved: the struggle of would-be aristocrat and commoner, white planter and black slave, newly arrived immigrant and native laborer, and states' righter and political centralist. They had experienced the War of 1812, lived through a war with Mexico, and now feared a new war between the states. Could a person's life have any significance when it was lived out in the near chaotic confusions and contradictions of the 1830s, 40s', and 50s'?

During the 1830s, serious popular song began to reveal the inner conflicts besetting the citizenry of the Jacksonian era. By the 1840s, serious song was offering a consistent explanation for their occurrence and a philosophic design to contain and resolve them. The fact that the messages that these songs delivered were all consonant was owing in part to a conscious effort on the part of the composers, who were forever sampling the popular temper. It was also owing to a selective process on the part of the public, which elevated to popularity those compositions that were found richest in meaning and most enjoyable as music.

Alongside serious song appeared comic song that looked everyday life square in the eye and refused to be cowed by adversity. It defied and laughed at misfortune, where common sense would have advised submission to fate. If disaster overwhelms you, comic song said, you must learn to pull yourself together and survive one way or another. The admission of defeat is the only unforgivable sin.

The antipodal relationship of serious and comic song illustrates the dichotomy in the contemporary American's mind and the paradoxical thinking that helped the individual to maintain sanity when confronting an oppressive reality.

Whereas in my earlier book, *Sweet Songs for Gentle Americans,* I described antebellum American song in terms of its composers, performers, publishers, and general characteristics, in this study I try to search out the recurring symbols in mid-nineteenth-century popular song and relate them to the exigencies of the antebellum decades and to the psychological needs of most humans. I pray my presumption remains on the side of accuracy and enlightenment.

Plate 3. *Farewell Old Cottage*. Youth's departure from Arcadia and entering into the world of experience. Note the luxuriant foliage of the trees in Arcadia and the blighted look of the tree that belongs to the outer world.

CHAPTER 1

Backgrounds

A turbulent era in American history opened with Andrew Jackson's election to the presidency and his passionate attack on privilege. It closed with Lincoln's election and the onset of the Civil War. From 1828 to 1861, new democratic beliefs and practices interspersed themselves aggressively among older aristocratic ways of thinking. At the same time, a regenerated but capitalistic America emerged phoenix like from the ashes of Biddle's Bank of America and a conservative mercantilism.[1] This was a critical time for the American people; a time of confusion, of conflict between old and new ways of living, thinking, and believing. One of the most heated conflicts involved the question of owning slaves. The forced servitude of an entire race, fiercely defended by white Southerners and as fiercely opposed by Northern abolitionists, became an increasingly divisive issue in American affairs. Until the last moment, few inferred that the outcome would be the tragic slaughter of Americans by Americans.

Inevitably, music reflected the social, economic, and political upheavals of these years. The once-dominant European-derived composition mirroring a narrow, leisured constituency was soon overwhelmed by a different type of musical work, one imbued with ideas favored by the common citizenry and exposed in the simplest verbal

[1] J. Perry Leavell, Jr., "Introduction," in James Fenimore Cooper, *The American Democrat* (1838), reprint (New York: Funk & Wagnalls 1969) xxi.

1

and melodic terms—the American popular song. More than the novel or play, the popular song touched the majority of Americans, for, as we shall see, it articulated their inmost concerns and aspirations.

It is important to note that songs composed by native Americans, exceedingly rare before 1815, rose in number after 1828 and reached flood stage in the late 1840s. These works swiftly became intimates in countless households where other forms of expression had no entrance. In the 1840s and '50s, men and women from every walk of life, laborer and slave to rich and mighty, enjoyed this music. While in amateur circles more women than men might have sung these songs, a considerable number of men did also perform them. Or they made up an enthusiastic audience when others sang. Moreover, it was mostly men who composed these popular compositions and performed them professionally.

To understand both the men and the women living in these years, therefore, we must explore the many-layered meanings in this art form they held so dear and wholeheartedly sponsored.

One major problem the United States government had faced after independence came was the encouragement of national feeling to supersede loyalty to one's district and state. In this matter, the War of 1812 and the election of Jackson, a hero of that war and a symbol of liberty for the common man, soon thereafter loomed large. These two events closed off the earlier age and introduced another during which people saw themselves and their tomorrows differently. More and more citizens thought about *their* nation and *their* American destiny. Conviction replaced the veiled vision of democracy from yesteryear. America had twice fought Europe's most formidable power (and the most oppressive to Americans) and come away undefeated. National greatness lay in the future. It is no accident, and is altogether fitting, that the song later to become our national anthem commemorated a hard-fought battle of the War of 1812 and celebrated "the land of the free and the home of the brave."

In the three decades after Jackson's election, at least on the surface, much appeared right with our fledgling nation. The unassuming manners and virtues hallowed by tradition still seemed honored among our largely rural population. Though they might educate

2

themselves at home or work, the ordinary citizens read—
newspapers and instructional books certainly, but also Shakespeare's
plays and the Bible. They attended whatever uplifting lectures came
their way and avidly discussed the sermons they heard on Sundays.
A consensus affirmed the necessity of an aware citizenry. It recognized the importance of civilized conduct as a requisite for the pres-
ervation of a government based on free elections. The land was astir
with numerous ventures promising rich rewards; its bounty shielded
most men and women from "the sore of pauperism" that afflicted a
contemporary Europe.[2] In 1832, William Cullen Bryant returned to
New York after a long absence and found the city doubled in population, the once-quiet harbor teeming with ships, the wharves laden
with goods, and "everywhere the activity and bustle of a prosperous
and hopeful people."[3]

New and powerful currents of industrialism, urbanization, and
immigration, however, had wrenched America from its customary
moorings. Factories and mills mushroomed in the countryside. Railroad trains and clipper ships rushed people and goods hither and
yon, nourishing infant towns and forcing the growth of old cities.[4]
Only the South, vised in a rural and slave economy, remained relatively fixed in its ways.

Even as the mouthpieces for industry insisted that modern tech-
nology was a helpmate of nature and a harbinger of widespread
prosperity,[5] others demurred. Hard times aplenty soon mocked the
notion of prosperity, especially during the prolonged depression of

---

[2]Ralph P. Boas, *The Social Backgrounds of American Literature* (Boston: Little,
Brown 1940) 80; Russell Nye, *The Unembarrassed Muse* (New York: Dial 1970) 2;
Louis B. Wright, *Culture on the Moving Frontier* (Bloomington: Indiana University
Press 1955) 197. The reference to the absence of pauperism in America comes
from Michel Chevalier, *Society, Manners, and Politics in the United States,* ed. John
William Ward (Ithaca, N.Y.: Cornell University Press 1969) 97.

[3]William Cullen Bryant, *Prose Writings,* 2 vols., ed. Parke Godwin (1884), reprint (New York: Russell & Russell 1964) I, 355.

[4]Daniel J. Boorstin, *The Americans: The National Experience* (New York: Random
House 1965) 6–20, 99; Leo Marx, *The Machine in the Garden* (New York: Oxford
University Press 1964) 208–10, 215.

[5]Marx, *Machine* 197–206, 220.

1837–1841. Many people had abandoned farm life for urban living and the lure of money wages. In the cities and towns, a landless proletariat, the numerous offspring of large American families, vied with Irish and German immigrants for low-paying jobs. Aggressive entrepreneurs took hardheaded advantage of laborers and national resources alike in their quest for profit. Frequently, exploitation and precarious financial existence left humble urban dwellers feeling helpless and spiritually dislocated, their standards of behavior and belief eroded, their social status ambiguous. In addition, the thousands of independent souls who were forever thrusting westward into the wilderness endured physical hardship and isolation that almost inevitably brought on inner disorientation.[6]

Caution must accompany our attempt to understand these human beings. We must remember that history is a chronology of important events usually seen through the eyes of prominent personages, but that popular song is a commentary on events in the voice of ordinary men and women. For example, around 1840 the song *A Jumping Epistle* appeared now and again in the repertory of journeying American music troupes. Its bitter summary of the times began:

> We are jumping through the world,
>   And some are jumping fast,
> For some by choice jump off the Dock
>   That it may be their last.
> The most are jumping to get rich,
>   But find their sad mistake,
> For if they get a note or two,
>   The Banks are sure to break.

---

[6]Sydney E. Ahlstrom, *A Religious History of the American People* (New Haven, Conn.: Yale University Press 1972) 475; Norman Ware, *The Industrial Worker, 1840–1860* (1924), reprint (New York: Quandrangle 1974) x–xi, 1; Rowland Berthoff, *An Unsettled People: Social Order and Disorder in American History* (New York: Harper & Row 1971) 127, 189–95; Robert Lacour-Gayet, *Everyday Life in the United States Before the Civil War, 1830–1860,* trans. Mary Ilford (New York: Ungar 1969) 6–8; William Charvat, *The Origins of American Critical Thought, 1810–1835* (New York: Russell & Russell 1968) 49–50; Arthur M. Schlesinger, Jr., *The Age of Jackson* (Boston: Little, Brown 1945) 92, 218–19, 264.

The destruction of savings, morale, and self was haunting the minds of contemporary Americans. The topical song quoted above embraced a reality they understood and could respond to.

About the same year another song, *No More,* by "a young Lady of Georgia," also appeared. It rebuked the sanctimonious pollyannas who promised a near-termination to the pain of separation and death, felt by so many families during this tense time.

> Oh tell me not of future peace,
> > Nor let my wand'ring fancy soar
> To realms where every doubt may cease,
> > And our fond hearts can part no more.
> This magic tale a while may charm,
> > But can it lasting peace restore?
> The transcient *[sic]* glow awhile may warm,
> > Then fades to think we meet no more.

The song's adherents refused to forget those they loved.

Few lives knew tranquility. A thousand cares wound tightly around every joy. Would there be a heaven, the unhappy wondered, a more promising hereafter on which to center their hopes?

> 'Tis a world of enjoyment and sadness.
> > It is chequered with doubts, hopes and fears;
> New attachments are now formed in gladness,
> > And old ones severed in tears.
> To our longings there sometimes are given,
> > As we pass thro' this life's fleeting scene,
> Some flashes and glimpses of heaven,
> > Tho' darkness and clouds intervene.

So went a composition published in 1840 by Oliver Shaw, the Providence, Rhode Island, composer.

Songs like these told persons something about themselves. The music aimed at assisting listeners along the road to self-knowledge, at the same time that it entertained them and assuaged their cares.

Writing about the antebellum years, Daniel Boorstin points to the great uncertainties permeating the nation, the "products of ignorance and progress." He claims these uncertainties engendered a vagueness about what our country signified that ultimately "was a source of American strength." While this conclusion is debatable, his next statement about mid-nineteenth-century Americans does underline a significant reason for American popular song's coming into existence in the Jacksonian years: "Their first enterprise was to discover who they were, where they were, when they were, what they were capable of, and how they could expand and organize. Their America was still little more than a point of departure."[7]

When I refer to the popular-song public, I commence by meaning the inhabitants of cities, large towns, and smaller villages contiguous to metropolitan areas. I refer only secondarily to rural dwellers, despite the fact that popular music was increasingly infiltrating into the hinterlands. We must keep in mind that however much the songs might sing the praises of field, forest, and mountain, they were invariably composed, published, and enjoyed by urbanites. A pervasive influence on their content was an inner and outer life seen through urban eyes and filtered through urban feelings.

SEARCHING FOR MORALITY

Any society in any age may see itself in the grip of change, affected by the dissolution of old values and the seeming absence of new values. The present, empty of moral principles, may seem given over to unrestrained passion and self-interest. Often it is the manner in which one society inquires into itself and then deals with its issues that sets it apart from the others.

Many citizens living in the United States of 1830–1860 thought their age unique, owing to the radical democratic premises underlying their society and the thoroughness of the change taking place around them. Prevalent was the worry over a nation submerging itself into utmost social and political confusion, and a people becoming spiritually footloose. How could one reconcile these contending forces?

Again and again the pages of authors like Cooper, Hawthorne, and Melville sound a threnody over the incertitude within them and

[7]Boorstin, *Americans* 219.

their contemporaries. A sense of loss, a search for meaning, and a yearning for stable values permeate their novels and short stories. Adding to their and other thoughtful Americans' discomfit were a few bold voices hinting that man was beastly, nature was immoral, and God was nonexistent—soon to crescendo with the writings of Darwin and Marx, and with the actions of American robber barons. The prospect frightened many. An unstable society of insecure humans who felt neither guilt nor responsibility, quite a few Americans insisted, meant a life without significance, a terrifying existence where one monitored the body's constant decay and anticipated inevitable extermination in an indifferent universe. Were the spiritual victories of good over evil, God over the Devil, immortality over death the fabrications of superstitious minds?[8]

Only a fraction of the populace read American literature. More to the majority's taste was something with a homely turn of expression. For this reason the disquiet of ordinary men and women translated itself more naturally into a commonplace symbolism that wandered from favorite song to favorite song. Thus, an Indian mother keening her child's death might embody the ultimate loss threatening every individual; the nonfeeling of onlooking whites might mirror the uncaring world. This is the theme of *The Burial of an Indian Girl*, words by Mrs. Sigourney and music by Sophia Baker, a song popular in 1845. The bereft mother bewails "her lost, her only one," while "pale faces gather round her." They "mark the storm swell high that rends and wrecks the tossing soul, but their cold blue eyes were dry."

On the surface, the protest concerns the relationship of Indian and white—underneath, that of individual and society. A special horror arises from the listener's contemplation of witnesses to misfortune who are incapable of loving, and of an outworld that inflicts

[8]For an examination of the psychological problems stated here, see Ernest Becker, *The Denial of Death* (New York: Free Press 1973) 68–69. For the reflection of these problems in American fiction, see Richard Chase, *The American Novel and Its Traditions* (Garden City, N.Y.: Doubleday 1957) 1–2; Randall Stewart, *American Literature and Christian Doctrine* (Baton Rouge: Louisiana State University Press 1958) 149.

7

suffering and death to no purpose. The solitary mother "watched, and toil'd and pray'd;" but "every dreary dawn reveal'd some ravage Death had made" on the girl's form. And no one "deplored her pain."

Essential to the understanding of antebellum popular song is the recognition that the nineteenth-century Americans who treasured it wished neither to define themselves only as highbred animals,[9] nor to extol the state of aloneness. They favored self-reliance so long as it rested upon the bedrock of right conduct and caring. Ingrained in the American memory was a stern Christianity that disvalued individualism for its own sake, a pioneering experience that required cooperation for survival, and a Calvinistic conviction that life's purpose lay in proving that one merited fusion with deity.[10]

Was there some way to refashion this common experience to meet contemporary conditions? This thought lies behind Emerson's observation of 1847, that "the moral must be the measure of health. If your eye is on the eternal, your intellect will steadily grow, and all your estimates, conclusions, and actions will have a genius and beauty which no learning or combined advantages of other men can rival."[11] His remark conceals an anxiety that the memory of the older America, however widespread, was dimming and the potential for moral collapse accelerating.[12]

---

[9]Susanne K. Langer, in *Philosophy In a New Key* (New York: Penguin, 1948) 31, writes that man has always aimed higher than animalism, and that for many, desire sublimated as moral sentiment is a sign "of the ultimate godhead in man."

[10]Stewart, *American Literature* 148–49, states: "On . . . the Christian side, writers of the nineteenth century like Hawthorne, Melville, and James were not satisfied with the prevailing romanticism, which inflated the individual. Hawthorne's stories illustrated the perils of "self-trust." Melville showed the catastrophic end of an irresponsible, devil-inspired individual." Becker, *Denial of Death,* 154, claims that individualistic living creates an unbearable isolation in all humans, and that moral living is an attempt "to get a place of special belongingness and perpetuation in the universe."

[11]Ralph Waldo Emerson, *The Journals and Miscellaneous Notebooks,* (Cambridge, Mass.: Belknap Press 1969–1975), X, ed. Merton M. Sealts, Jr. (1973), 17.

[12]See, for example, Ronald G. Walters, *Sexual Advice to Victorian America* (Englewood Cliffs, N.J.: Prentice-Hall 1974) 11. Harvey Wish, *Society and Thought in Early America, Vol. 1 of Society and Thought in America,* vols. (New York: Longmans,

Van Wyck Brooks speaks of the "thirst for truth" and "passionate dream of perfection" driving Emerson and others like him. Note Hawthorne's supreme estimation of moral perfection when he jotted an idea for a story into his notebook, in 1839: "A person to be the death of his beloved in trying to raise her to more than mortal perfection; yet this should be a comfort to him for having aimed so high and holily."[13]

That many agreed with Emerson and Hawthorne is demonstrated in a song from around 1854. The lyric of *Better Times Are Coming* indicates that aiming high and achieving perfection meant a behavior required by moral necessity (doing one's "duty"), an acceptance of responsibility for others (aiding "each poor and suffering brother"), and a conquest of passion (replaced by "the power of reason"). Actions such as these "serve to guide to man's divinest season."[14]

The far-flung sponsorship of songs like the one above confirms William Charvat's comment on people's attitudes toward creative works during the antebellum years. An essential function of these works, he asserts, is to promote a healthy society by demonstrating the wretchedness in a life subjected to selfishness and base appetite, and the wholesome beauty in one guided by virtue and duty.[15]

Whenever a composition illustrated some form of decency and appealed to the masses, then potentially virtuous but unthinking men and women were persuaded to selfless thought and concern for

Green, 1950) 235, writes of the desire to contain undirected individualism, especially as manifested in the "murderous habits of the frontier."

[13]Van Wyck Brooks, *The Flowering of New England* (New York: Dutton 1952) 62-63; Nathaniel Hawthorne, in Vol. XVII of *The Complete Works* (Boston: Houghton Mifflin 1884) 210.

[14]*Better Times Are Coming,* written by H. Dumbleton (New York: Waters 1854). In a letter to George B. Loring, written 11 April 1842, James Russell Lowell states: "You say that life seems to be a struggle after nothing in particular. But you are wrong. It is a struggle after the peaceful home of the soul in a natural and loving state of life"; *Letters, Vol. I,* ed. Charles Eliot Norton, in Vol. XIV *of The Complete Writings of James Russell Lowell,* (New York: AMS 1966) 86.

[15]See Charvat, *Origins* 7-16; also Russell B. Nye, *Society and Culture in America, 1830-1860* (New York: Harper & Row 1974) 118.

fellow human beings.[16] In such moments, the answer to the question, What is man? might more truly be "a little lower than angels." It is important to note that songs similar to those quoted appealed to a broad spectrum of Americans, sophisticated and unsophisticated. They could remain vividly in the memory and perhaps redirect potentially disruptive emotion to virtue. In this regard, the evidence both of contemporary writings on music and of composers' views is compelling.[17]

THE POPULAR PERCEPTION OF ELITE CULTURE

A small elite group, distinguished by education, profession, and affluence, had always existed in America. It alone had some measure of freedom from work. After 1825, the wealth and leisure time of this group increased dramatically. At the same time, awareness and suspicion of American society's upper echelon grew among our less affluent and less educated citizens.[18] They saw the fortunes and power of the mighty taking on an oppressive edge. By the 1840s, for example, 4 percent of the population owned around 65 percent of the taxable land in major cities.[19] America, ostensibly a democracy, seemed increasingly to take its direction from an authoritative mi-

---

[16]This is an echo of Emerson's feelings about the purpose of all art; see *Journals*, VII, ed. A.W. Plumstead and Harrison Hayford (1969), 222, 528; X, 10.

[17]A moral judgment of song is already being made in the Boston *Euterpeiad* (27 April 1822), 219, in an article entitled "Use and Abuse of Music." It recurs in a criticism of songs of Thomas Haynes Bayly, in the New York *Euterpeiad* (15 July 1830) 51. The strong desire to entertain and at the same time influence every class of American is stated again and again by song composers like Isaac B. Woodbury, Henry Russell, and George F. Root; see, for example, Russell, *Cheer! Boys, Cheer!* (London: Macqueen 1895), Root, *The Story of a Musical Life* (Cincinnati: Church 1891), and the pages of the several music periodicals published during the 1850s. For example, Russell, p. 12, writes: "All my songs were written earnestly, and with a beneficent object." He claims to have attacked slavery, shown the evils of immoral acts, and advocated a variety of social reforms in his songs.

[18]Schlesinger, *Age of Jackson* 32–33.

[19]Howard P. Chudacoff, *The Evolution of Urban Society* (Englewood Cliffs, N.J.: Prentice-Hall 1975) 45.

nority that controlled the economy and employed thousands of persons in mines, factories, and mills. They heard individuals from moneyed circles equating the common lot of humanity with machinery that one would use and then cast aside when "old and useless." A voice here and there criticized free public education and aid to the poor for the dangerous ideas that these might encourage.[20]

The public noticed dandies and their fashionable ladies emerging from the group of rich urbanites. These pretty pretenders to gentility had hastened to take on the airs of European aristocracy. They chased after every current transatlantic fashion and pronounced anything American to be vulgar and unworthy of serious consideration.[21] In music these *au courant* creatures enrolled under imported instructors to learn British, French, and Italian vocal and piano compositions. By the 1850s, German *Lieder* and sonatas began to find a welcome in select homes. Worried over this trend to foreignness, a correspondent to *Dwight's Journal of Music* wrote, in 1859: "There is danger lest fashion or exclusive cliques in our principal cities should succeed in introducing certain styles of music to the exclusion of other kinds equally good. . . . We must . . . remember that all music is not either German or Italian."[22]

The American public viewed this group's leisure activities as manifestations of a dangerous trend toward aristocracy.[23] The advocates for foreign music, critics claimed, evidenced a "lack of some earnest and noble purpose in a life they found it difficult to fill with aught beside frivolity." These spoiled members of the fashionable *haute monde* were seen as corrupters of the home, enemies of democratic institutions, and deniers of Christian principles. They denomi-

[20]Berthoff, *Unsettled People,* 202; Rush Welter, *Popular Education and Democratic Thought in America* (New York: Columbia University Press 1962) 125–33.

[21]Chevalier, *Society, Manners, and Politics* 96; Francis J. Grund, *Aristocracy in America* (1839), reprint (New York: Harper & Row, 1959) 10; George W. Curtis, *The Potiphar Papers* (New York: Putnam 1853) 30–31.

[22]The quotation is from a letter written by "L.D.P.," appearing in *Dwight's Journal of Music* (15 January 1859) 329. See also the New York *Musical Review and Gazette* (12 January 1856) 3; Grund, *Aristocracy* 268.

[23][Donald G. Mitchell], *The Lorgnette,* 2nd ed., (New York: Stringer & Townsend 1850) I, 221; Chevalier, *Society, Manners, and Politics* 200; Russell, *Cheer!* 116–117.

nated themselves patrons of Italian opera and music of similar ilk. But they also squandered "thousands upon equipage and laces, deaf to the low cries of a hundred mothers going supperless each night to their straw pallets."[24]

As never before in America's cultural history, those Americans who kept abreast of European cultivated tastes made a distinction between the music they preferred and the simple American songs that were proliferating by the thousands after 1840. While some sophisticates might champion Donizetti and Bellini, and others, Beethoven and Mendelssohn, all pronounced the native compositions as trash, works of mediocrity and certainly not of genius.[25] Presumably, they did not repudiate those popular songs that were adapted from the Italian (and to a lesser extent from the German and French), simplified, and supplied with an English text. Indeed, one should add that several such songs won a widespread following among all classes.

Abetting the anticommoners were educated British, French, and German writers, some of them visitors to America, who excoriated the manners and culture encouraged by republicanism. Oblivious of their own countrymen's limitations, they vilified the American public for lacking the fastidiousnes of the European upper class.

Angered at French obtuseness, Louis Moreau Gottschalk, composer and pianist from New Orleans, exploded with: "There certainly is an intelligent class who read and who know the truth; but it

---

[24]The first quotation is from Junius Henri Browne, *The Great Metropolis: A Mirror of New York* (Hartford: American 1869) 35; the second is from [Mitchell], *Lorgnette* 2nd ed. I, 115, 224–25. Charles Hamm, in *Yesterdays* (New York: Norton 1979) 69, writes: "From the beginning, Italian opera had appealed largely to America's 'beautiful people'." See also Gordon Milne, *George William Curtis and the Genteel Tradition* (Bloomington: Indiana University Press 1956) 200; Bernard Wishy, *The Child and the Republic* (Philadelphia: University of Pennsylvania Press 1968) 14; Carl Bode, *The Anatomy of American Popular Culture* (Berkeley: University of California Press 1959) 75; Curtis, *Potiphar* 23.

[25]Root, *Story* 54–55, 96; John Tasker Howard, *Stephen Foster: America's Troubadour* (New York: Crowell 1953) 180; Nye, *Society* 78; New York *Musical Review* (2 February 1854) 42; *Dwight's Journal of Music* (28 May 1853) 62; (24 June 1854) 54; (13 January 1855) 118.

12

is not the most numerous, nor the most interested in doing us justice. Proudhomme . . . sees in the pioneer of the West only a *heroic assassin,* and in all Americans *half-civilized savages.* From Talleyrand, who said that *'l'Amérique est un pays de sales cochons et de cochons sales'* (America is a country of dirty and filthy swine), to Zimmerman, director of the piano classes at the Paris Conservatoire, who, without hearing me refused to receive me because *'l'Amérique n'était qu'un pays de machines vapeur'* (America was only a country of steam engines), there is not an eminent man who has not spat his petty spite upon the Americans."[26]

Americans took offense at Parisian writers who encouraged our talented musicians to escape from their cultural wasteland to a more appreciative Europe, and at Germans who denominated our taste for ballad singers and minstrel men as an addiction to the cheapest humbuggery. One musician from Germany, Herman Saroni, even told us we erred in our musical setting of English words. Reviewing "Wherefore, Nellie, Look So Lovely," by Saunders, he wrote, in 1851, that the song was "an excellent illustration of the extent to which a folly can sometimes be carried." He refers here to the "shortening of one syllable and giving an undue accent to the next one," as in the following:

[26]Louis Moreau Gottschalk, *Notes of a Pianist* (1881), ed. Jeanne Behrend (New York: Knopf 1964) 51–52. This observation was made February 1862 in New York City. For other comments, see James Russell Lowell, *Fireside Travels* (1864), in Vol. I of *Complete Writings* 325; Max Maretzek, *Crotchets and Quavers* (1855), reprinted as Part I of *Revelations of an Opera Manager in Nineteenth-Century America* (New York: Dover 1968) 57–58; Constance Rourke, *The Roots of American Culture and Other Essays* (New York: Harcourt Brace 1942), 43–44; Francis Hodge, *Yankee Theatre: The Image of America on the Stage, 1825–1850* (Austin: University of Texas Press 1964) 12–17.

Saroni, of course, associated accent with note duration, which was not necessarily an American equivalence.

When, in 1854, the London *Athenaeum* sniffed at democracy and its music and wondered at the prospects for any real culture in America, the editors of the New York *Musical Review* replied tartly: "In the artistic sense of the term, we do not mean to have it [music] of 'high quality', Mr. *Athenaeum*. A plough is valuable just in portion as it answers the purpose for which it is made. So with our music. We hold that to musically educate any people they must have music that they can sing. This, we think, we are furnishing; and if Beethoven or Mendelssohn were alive and should offer to write music for our pages, unless we believed that they fully understood the object we have in view, we should respectfully decline their services."[27]

A consequence of the attack of Europeans and native "aristocrats" was their incorporation in the popular mind into a hierarchy of villains, corrupt antidemocrats all. They skulked and simpered their way through popular novels like George Lippard's *The Quaker City* (1844), plays like Mrs. Anna Mowatt's *Fashion* (1845), and songs like *Rough and Ready* (1847).

A special dislike for opera singers developed. Most Americans considered them entirely the creatures of the moneyed classes: pampered, vain, jealous, impudent, and immoral.[28] An affluent and fashion-minded minority imported them and sponsored their productions. In part, opera attendance was in imitation of the habits of aristocratic Europeans. A subscription to a box established a lady or

[27]See, respectively, the New York *Musical Review* (6 February 1858) 36; *Dwight's Journal of Music* (8 December 1852) 83; *Saroni's Musical Times* (16 August 1851) 223; and the New York *Musical Review* (16 February 1858) 57–58. That English writers continue to misconstrue the mid-nineteenth-century American popular song is made evident in Wilfred Meller's *Music in a New Found Land* (New York: Knopf 1965) 247–49, where he writes: "Foster's music is a quintessence of the common man's nostalgia . . . his fear of experience." Meller finds "something a little horrifying" about *Beautiful Dreamer*, since "feeling is knowingly indulged in so that it sullies at the same time as it reveals the aspiration of the common heart." The error of Meller's conclusions will be demonstrated repeatedly as we continue our examination of popular song's meaning.

[28]New York *Musical Review* (19 January 1854) 27; Grund, *Aristocracy* 159; Maretzek, *Crotchets* 158.

14

gentleman as a person of taste and high social position. One attended in order to gossip, "to see and be seen," attired in the latest fashions. An understanding of the music was of secondary importance to many attendees—at least this was a claim of many contemporary American writers.[29] And this was a class whose foibles the popular song writers mercilessly lampooned in compositions like *Gumbo Chaff* (1836):

> I learn'd to talk de French oh! a la mode de dancy,
>   Kick him shoe, tare him wool, parle vo de Francey,
> Bon jaw Madamselle, Stevadors and Riggers,
>   Apple jack and sassafras and little Indian niggers.

A further reason for dislike—foreigners charged extortionist fees for their services, forcing ticket prices to soar upward. On 21 May 1853, *Dwight's Journal of Music* quoted from the Newark *Mercury:* "More Operatic Robbery—It seems that Mario and Grisi have contracted with Mr. Hackett to visit this country in the autumn. . . . It is stated that the two together are to receive $2,500 for every night of their performance . . . so that from $3 to $5 a ticket must be charged."[30]

By 1848, "New York itself was divided into parties. One class of society in it which consists of the 'upper tendom,' and bears a spurious sort of consanguinity with the *Faubourg St. Germain* and the West End upon . . . [the other] side of the ocean, was taught to regard the opera, or I should say, any opera so long as it was Italian, as one of the paramount necessities of life. Another and a larger class remained, who were more democratic in their tendencies. Partly because the opera was an expensive amusement, suiting more particularly those who have long purses . . . these look upon it as an antirepublican institution, and unhesitatingly condemn it."[31]

---

[29]Joseph N. Ireland, *Records of the New York Stage, from 1750 to 1860,* 2 vols. (New York: Morrell 1867) II, 464; [Mitchell], *Lorgnette,* 2nd ed. I, 149–51, 154; Browne, *Metropolis* 177; Maretzek, *Crotchets* 67, 70.

[30]See also *The Family Minstrel* (16 March 1835), n.p.

[31]Maretzek, *Crotchets* 25–26. Charles Hamm, in *Yesterdays* 69, quotes both Walt Whitman and Philip Hone, former mayor of New York City, as testifying to this split in American society.

The condemnation came to a head in May 1849, when the Englishman Macready was appearing on the Astor Place Opera House stage. This actor was seen as allied with the rich and disdainful of the American masses: "A portion of the public, called by the 'Upper Ten' the 'Lower Class,' declared that they would permit *no* English actor, *no* Italian Opera, and *no* aristocratic theatre in New York, they being a free and enlightened people." The "Upper Ten" said they would "have whatever amusement they chose to pay for." On 10 May, a threatening mob, numbering over 15,000 persons, gathered before the doors of the opera house. They became unruly. The state militia was ordered to fire upon them. About thirty people died.[32]

When the New York Astor Place Opera House was leased to William Niblo, he gave the wealthy subscribers not the expected operas, but performances by trained dogs and monkeys. Sued because only "refined" and "respectable performances were permitted," Niblo testified with tongue in cheek that the "dogs and monkeys had, in their younger days, appeared before princes and princesses, and kings and queens." Moreover, several witnesses declared under oath "that the previously mentioned dogs and monkeys behaved behind the scenes more quietly and respectably than many Italian singers."[33] From that day, opera became a subject for ridicule and a stranger to the popular affections.

The hopes of the few Italian residents of New York died; their beloved musical theater would remain the plaything of an exclusive class, walled off from the common citizenry. Meanwhile, the Italian operas that Americans did hear in the larger towns would continue to be "Englished" versions, sometimes having slight resemblance to the originals, sung by traveling English companies such as the well-received Seguins Troupe. Arrangers might extract an infectious melody from an "Englished" opera, modify it, and add a simple accompaniment and a text conforming to American tastes. Issued as a popular song, it might have an extensive sale. But no song lover inquired or cared about its origin. To the public, the solo vocal piece was an Americanized product having no history beyond itself.

[32]Maretzek, *Crotchets,* 57–58.
[33]Maretzek, *Crotchets,* p. 214.

CULTURE FOR THE MILLIONS

The American songs that began to emerge in the late 1820s can be denominated as our first genuinely popular music because their creators, publishers, and first performers had the majority of the public in mind for customers—rather than a select few, as had heretofore been the case. By the 1850s, such compositions were consciously shaped to accommodate a common mental grasp and taste. The artificial conceits of the earlier songs—with their upper-class ladies and gentlemen disguised as bucolic or seafaring swains and lasses, and their elegant wordage—disappeared. No longer was enjoyment hindered by melodies with uneven, unpredictable phrase lengths and with chromatic alterations, or by lyrics with surface sentiment. Amateur singers preferred the artless charm of the new melodies. This, coupled with the simple emotional appeal of the new lyrics, enabled contemporary American song to have a general currency among the educated and uneducated alike.

A mass market for music had come into existence. The census of 1820 counted about 9.5 million people in the United States, the census of 1860, about 31.5 million. The extra millions had dispersed themselves from the Atlantic seaboard to the territories beyond the Mississippi. What is more important, this mass market could be easily reached. The era of canal building had begun with the opening of the Erie Canal in 1825; of railroad networks, with the start of the Baltimore and Ohio in 1828; of steamships, with the success of Fulton's *Clermont* in 1807. More and more roads were constructed. Improved printing presses spewed forth inexpensive song editions. A more reliable postal service could deliver music almost anywhere in settled America. In short, beginning with the 1820s, the time was ripe for the flourishing of a native music shared by a majority of the people.

By the mid-1830s, contemporary men of letters had awakened to the popular culture burgeoning about them. In 1838, James Fenimore Cooper complained of how "everything" now had to reflect "the common mind." Writers in *The Democratic Review* of 1825 rejected John Quincy Adams's suggestion that creative works "must be aristocratic" and insisted that current literature and the arts had to fit "the New Man in the New Age" by reflecting "the animating spirit of democracy" and "the thinking heart of humanity."[34] Ralph Waldo Emerson, in his Phi Beta Kappa address of 4 July 1837, recognized the recent "elevation of what is called the lowest class," which had assumed "a very marked and as benign an aspect" on American creative efforts. He told his listeners: "Instead of the sublime and beautiful; the near, the low, the common, was explored and poetized. That which had been negligently trodden under foot . . . is suddenly found to be richer than all foreign parts. The literature of the poor, the feelings of a child, the philosophy of the street, the meaning of household life, are the topics of the time. It is a great stride. It is a sign—is it not? of our new vigor. . . . I embrace the common, I explore and sit at the feet of the familiar, the low. Give me insight into today, and you may have the antique and future worlds. What would we really know the meaning of? . . . The ballad in the street."[35]

After some 25 years of pruning out complexity and polishing the remanent strands of music and text, composers evolved a genre recognized by musicians living in the 1850s as "the people's song" or a "music for the millions." Note one writer's distinction between this new type of song and artistic music: "By artistic music we mean such as requires a comparatively high degree of musical development both in the power of appreciation and in the skill of performance; and by the people's song we mean a style so simple and easy (yet pure and chaste) as is ever within the reach of all, including the uncultivated and unlearned."[36] Advertisements and reviews of new music in the periodicals of the fifties commenced separating out for their readership the music intended for the sophisticated and musically trained minority and that for the commonalty. The former category included operatic arias, German art songs, and the more ambitious works of British composers; the latter, American and some

---

[34]Cooper, *American Democrat* xxv; Nye, *Society* 79.

[35]Ralph Waldo Emerson, *Essays and Poems* (New York: Harcourt, Brace 1921) 303–04.

[36]New York *Musical Review* (14 July 1855) 228.

British sentimental and comic ballads, as well as the dialectical American minstrel songs.[37]

Sifting through the thousands of songs published between 1828 and 1860 in the United States, I tried to get a sense of the common themes flowing through them. The enormous collections in the Houghton Library of Harvard University and the Brown holdings at the Boston Public Library, in particular, were closely examined. In addition, the songbooks, songsters, penny ballad sheets, and privately bound sheet music volumes held in the above-named libraries, as well as those in the Boston Athenaeum and in the library at Old Sturbridge Village, were studied. While the holdings in these four libraries are mainly representative of northeastern America, quite a few of the privately bound volumes had been owned and put together by individuals from the South and Midwest. They demonstrate that the song preferences of Americans from every part of the country were similar. Especially after 1840, this body of song comprised, on the whole, the productions of American composers, who set either native poetry or, sometimes, the lyrics of congenial British writers like Felicia Hemans and Eliza Cook. The occasional non-native-born composer whose works are examined had lived sufficient years in America so that he identified himself with American popular musicians.

Indifferent to originality and to the realization of an artistic personality, these musicians would readily have admitted, as Emerson did admit, to "a good many commonplaces which often turn up in" their writing, which they "have used so often" that they have "the right of the strong" for claiming them. These composers wished to accommodate their works to standards they and most other Americans valued, even if a high degree of conformity resulted.[38] So long as a song made an artless but attractive appeal to sense and feeling,

[37] See, for example, the New York *Musical Pioneer* (1 January 1856) 52; New York *Musical Review* (29 December 1855) 436; (19 May 1855) 167; (16 June 1855) 199; (26 January 1856) 39.

[38] Emerson, *Journals* X, 142; George Boas, "Preface," in George Boas, *Romanticism in America* ed., (New York: Russell & Russell 1961) vi.

thereby winning a wide appreciation, it remained impervious to criticism from the fashionable and aesthetic minority.[39]

Coincident with Jackson's first presidential term began the flood of indigenous minstrel tunes (like *Jim Crow, The Coal Black Rose, Ching A Ring Chaw,* and *My Long Tail Blue),* followed about a decade later by the incredible proliferation of American serious ballads (like *No More, My Bark Is On The Sea, The Betrothed,* and *Years Ago).* The comic songs dwelt on man's outer world, either setting forth its illogicalness in ironic, mock-tragic, and sardonic tones, or urging a light-hearted and unbuttoned celebration of sheer physical existence. In contrast, the serious compositions probed inner world of the human being, often in symbolic manner. Through a grave contemplation of life's significance, they attempted to excite awe and veneration. They infused the most deeply felt human experiences with an ultimate meaning and imposed a spiritual order on the seeming confusions that disturbed every man and woman. Keeping in mind what has just been stated, we can understand why Abraham Lincoln's taste, as Kenneth Bernard describes it, went "from the nonsensical and ludicrous to the sad and mournful—from 'Hossen Johnny' and 'The Blue-Tail Fly' to 'He Doeth All Things Well' and 'Twenty Years Ago'." Lincoln was "especially fond of sentimental songs" and "laughed heartily at minstrels and appreciated the comforting solace of 'Rock of Ages'."[40]

Lincoln's generation required no excuse to sing comic ditties. Their rhythms had a buoyant infectiousness. Impudent lyrics hit straight to the mark. Jaunty melodies produced happy elation, a sense of visceral and kinetic well-being.

The serious ballads, on the other hand, were valuable educational tools. The enlightened among Lincoln's generation, as well as the song composers themselves, were agreed that a true preparation for

[39]"On Melody," Boston *Euterpeiad* (30 September 1820) 107; "Musical Review," *Dwight's Journal of Music* (26 June 1852) 93; "Popular Melodies," *The Singer's Companion* (New York: Stringer & Townsend, 1854) 161.

[40]Kenneth A. Bernard, *Lincoln and the Music of the Civil War* (Caldwell, Idaho: Caxton 1966) xvii–xviii.

living encompassed more than learning to read, write, and cipher.[41] Somehow or other, they wanted to instill in the popular mind the idea that the quality of an American's life was of paramount importance, that a system of values merited one's allegiance, that a penetration into the heart of problems involving suffering, decay, and death was intrinsically satisfying in the long run, however simply the concepts had to be put and understood, and that an aware citizenry could change America into a better country.

Certainly the America they saw about them urgently needed to be brought to a higher standard of goodness. They accepted the notion that emotions, agreeable or not, have essential human functions, for they help people cope with vital personal and collective problems. Civilized existence necessitated a control over feelings like love and guilt in order to channel them toward altruism and social commitment.

Serious popular song was central to the educational endeavors of the time. It was felt that music, more than any other medium, could affect and influence ordinary people. Why? Because the mass of Americans tended to trust their feelings; song conveyed to them those feelings and commonplaces they had faith in. People desired enjoyment; a loved melody could persuade them to cherish the lyric's message. They felt comfortable only with the familiar; song presented individuals, situations, and sentiments that were recognized by all.[42]

Prominent educators and social-minded leaders were confident that music could shore up humanity's ethical and emotional being, teach democratic principles, and encourage allegiance to an undi-

[41]See, for example, [Mitchell], *The Lorgnette,* 10th ed., (New York: Scribner 1853) II, 104–05; Henry Wadsworth Longfellow, *Letters,* 2 vols. (Cambridge, Mass.: Belknap Press, 1966) I, 361.

[42]For the general attitude about the need for this sort of education, see Emerson, *Journals,* VII, 382–83; Charvat, *Origins* 53. For the references to music as an essential part of this education, see John W. Moore, *Complete Encyclopaedia of Music* (Boston: Ditson 1854) s.v. "Ballad"; Thomas Hastings, *Dissertation on Musical Taste* (New York: Mason Brothers 1853) 190.

vided national society. For these reasons, they encouraged music's use in the home and school. When, in 1857, Lowell Mason pioneered music education in the Boston Public Schools, an evaluating committee issued a report urging the continuation of this instruction. The object of "popular instruction" in music, the report read, is to train pupils "for usefulness and happiness in coming life." Teaching of this sort benefits the person and the nation. Schools must not limit themselves to developing the intellect only, "when for all the true purposes of life, it is of more importance . . . to feel rightly, than to think profoundly." Singing "seems best fitted to supply that direction."[43] Public music education caught on and spread through out the country. A major part of its curriculum consisted of popular song.[44]

The songs taught to the young were also enjoyed by adults. They edified convicts at Sing Sing Prison, the president and the ranking politicians in Washington, and "all the poor and laboring classes" who enjoy music as much as "the Monied Class" and who can profit "by its good influence as much if not more."[45]

Asa Hutchinson, member of the Hutchinson Family Singers, is quoted above. How can we characterize popular musicians like him, whether composer or performer? First, they came neither from the uppermost nor from the bottommost segments of society, but from the broadly spread out group in between. Nor, usually, were they trained musicians or foreign-born. Second, they believed in the virtues extolled by the middle class and aspired to by the lower class. George F. Root, a successful composer and performer who had grown up in a Massachusetts village, came to identify completely with the American majority: "I saw at once that mine must be the

[43]Arthur Lowndes Rich, *Lowell Mason* (Chapel Hill: University of North Carolina Press 1946) 22–23.

[44]This is established beyond doubt in my book *Sweet Songs for Gentle Americans: The Parlor Song in America, 1790–1860* (Bowling Green, Ohio: Bowling Green University Popular Press 1979).

[45]New York *Musical World* (31 October 1852) 137; New York *Musical Review* (31 August 1854) 307; Boston *Musical Gazette* (1 March 1847) 22; Carol Brink, *Harps in the Wind: The Story of the Singing Hutchinsons* (New York: Macmillan 1947) 40, 78, 82.

'people's song'." At first he wondered whether he should sign his own name to his songs: "When Stephen C. Foster's wonderful melodies . . . began to appear and the famous Christy's Minstrels began to make them known, I 'took a hand in' and wrote a few, but put 'G. Friederick Wurzel' (the German for Root) to them instead of my own name." Shortly thereafter, Lowell Mason taught him to take pride in his activities and to feel he carried on an urgent educational mission. As a result, Root writes: "[I] went more among the people of the country. . . . I saw these things in a truer light, and respected myself, and was thankful when I could write something that all the people would sing."[46]

The "something that all the people would sing" necessitated a composer's constant monitoring of the tastes of the "numerous and discerning public" so that he could aim not "at what is new" or at displaying his "own powers," but rather at developing "the real beauties of the art." The popular composer, always aware of the limitations of his auditors, consciously simplified the music and set texts with directly apprehensible themes.[47]

Marion Dix Sullivan, composer of one of the biggest hits of the 1840s, *The Blue Juniata* (1844), writes in the "Author's Preface" to a collection of her songs, published in 1855, a few paragraphs on the popular composer's understanding of what the musician's relationship to the public consisted of: "To my friends of the forest and the mountain, the river, the lake, and the sea shore—of the poor—of the laboring—and to EVERY child, the 'Juniata Ballads' are affectionately and respectfully dedicated. They are to be sung to the oar, the loom, and the plow—through the forest, over the prairie, and in the small log-cabin by the light of a pine-knot.

"They are written as they came to the mind of the composer, often unsought and undesired: the melody and the words together. The latter may not be poetical, but they at least harmonize with the

---

[46]Root, *Story* 83. Further discussion of Root's relation to Foster and to "people's song" may be found in William W. Austin, *"Susanna," "Jeanie," and "The Old Folks at Home"* (New York: Macmillan 1975) 261–69.
[47]Boston *Euterpeiad* (27 January 1821) 175; Root, *Story* 99–96.

former. Most of them commemorate in the mind of the writer some event, or place, or circumstance. . . .

"If I knew which were the heavy and uninteresting songs in the collection, I would leave them all out; but as I do not, I will trust those to whom it is frankly offered, to do that favor for me."[48]

Note to whom she directed her music; note her claim that her songs came to her naturally; and note also the cheerfulness with which she concedes the right to judge the ultimate worth of her compositions to the song lovers themselves.

It was up to the composer, aided by the performer, to stir listeners to a favorable response to a song. A prime goal was less to write a work of enduring artistic merit, but more to write one in which the text's message and the melody's charm would win over a large audience. For this reason, the composer and singer resorted to every movingly expressive strategem under their control, trusting more in an arousal of sentimental feeling than an appeal to reason, and placing their hope on scenes making a bald bid for tears or laughter, on rhetorical repetition in the music, and on eloquent delivery in order to gain instant and unquestioning approval.

Very few of these musicians had received thorough musical instruction. To the admirers of artistic music, they did not seem particularly gifted. Yet they did show good judgment in estimating the desires and needs of their countrymen, and they did exercise prudence in their public appearances. Song lovers perceived many of them as sincere, honest, unaffected, and moral beings. A Lowell factory girl writes of the Hutchinsons: "In the evening we had the Hutchinsons, from our own Granite State, who discoursed sweet music, *so sweetly.* They have become great favorites with the public. It is not on account of their fine voices only, but their pleasant modest manners—the perfect sense of propriety which they exhibit in all their demeanor."[49]

---

[48]The preface is quoted in full in the New York *Musical Review* (1 December 1855) 412. *The Juniata Ballads* is a collection of fifty songs. When published, it was offered for purchase at 25 cents per copy.

[49]The quotation is from *The Lowell Offering,* IV (August 1844) 238. See also *Dwight's Journal of Music* (28 May 1853) 62; New York *Musical Review* (7 February 1857) 34; Henry Phillip, *Musical and Personal Recollections,* (London, 1864) I, 285–87.

Even some blackface minstrels made certain their audiences understood that they, too, had a "perfect sense of propriety." However frantic their stage antics, however bizarre their costumes, and however ludicrous their ditties, they let people know that outside the theater they led moral and dignified lives. For example, although the sheet music covers of the songs they popularized may show them dressed in grotesque clothing, underneath this depiction is often found a second view of these same men, now in somber suits and affecting sedate poses.

What is more, whether ballad concert or minstrel show, theatrical performances were inexpensive to attend. Instead of the usual $1.00 to $2.00 admission charge of Italian opera singers and British recitalists, the charge for attendance at concerts given by Americans was 25 cents, 15 cents, and sometimes as low as 12.5 cents, thus enabling anyone save the truly destitute to enter. Only rarely did admission to popular performances touch on 50 cents.[50]

THE IMPERFECT DEMOCRACY

The years 1830–1860 enclose a period in which a fresh recognition of social ills grew, and reform movements began to be formed to fight for their rectification, despite the lethargy or prejudices of those satisfied with the *status quo*. A Christian awareness of right and wrong and a sensibility to one's own religious transgressions formed prominent components of the sometimes unpredictable American character. While awareness did not always produce right behavior, it often brought on a sense of guilt. The instances of moral relapse and apathy were assuredly numerous, as they ever will be with humans. Yet, a number of these nineteenth-century Americans could rightfully claim themselves persons of conscience.[51]

[50]William B. Wood, *Personal Recollections of the Stage* (Philadelphia 1855) 15–18, 456; Nye, *Muse* 145–46; Boston *Musical Gazette* (20 July 1846) 97; New York *Musical World* (31 October 1852) 137.

[51]A characteristic feature of these years, as well as a strong trend during them, was the large number of reform organizations that claimed a Christian necessity for their activities.

The injustice done to Indians, the horrors of slavery, the subjugation of women, the suffering of the penniless, the abuse of alcohol, the addiction to gambling, and the indifferent treatment accorded the orphan, the insane, and the blind became the subject of many popular songs. These were areas of concern both to reformers like Dorothea Dix, Samuel Gridley Howe, Horace Mann, Josiah Quincy, Margaret Fuller, and William Lloyd Garrison,[52] and to some of our popular musicians, who gave musical vent to their troubled thoughts: the Hutchinson Family, the Baker Family, Wood's Minstrels, Isaac B. Woodbury, B.R. Hanby, Stephen Foster, L.V.H. Crosby, to name a few.

The comprehension of the disorders in society was imperfect, it is true. But it requires years to recognize a problem and further years, first, to see that problem in all its dimensions and, second, to discover a solution of even partial effectiveness. Still more time is necessary to have the problem understood and solution supported by a majority. At least during these years, a feeling of urgency did drive the reformers to reexamine social wrongs without attributing them exclusively to sloth, sin, inferior creation, or God's hidden ways. This in itself was a momentous advance for humanity.

In what immediately follows, I examine songs on social problems for their literal meanings, not for their universal implications (where they can be reinterpreted to encompass everyman's lot). The latter aspect will be studied later.

The popular-song writers of these years were inclined mostly to condemn the white man's cruelty toward the Indian. Scarcely a song hints at an opposite viewpoint. Even as the Eastern tribes were slaughtered or driven westward, the notion of the noble savage, "the child of nature" as contrasted to the corruptly civilized white man, persisted from the times of Montaigne and Rousseau. Several plays, like Robert Roger's *Ponteach* (1776), musical dramas like Barker and Bray's *The Indian Princess* (1806), and adventure novels like the Leather stocking tales of James Fenimore Cooper, perpetuated this image in America. "The solitary savage feels silently, but acutely. His sensibilities . . . run in steadier and deeper channels" than those

[52]Berthoff, *Unsettled People* 256–59; Boorstin, *Americans* 43–48, 377.

26

of the white, wrote Washington Irving. Indians belong to "a race possessing magnanimity, generosity, benevolence, and pure religion without hypocrisy. . . . They have been most barbarously maltreated by the whites, both in word and deed," wrote Longfellow.[53]

Guilt feelings guaranteed no swift rectification of injustice. After all, in years when people with no property and little money greatly outnumbered those comfortably situated, cupidity easily smothered benevolence. And because the harried Indian lived in lands separated away from most settled Americans, distance discouraged right action. Moreover, frontier settlers and army commanders, eager to dispossess the Indian of his homeland, nursed a venomous hatred of every aborigine. They sent false and self-serving reports eastward, which told of the brutality and utter untrustworthiness of the red man.

The wonder is hardly a song that became widely accepted took up the theme of the Indian's alleged perfidy. Most portrayed the Indian as the victim.

On the other hand, these songs were never intended to be reform tracts. Thus fashioned, they would have ceased to entertain. Instead, they pictured the Indian's plundered patrimony, courage, dignity, and anguish in lyrics relating the red man's reality to universal motifs of suffering and redemption.[54] Interestingly, the admission to some Indian ancestry was not accompanied by any condemnation by whites. The composition *Bell Brandon,* for example, depicts an exemplary white American heroine: "They said the life current of the Red Man ting'd her veins from a far distant spring."[55]

In a typical composition, two Indian lovers, children of nature and without guile, are murdered "by the foeman/Who came o'er the billow/And stole the broad lands/Where their children reside."

---

[53]Rourke, *Roots* 64–74; Washington Irving, *The Sketch Book,* new ed., 2 vols. (London: Murray 1821) II, 151–68; Longfellow, *Letters* I, 56.

[54]Constance Rourke, *American Humor* (Garden City, N.Y.: Doubleday, 1953) 98, states that a similar depiction took place on the American stage.

[55]*Bell Brandon,* words T. Ellwood Garrett, music Francis Woolcott (St. Louis: Balmer & Weber 1854). The date given here, and in all the songs that follow, indicates the year of copyright.

Or a brave warrior dies defending his inheritance against the "pale foe," a foe who then "hurried . . . his tribe westward," coercing family and friends to abandon "their abodes." Though "forced to roam" and driven "far away to a western" land, another warrior continues to yearn for his "forest home" and still dreams of discovering a new "peaceful" home free of the presence of whites. While he lives, however, his permanent condition is loneliness, for "the steel of the white man" has ruthlessly destroyed everyone he loves: his "father who watched over" his youth, his "mother who taught" him "the precepts of truth," and his "sister, the pride of the vale." He prays to follow them soon, called by "the Great Spirit . . . to the bright blissful shores, and the fair forest shade/Where the steel of the white man will never invade."[56]

The bondage of black Americans was less universally condemned in song. Northern opinion about slavery seemed ambivalent at best. The Southern position that the slave lived better and happier than the Northern factory worker had advocates among a few well-known writers and composers, most of them from the South. Edgar Allan Poe insisted that blacks looked peculiar, thought differently than whites, and should remain enslaved because "it was the will of God it should be so." John H. Hewitt, in his song *Aunt Harriet Becha Stowe,* sneered at abolitionists, whom he portrayed as greedy for money, indifferent to the starvation of the Northern poor, and unwilling to accept the Southern contrast of kind masters, gentle mistresses, and grateful blacks contentedly singing in chorus: "Lor bress de Southern Ladies, and my ole southern home."[57]

Nonetheless, a number of American popular composers, publishers, and performers were Northerners disinclined to propagate the Southern catechism. "Get off the track," the Emancipation

---

[56]See, respectively, *The Indian and His Bride,* w. George P. Morris, m. Francis H. Brown (New York: Firth, Hall & Pond 1844); *The Indian Warrior's Grave,* w. and m. Marshall S. Pike, arr. J.P. Ordway (Boston: Ordway 1850); *The Indian's Dream,* w. W.B. Farrell, m. Frank Howard (Boston: Marsh 1848).

[57]Edgar Allan Poe, in *The Complete Works,* (New York: AMS 1965) VIII, ed. James A. Harrison 265–75;*Aunt Harriet Becha Stowe,* w. Charles Soran, m. John H. Hewitt (Baltimore: McCaffrey 1853).

Train is unstoppable, warned the Hutchinson Family, singing a work by Jesse Hutchinson. Another of Jesse's compositions, *The Bereaved Slave Mother,* describes a loathsome "Master" whipping a mother and snatching away her babe to sell on the block. The text closes with a plea to all "kind mothers" to heed "the cries of the Slave." The same theme is explored in L.V.H. Crosby's *The Slave Mother.* An indignant Benjamin Hanby watched an auctioneer sell a wife, tearing her away from her husband. Deeply depressed by the sight, he composed *Darling Nelly Gray:* "The white man bound her with his chain/They have taken her to Georgia for to wear her life away/As she toils in the cotton and the cane."[58]

As with the Indian, the slave's release from sorrow came in death. When the "poor unhappy slave" dies, in *Poor Old Slave,* he is at last fortunate since he has no master to fear. An enthusiastic William Lloyd Garrison, publisher of *The Liberator,* delighted in the broad acceptance of sentimental ballads like these, for he was convinced they served the cause of democracy and increased the moral elevation of the American people.[59]

In recent years, a proper liberal stance has required the condemnation of antebellum minstrel shows and their songs as openly racist. Books like Robert Toll's *Blacking Up* and Sam Dennison's *Scandalize My Name* come immediately to mind.[60] While I advocate no completely opposite view, I do suggest that truth is handicapped by this extreme position. I am convinced that many minstrel songs, especially those of the late 1840s and '50s, have underlying agenda, hid-

---

[58] *Get Off the Track,* by Jesse Hutchinson (Boston: published for the author 1844); *The Bereaved Slave Mother,* w. Jesse Hutchinson, adapted to a familiar air (Boston: Ditson n.d.); *The Slave Mother,* w. and m. L.V.H. Crosby (Boston: Ditson 1853); *Darling Nelly Gray,* w. and m. Benjamin R. Hanby (Boston: Ditson 1856). Hamm, *Yesterdays* 142–61, discusses the Hutchinsons' songs in detail and, 136–37, Hanby's *Darling Nelly Gray.*

[59] *The Poor Slave,* w. and melody G.W.H. Griffin, arr. "E.M.F." (Boston: Reed, 1851). E. Douglas Branch, *The Sentimental Years, 1836-1860* (1962), reprint (New York: Hill & Wang 1965) 180.

[60] Robert C. Toll, *Blacking Up: The Minstrel Show in Nineteenth-Century America* (New York: Oxford University Press 1974); Sam Dennison, *Scandalize My Name: Black Imagery in American Popular Music* (New York: Garland 1982).

den and subtly overt, that set forth slavery's reality. Charles Hamm, in *Yesterdays* (126, 211-212), states that the early minstrel song, from the late 1820's and the '30's, portrayed blacks as simpleminded grotesques, without any of the finer feelings. He claims that Stephen Foster's *Old Uncle Ned* (1848) and *Nelly Was a Lady* (1849) were two of the first minstrel songs to depict blacks as human, and that Foster's *Oh! Boys, Carry me 'Long* (1851) was one of the earliest minstrel songs to complain about slavery. In my own book *Sweet Songs for Gentle Americans,* I devote an entire chapter, Chapter 5, to the changing characteristics of the minstrel songs.

To Hamm's statement I would add that Foster's *Way Down in Cairo,* published in 1850, recognized the starvation that slaves often had to endure: "Now we libs on de fat ob de land,/Now we libs on de lean./When we hab no cake to bake/We sweep de kitchen clean./I hear my tree lub weep/ . . . [because] Dis nigga's guine to die." Foster's *Oh! Boys, Carry Me 'Long,* however, does make hatred of slavery more explicit. Here, death means "no more trouble. . . . I's guine to roam/In a happy home/Where all de niggas am free."

The tone in the pre-1850 minstrel song is normally unsentimental, unlike that of the songs mentioned above. There are no pathetic implications, for example, in the song *Ching A Ring Chaw,* which suggests that the shrewd black should escape to Haiti, where a revolt against the French had made the blacks free and the island independent. Here he can become a true equal and no longer experience hard labor, whippings, hunger, crying, and the need to steal in order to survive. Most such minstrel songs mock the "loved Master" fiction of white Southerners. The Master is a liar: "Massa an Misse promise me/When dey died to set me free./Now dey boss am dead and gone/Left ole Sambo hoeing out corn." The Master sells humans as if they were animals: "Oh! dars de wite man comin/To tear you from my side." Like a slave's wishful dream, *De Blue Tail Fly* has the Master bitten by a fly, torn by a brier, and eventually killed by his horse: "Dey say all tings am for de best," concludes the smiling singer.

In *Gumbo Chaff,* the Master has died and "gone to de debil/For when he live you know he light upon me so,/But now he's gone to tote de firewood way down below." Most astonishing of all, *Settin' On a Rail* mentions poison as a means for easing the Master's way to hell: "My ole Massa dead an gone,/A dose ob poison help him on./ De Debil say him funeral song,/Oh bress him let him go/. . . An joy go wid him to."[61]

The question of women's emancipation produced even more mixed reactions than did that of slavery's abolishment. Hardly any undisguised songs on the rights of women seem to have won acceptance beyond the circle of the dedicated few. The frequent performance of such songs by the Hutchinson Family was tolerated mainly because audiences admired the singing and expected to hear other works more to their liking. In contrast, songs ranged on the opposite side of the issue were more common. Less hostile than most was one composition telling a woman her right was to receive equal pay for equal work but not to ignore her home in the pursuit of fashion; her right was to speak her mind when advising her husband, but not to gain her ends by pouts, sulks, and sighs; and her right was to hold one man's love exclusively, but not to flirt with empty-headed young men.[62]

On the opposite side, Mrs. Rowson had tried at the turn of the century, in plays like *The Female Patriot* and *Columbia's Daughters,* and in poems meant for music, like "The Rights of Women," to enlist reasonable men for women's succor, in general, and suffrage, in particular. Hardly a male rallied to the cause. Later in the century no songs had the currency of Fanny Fern's essays against the "defilement and brutality" endured by "long-suffering, uncomplaining mothers" subject always to some form of "legal compulsion"; or of Lydia Maria Child's praise of women's vital contributions to every

---

[61] *Way Down in Cairo,* w. and m. Stephen C. Foster (New York: Firth, Pond 1850); *Oh! Boys, Carry Me 'Long,* w. and m. Stephen C. Foster (New York: Firth, Pond 1851); *Ching A Ring Chaw* (Baltimore: Willig c. 1833); *Jenny Get Your Hoe Cake Done,* as sung by J.W. Sweeny (New York: Firth & Hall 1840); *Lucy Neal,* w. and m. J.P. Carter (Boston: Keith 1844); *De Blue Tail Fly* (Boston: Keith 1846); *Gumbo Chaff* (New York: Firth & Hall c. 1836); *Settin' On a Rail* (New York: Hewitt c. 1837).

[62] *Women's Rights,* by Kate Horn (New York: Waters 1853).

civilization.[63] Regrettably, the currency I speak of developed only among the literate.

To most Americans, acquiescence to the demand for women's rights meant increased familial incohesion, of women thinking of and acting for themselves alone and not the family—a consequence viewed with horror. They wished only for songs that skirted this issue. The most that the really popular compositions would admit to was the possible future unhappiness of a bride, since she would now be completely dependent on her new and still untested husband— hinting that on her own she was a nonperson and that as wife she gained either fulfillment or emptiness, owing either to her partner's virtues or to his vices. Relief, other than dying, went unmentioned for the marital sufferer.

None of the favorite compositions explored solutions to social tragedies. Instead, they transcribed dramatic segments of experience into musical forms that move listeners with their pathos. In Dexter's *The Beggar Boy's Appeal,* a fatherless child has wandered the city streets all day, searching for milk and bread for his starving mother and sister. He spies a well-off woman: "Stay lady, sweet lady/O pass me not by," he begs, but is coldly ignored. "Farewell to thee, lady! Still drear is my lot," he cries after her. "No kind heart to pity, no soft hand to save/Ay, would with my father I slept in the grave." In *Hard Times Come Again No More,* Stephen Foster begs his listener to pause from the enjoyment of life's pleasures and give thought to the "frail forms fainting at the door," and the "pale drooping maiden who toils her life away/With a worn heart whose better days are o'er." Septimus Winner suggests that more than thought should be given, in *Cast Thy Bread Upon the Waters.* Along with pity, donate money, he urges, for "he that giveth to the poor/Only lendeth to the Lord."[64]

---

[63]Rourke, *Roots* 82–85, [Mrs. Sara Payson Parton], *Folly As It Flies,* by Fanny Fern (New York: Carleton 1868) 67; Sidney Herbert Ditzion, *Marriage, Morals, and Sex in America* (New York: Bookman Associates 1953) 240; Browne, *Metropolis* 636–39; Ann Douglas, *The Femininization of American Culture* (New York: Knopf 1977) 69; Wright, *Culture* 225.

[64]*The Beggar Boy's Appeal,* w. Mrs. S.M. Humphrey, m. E. Dexter (Boston: Reed 1854); *Hard Times Come Again No More,* w. and m. Stephen C. Foster (New York: Firth, Pond 1854); *Cast Thy Bread Upon the Waters,* by Septimus Winner

Composers zeroed in on one major contemporary evil, drunken-ness, and advocated total abstention. (Of course, a number of songs also sprang up, mostly comic, praising the opposite.) The consump-tion of alcohol was regarded as a symptom of society's disintegration and a principal participant in the home's destruction. Typical was the woe of one of alcohol's victims, little Katy. *Hot Corn,* a song based on a news item in the New York *Tribune,* depicts Katy as sad, weak, pallid, and near death; she pleads with passersby to buy her hot corn. She fears returning to "Her wicked mother madly burning,/ Passion beaming from her eyes,/For life's poison she is yearning./ 'Give, oh give me drink', she cries!"[65]

The little Katys were everywhere in urban America. What was to be done to relieve their plight and redress their grievances? Become "teetotalers" and sign "the Temp'rance pledge," sang the Hutchin-son Family. Alcohol is a tyrant whose downfall brings freedom, sang Ossian Dodge. Reform and shout the "joyful cry, We're Free, We're Free!" Dodge urged.[66]

Notwithstanding what has just been said about compositions on themes of social problems, the preponderance of popular songs con-centrated on the inadequacies in individual lives. In the main, peo-ple were too busy coping with their own problems to devote more than passing attention to the little Katys. Although they might live in cities, they had been born in rural areas and had grown up on farms or in villages. Despite the increasing attention to public education, their schooling had frequently been minimal. Nor had their lives

---

(Philadelphia: Lee and Walker 1855). Robert Marshall Copeland, in *The Life and Works of Isaac Baker Woodbury, 1819–1858* (Ph.D. dissertation, University of Cincin-nati, 1974) 118–19, writes that on 8 August 1853 the New York *Tribune* reported on a pitiable child, Katy, forced to sell hot corn on the streets owing to an alcoholic mother. Within a month, several pathetic songs describing the plight of the little girl were published, with titles like *Katy's Cry* and *Sorrowful Katy.*

[65] *Hot Corn,* w. James Simmond, m. Quos [A. Sedgwick] (New York: Waters 1853). The sheet music refers to the *Tribune* story of 8 August 1853 as the basis for the song; see also note 64.

[66] *The Old Granite State,* sung by the Hutchinson Family (n.p., New York copy-right 1843 by John Hutchinson); *The Temperance Shout of Liberty,* w. Ossian E. Dodge, m. arr. Isaac B. Woodbury (Boston: Keith 1843).

been easy. Helplessly, they watched a vast transformation of their society, and struggled to understand its implications. They saw that the changing emphasis from agriculture to industry was having a disastrous effect on personal interrelationships. Men spent longer and longer hours away from home. Women, who were accustomed to confining their activities to their household and to ceasing to earn wages after marriage, grew more and more psychologically dependent on themselves alone. In the countryside where they had been raised, a person was accepted and esteemed if from an upright family and active in a communal group. In the urban neighborhood it seemed that no one wished to offer any affection and support, and that the individual belonged to nothing. A restless anxiety gripped men and women alike. Was there meaning in lives such as theirs?

This is the background to a statement by Henry Tuckerman on the need for "the poetic element" to "relieve the sternness of necessity, to lighten the burden of toil, and throw a sacredness and hope even around suffering"; and to another by Edward Everett on how the songs of George F. Root have given "strength, courage, and life . . . to us all." The protagonist in the song *Farewell, My Lilly Dear* sings: "When I'm sad and weary/I'll make the banjo play."[67] And Zadoc Long, a Mainite and a lover of song and violin playing, wrote into his journal, on 30 September 1848, a heartfelt paean to music:

> My muse has no bright wings to soar—
> No warblings magical to pour
> On highly polished ears, I know;
> But croaks in accents trite and low.
> Her numbers still to me are full
> Of comfort inexpressible;
> They help along the toilsome day,
> Drive melancholy thoughts away,
> Dispel my cares, relieve my pain,
> And keep the Devil from my brain.[68]

---

[67]Henry T. Tuckerman, *The Optimist* (New York: Putnam 1852) 27; Root, *Story* 212; *Farewell, My Lilly Dear,* w. and m. S.C. Foster (New York: Firth, Pond 1851).

[68][Zadoc Long], *From the Journal of Zadoc Long, 1800-1873,* ed. Peince Long (Caldwell, Idaho: Caxton 1943) 166.

It was natural that Americans would turn to music. As the psychologists Hans and Shulamith Kreitler tell us, the desire for aesthetic experience of this sort is motivated by prior tensions: "The work of art mediates the relief of these preexisting tensions by generating new tensions which are specific," and which absorb and combine with those of the listener to provide a pleasureful release.[69]

How is this accomplished? The serious songs show us lonely people aching for companionship and seeing only strangers in alien settings. The lyrics use physical solitude to mirror the isolation of mind and feeling. Applicable to American song is what R.W.B. Lewis writes regarding mid-nineteenth-century literature: "Whitman's image of the evergreen, 'solitary in a wide, flat space . . . without a friend or lover near', introduced what more and more appears to be the central theme of American literature . . . loneliness." Writing about the Californians who valued Foster's songs, William Austin points out that they lived in "a fragmentary, temporary society of men without women, children, or old folks, a society of men assembled from many origins."[70] The songs caught their innermost feelings.

Carl Jung has written that if a person "knows his problem to be general and not merely personal it makes all the difference."[71] Popular songs did generalize personal loneliness. By so doing, they answered people's needs through providing an artistic crossroads where Americans could meet, agree on essentials, and inwardly relive and integrate their most intense remembrances. Individually and in consort, they sang:

[69]Hans and Shulamuth Kreitler, *Psychology of the Arts* (Durham, N.C.: Duke University Press 1972) 16-22.

[70]R.W.B. Lewis, *The American Adam: Innocence, Tragedy and Tradition in the Nineteenth Century* (Chicago: University of Chicago Press 1955) 49. On loneliness, see also Ethel Mannin, *Loneliness* (London: Hutchinson 1966) 9; Nils Bruzelius, "Feeling Lonely," reprint of a report from the 1978 meeting of the American Psychological Association, Boston *Sunday Globe* (3 September 1978) 1, 13; Austin, *"Susanna,"* 30.

[71]Carl Jung, *Analytical Psychology* (New York: Random House, 1968), 117. The author died in 1961.

Like a doomed shade I wander,
　To dark despair a prey,
As streams thro' vales meander
　Where sun ne'er sheds a ray;
Each tree around seems bending
　To the breeze that bears my moan,
While pining echo mocks my sigh,
　And cries, 'alone, alone.'[72]

They felt the better for it, as they discovered "the central areas of what they themselves" were and how these areas represented "the emotional core of their culture."[73]

What they were was viewed from two perspectives, as set forth in two main categories of popular song: the one serious, inner-directed, emotional, fanciful, and concentrated on an idealized world; the other comic, outer-directed, earthy, ebullient, and concentrated on the world as it is. On the one hand, song embodied the unswerving inclination of the human spirit to discover its true identity by merging into a cosmic order; on the other, the realization that however much a person huffs and puffs, he remains a funny, pathetic creature of no significance. As James Russell Lowell writes in *The Biglow Papers* of 1848: "We are inhabitants of two worlds"; one, "in virtue of our clay, this little ball of earth"; the other, "an invisible and holier fatherland . . . that ideal realm which we represent to ourselves under the names of religion, deity, and the like."[74]

Either way, serious or comic, a person could say to himself—this is what I have experienced and this is what we all have experienced. The mind's leap from "I" to "we" went from isolation to union with countless others, from the particular to the universal.

---

[72]*Alone, Alone,* w. S.S. Steele, m. T. Comer (Boston: Prentiss & Clark 1847).

[73]W. Lloyd Warner, *The Living and the Dead: A Study of the Symbolic Life of Americans* (New Haven, Conn.: Yale University Press 1959), 504. Warner is referring not just to popular song but to all the popular arts; see also Gary Alan Fine, "Popular Culture and Social Interaction," *Journal of Popular Culture* XI (Fall 1977) 460.

[74]In Vol. IX of *The Writings of James Russell Lowell* (Boston: Houghton Mifflin 1894) 68-69.

THE SENTIMENTAL VIEW

Favorite mid-nineteenth-century songs do establish a standard in aesthetic values, as well as a discrimination among them, that indicates at least for the time of the songs' popularity, a consistent notion of beauty in the American public's mind. This beauty took on a shape dictated by the way men and women converted their participation in contemporary events into ideas and convictions, and by the way they responded emotionally to the sum total of their lives. For perhaps the first time, the large majority of Americans could declare through their popular songs: This is how *we* perceive the beautiful; this is what *we* believe to be aesthetically important.

Usually these songs made their appeal to a relatively unsophisticated audience, but by no means an uncritical one. Indeed, comparatively few musical compositions aimed at the masses achieved success. Every composition had to prove its validity by showing that it imparted a kind of knowledge that objective thought processes ignored, and one to which the listener reacted with: Surely, this is what life is about. Although a popular song might contain a number of commonplaces, these were permeated by a fulfilling humanness that elevated the composition to a position of excellence, as far as its following was concerned. That this is not the perception of some respected twentieth-century writers on American music is made clear in Gilbert Chase's *America's Music.*[75]

Chase finds the serious songs from this period to be overly sentimental, trite, and artificial, "more silly than pathetic, more ludicrous than impressive." A song like Henry Russell's *Woodman! Spare that Tree!* is declared devoid of "the genuine emotion, the organic

---

[75]Gilbert Chase, *America's Music,* rev. ed. (New York: McGraw-Hill, 1966) 165–66. For a general discussion of taste, attitude, and fashion as related to creative works, see Henry Alonzo Myers, *Are Men Equal?* (Ithaca, N.Y.: Cornell University Press, 1955) 25–26; E.E. Kellett, *Fashion in Literature* (London: Routledge & Sons 1931) 14–18, 78–80; Harold Newton Lee, *Perception and Aesthetic Value* (New York: Prentice-Hall 1938) 123–37; Susanne K. Langer, *Feeling and Form* (New York: Scribner's 1953) 395.

vitality, the timeless and impersonal [note!] quality of, for example, the old folk ballads.'' Chase's sensibility, however, is not that of the nineteenth-century American. He judges sentimental song from the viewpoint of a later age, when emotionality in music was suspect and bourgeois taste discredited.

Very few antebellum men and women would have agreed with him. They would have admitted to the role of fashion, artificiality, and insincerity on the part of some people, but would also have insisted on the primacy of emotion simply stated in their songs. Because some people were shallow, because some songs were trite— this did not prove the entire genre to be so. Perhaps it is more to the point to try to see matters through their eyes.

The antebellum demand for ready communication necessitated repetitious truisms, the stripping away of extraneous details in word and melody, and concentration on the essential meaning of a work. However endowed with a glow of reality, the theme remained unindividualized and undeveloped. However effectively communicated, emotion seemed the result of dramatic formalism.[76] At a premium were economy of utterance, concentration on a single incident and feeling, sensitivity to the "universals of human nature" exemplified in "the humblest of our fellow-creatures," and representations just sufficiently natural to "strike the deep chords of the heart."

Unlike the romanticism in English song, that in the American product abstained from an immoderate fantasizing, showed no passion for primeval nature, took no delight in medievalism, preferred not to exalt aristocracy, however virtuously depicted. On the other hand, both William Austin and Charles Hamm underline the considerable influence exerted on Americans by one British source, Thomas Moore's *Irish Melodies and National Airs* (first issued in 1808 and continuing to appear over three decades). Moore and, later, American composers like Foster took as their "most frequent subject," according to Austin, a dream of security, of a vaguely defined home from the past, of a friendless present. Hamm confirms Austin's view. Moore's "persistent theme," he writes, "of nostalgia, of longing for a lost home, childhood, and friends, struck a responsive

[76]R. Chase, *The American Novel* 13, writes on this point in relation to the American novel of romance.

chord among nineteenth-century Americans." The subject matter and the popularity of Moore's songs is also alluded to in my *Sweet Songs for Gentle Americans.*[77]

Stephen Foster's *Old Folks at Home* (which owes much to Moore, less to other British song writers) tells of a humble American, a democratic everyman, forced to wander "all up and down de whole creation." Distant from "de old folks," he feels "sad and dreary," and dreams of returning to "de little farm" and "little hut . . . dat I love." The words are put to a simple diatonic musical phrase that returns several times with hypnotic monotony. In contrast, the British composer Michael Balfe, in *I Dreamt that I Dwelt in Marble Halls,* has a heroine, stolen from her castle by untamed gypsies, dream of "marble halls, with vassals and serfs." She can "boast of a high ancestral name," of knightly suitors "upon bended knee." The tune repeats its phrases less than does Foster's, modulates to the key of the dominant and mediant, introduces some difficult-to-sing chromaticisms, and indulges in unfacile skips.

This is not to say that Balfe's songs were unpopular in America. They were enjoyed by a considerable number of men and women. When it came to native song, however, the public would accept neither an artificial elevation of theme, nor a violation of democratic principles, nor a complexity in the music. Moreover, our native composers saw their task as distinctly different from that of British musicians. Balfe's sort of dream appears hardly at all in their compositions; Foster's is often reproduced.[78]

---

[77]The quotations are from Tuckerman, *Optimist* 105–06, where contemporary lyric poetry is discussed. But also see the "Memoir of the Author," by H.B. Wallace, in George P. Morris, *Poems* (New York: Scribner, 1860) 23–24, where the same characteristics are claimed for Morris's songs. To read about the nature of nineteenth-century American romanticism, see Daniel Hoffman, *Form and Fable in American Fiction* (New York: Oxford University Press 1965) 353–54; Emerson, *Essays* 274–75; Rourke, *American Humor* 161–62; Nye, *Society* 23, 74–75; Charvat, *Origins* 59–60. On Moore, see Austin *"Susanna"* 131–32; Hamm *Yesterdays* 61; Tawa, *Sweet Songs* 6, 33, 57, 79, 104–05, 141, 149.

[78]*Old Folks at Home,* w. and m. Stephen C. Foster (New York: Firth, Pond 1851); *I Dreamt that I Dwelt in Marble Halls,* w. Alfred Bunn, m. Michael Balfe (Philadelphia: Ferrett 1845). Although the Balfe song was successfully sung in America's cities, it was purchased mainly by the more well-to-do and educated Americans, as evidenced in the private song collections of these years.

Despite the warm winds of romanticism fanning their sensibilities, the men and women from these years had been taught under ordinary circumstances to avoid public display of emotion. For them to appear moved sympathetically by something or someone sometimes caused discomfit. Frank revelations of personal feeling, despite the yearning to do so, could bring on acute embarrassment. Here, in part, lies the explanation for the strong current of sentimentality in popular song. Sentiment becomes an essential ingredient in any composition meant for a listener whose culture denies any direct outlets for the expression of inner feeling, but yet, that also proclaims the validity of the imaginative and emotive components of experience. He could allow himself to appear affected by song, since to do so was not an isolated or individualized action, but one motivated from the outside, sanctioned by others and shared with them. In short, the reaction to song was both private and communal, therefore safe. The inviolateness of inner being was thus maintained even as the spirit was purged of its turmoil.

It is no wonder that the nineteenth-century American fervently espoused the idea of song as a structure that incarnates human feeling. However overly sentimental we may find this music today, at that time the sentiment was considered true and justifiable because it was felt universally and recurred in everyone's experience through a lifetime. Furthermore, it was believed that the "intense feeling" derived from song gave "us more entire command over some thought or power within us. Every inundation of passion enriches and gives us a deeper soil."[79] An admonitory example of what might happen when the "head" predominates, and intellect freezes the "heart" and denies its emotions, is contained in Hawthorne's story "Ethan Brand"; Brand's end is suicide.[80]

The accepted manner for displaying the emotionality elicited by this music was through shedding tears, whether in joy or sorrow or, as often as not, both together. The song *Ben Fisher* gives a picture of

[79]"Expression," *The Atlantic Monthly* VI (1860) 576.
[80]This aspect of "Ethan Brand" is taken up in Randall Stewart, *Literature and Doctrine*, 95–96.

total harmony and happiness. Yet:

> I fancied a tear in Ben's eye . . .
>   I could not tell why, the man should cry,
> But he hitched up to Kate still nearer,
>   He leaned his head on her shoulder there,
> And he took her hand in his.[81]

Contemporary music lovers intuited the reason for his weeping. Underlying the words is Ben's awareness of his and Kate's mortality, even in the moment of perfect joy. They knew that he who loves intensely, as does Ben, must also accept the inevitability of pain brought on by the beloved's decay and eventual death.

Weeping over a song was the outward sign of emotional repression released and therapeutic relief from anxiety achieved. Arthur Koestler also adds that another basic element in weeping of this kind is "a craving to transcend the island boundaries of the individual, to enter into a symbiotic communion with a human being or some higher entity, real or imaginary, of which the self is felt to be a part." The reaction gratifies and ennobles, since the weeper ceases thinking of himself only and identifies with others, knowing he feels both his and their mourning or rapture.[82]

The large dollop of nostalgia that was splashed into most songs also encouraged weeping. The remembrance of former felicity in a time and place inhabited by loved ones, a place where one had felt wanted and secure, is the essential ingredient in such songs. Looking back at the kind of pastoral democracy envisioned in nostalgic song lyrics was, at least for one resident of Pittsburgh, a dwelling in a moment "of unaffected" contentment "and gaiety, when . . . all was peaceful heartfelt felicity, undisturbed by the rankling thorns of envy," and the equality displayed "a tie that united all ranks and conditions in our community."[83]

American singers' and listeners' eyes were undoubtedly bedewed

---

[81]*Ben Fisher,* "A Home Picture," w. Francis D. Cage, m. L.V.H. Crosby (Boston: Ditson 1853).

[82]Arthur Koestler, *The Act of Creation* (New York: Macmillan 1964) 278, 299.

[83]Berthoff, *Unsettled People* 179.

by the lyric of *Ah! Sing Again.* Set to a winsome melody, the words
went:

> Ah! sing again,
>> And let it be a measure sweet and low,
>
> Not one that giveth pain,
>> But such as we have oft heard long ago,
>
> When fortune ne'er denying,
>> Did give us home and friends that made it dear
>
> And time so quickly flying,
>> Was bringing us new joys with ev'ry year.
>
> Sing of the past,
>> When all the joyous dreams of youth now gone
>
> Their brightest pictures cast
>> Around our hearts while bidding us speed on;
>
> Yet though these scenes have fled, love,
>> And those bright days are now forever flown,
>
> Still by thy sweet song led,
>> Again those happy years seem all my own.[84]

The imaginative re-creation of a vanished age in musical terms
must be understood as sounding within the music lover's environment of sometimes persistent uncertainty and brooding discontent
over his present state. The mostly unconscious but incipient threat of
loosing one's bearings caused a Camelot—that fleeting, joyous time
that each one of us believes once existed—to rise up in the past in
order to provide a means for the self's continuing spiritual cohesion.
It is no wonder that nostalgia was a persistent accoutrement of popular song.

The ache to be remembered somewhere by someone was often a
coefficient to nostalgia. This was especially true for the nineteenth-
century Americans who experienced solitariness when first they
moved away from their rural communities and when they pursued
their incessant travels westward or overseas in pursuit of opportunity. That wherever they went no one knew or cared who they were
or what they felt haunted the minds of these newly uprooted ones. To

---

[84] *Ah! Sing Again,* ballad composed by H. Avery (Boston: Ditson 1857).

cease to exist in another's thoughts was to become a nothing. Therefore the kithless wept at the meaning of *'Tis Sweet to be Remembered:*

> 'Tis sweet to be remembered
> In the turmoil of this life,
> While toiling up its pathway—
> While mingling in its strife.
>
> . . . . .
>
> What though our path be rugged,
> Though clouded be our sky,
> And none we love and cherish
> No friendly one is nigh
> To cheer us in our sorrow,
> Or share with us our lot;
> 'Tis sweet to be remembered—
> To know we're not forgot.[85]

The people I am describing scarcely desired to stand aloof from
their strongest feelings and regard them with knife-edged objectivity.
Such objectivity, nevertheless, can be a necessity in the humorous
handling of a subject. Interestingly, when their comic songs resorted
to derision, they gibed at indulgent husbands, scolding wives, egotis-
tical bachelors, predatory spinsters, and the like; but never at their
vision of the past and need to be remembered. Nor did any composition laugh at the traveler's longing for home, the intertwining devotion of father, mother, and children, or the menace of suffering and
death. These were the subjects of serious songs alone. The flip
speech and jaunty tune of the comic minstrel composition, Americans felt, were better directed at the foibles of superficial people with
shallow sensibilities, not at the convictions drawing humans of good
will to one another. Above all, their comic works avoided any mock-
ery of deep love freely given and honorably returned. Love's proper
tone was that of *Some One to Love,* where affection stands a stalwart
against the world's painful vagaries:

---

[85] *'Tis Sweet To Be Remembered,* w. John S. Adams, m. George O. Farmer (Boston: Ditson 1849).

43

Some one to love in this wide world of sorrow,
   Some one whose smile will efface the sad tear;
Some one to welcome the light of tomorrow,
   Some one to share it when sunshine is here.
Oh, the world is a desert amid all its pleasures,
   And life seems bereft of the only true zest,
If we fail in possessing with all its proud treasures,
   The best of all blessings, some dear kindred breast.

Some one to love whose affection will cherish
   The sweet bud of hope when 'tis blighted with care;
Some faithful heart that will ne'er let it perish
   By sinking forever in depths of despair.
'Tis an angelic radiance, a beacon to guide us,
   Resembling those lamps that are shining above,
'Tis a guardian from heaven, a light to decide us,
   Teaching us lessons of wisdom and love.[86]

To later critics who satisfy their emotional needs differently and apply judgmental standards relative to their own age, texts like the above may seem to suggest sentimentality that overleaps genuine feeling to land in the ditch of bathos. Inordinate self-indulgence besmerches idealized feeling. Yet when we accept the impossibility of aesthetic absolutes and agree that the valuation of works of art depends on the nuances of human cognition, then what seems trite, insincere, or excessive to one society may hold the essence of truth to another—with equal validity, as far as the researcher is concerned. So it is for nineteenth-century popular song in America.

   The composers claimed only a modest corner of expressiveness for their musical creations. Through their songs, they tried to speak gratifyingly about rectitude and the human condition. Owing to their Christian beliefs, none depicted man as sinless. Nonetheless, they persevered in portraying the human being, however flawed, as a figure originally shaped by God. On this, they and their audience were agreed. As dangerous sickness was to the physical organism, so moral deterioration was to the spirit—a disease requiring doctoring

[86]*Some One to Love,* w. James Simmonds, m. J.R. Thomas (New York: Hall 1854).

with music, among a host of specifics, in order to achieve a healthy state.

The sentimental approach to God necessitated that the older Puritan tenet of utter human depravity be tempered with hope for divine forgiveness. Suffering was finite, limited to earthly existence. When complete virtue was achieved, there also came as complete a felicity as was possible for any human being. Absolutely fallacious to these Americans was the thought that commitment to moral excellence and God overloaded man's essential being. Man could achieve a large measure of goodness if he but tried.

A whole-souled faith breathes from Isaac B. Woodbury's *Broken Hearted, Weep No More,* a song overflowing with feeling, whose theme is omnipresent in the various popular writings of the 1850s:

> Broken hearted, weep no more!
>   Hear what comfort He hath spoken,
> Smoking flax who ne'er hath quenched,
>   Bruised reed, who ne'er hath broken;
> Ye who wander here below,
>   Heavy laden as you go,
> Come with grief and sin oppressed,
>   Come to me and be at rest.
>
>   . . . . .
>
> Broken hearted, weep no more,
>   Far from consolation flying;
> He who calls hath felt thy wound,
>   Seen thy weeping, heard thy sighing:
> "Bring thy broken heart to me;
>   Welcome off'ring it shall be:
> Streaming tears and bursting sighs,
>   Mine accepted sacrifice."
> Turn and live?—why will ye die?[87]

Note that the grief and sin crushing man down are not seen as inherent to his inmost substance, but as things apart. In accord with

[87]*Broken Hearted Weep No More,* m. Isaac B. Woodbury (New York: Firth, Pond 1852).

45

the prevalent sentimental perspective, God watches, feels, and ultimately bestows His grace to comfort the dispirited. The sufferer becomes an immolated victim consecrated to a merciful Deity. Implicit is the message that Job-like resentment must give way to humility, submission to divine will, and an acknowledgement of human life on the conditions God alone imposes.

Clearly, the serious view portrayed in popular song was a melancholy one. Melancholia, however, turns into an avenue leading to self-understanding, inner harmony, and the soul's maturation. It has a beneficent effect on the listener, whether felt as the concomitant of blighted love, distant isolation, poverty, oppression, or loss through death.

An incredible number of mid-century popular songs, for example, had death snatch an innocent young woman from the presence of her suitor. The ensuing sadness brought wisdom, not bitterness; the youth, a person of sensibility, by yearning for his beloved realizes a higher truth:

> Beneath the churchyard turf and flowers,
> All cold, and still, and pale;
> Lies one I loved in by gone hours
> The fair young Jenny Dale.
>
> . . . . .
>
> And now the wild birds come and sing,
> Above her little grave;
> The breezes there their music bring,
> And wild flowers o'er her wave;
> And I am often there alone,
> To think of her and weep;
> And there the low winds seem to moan,
> Why did'st thou fall asleep?

He must ask the question of the last line in order to achieve insight.

> O, let her dwell on that bright shore
> I would not call her back . . .
> For she is happier there, I know . . .
> Than I could make her here below. . . .

Sleep on, sweet Jenny Dale . . .
Thy life on earth was short and brief,
But we'll soon meet with God.[88]

His sweetheart has died. Yet he has grasped a truth similar to the one set forth in the Tupper-Thomas song *All's for the Best,* published by William Hall of New York: "All's for the best! be sanguine and cheerful;/Trouble and sorrow are friends in disguise./Nothing but folly goes faithless and fearful;/Courage for ever! is happy and wise."

Although *All's for the Best* suggests pollyannaism, its optimism is not blind. Nor does it deny the probability of pain. Trouble, sorrow, and fear do exist; at the same time, faith must bear up the afflicted. Suffering is for a purpose. To cope calls for mental and moral strength and the conviction that a just conclusion will eventuate. Weeping lasts but a little while; eternity lies ahead.

THE SYMBOLOGICAL REPRESENTATION OF DEMOCRATIC AND OTHER VALUES

Emotional response was triggered, first, by the shape, structure, and sound of lyric and melody; second, by the obvious meanings of the words; and third, by the additional significations conveyed to listeners through a symbolism they held in common. The third kind of response interests us here. Certainly, in the crisis years preceding the Civil War, the continuance of the American society required some degree of solidarity and a conviction that certain specific ways of conducting one's life accorded with national custom and feelings of rightness. Popular song's importance derived from its ability to charm even as it expressed this national consensus.

As will be shown in the chapters that follow, serious song surveyed the space separating man as he was from man as he should be. It explained the failure in humans and the world at large to come up to ideal expectations. It pictured the spiritual progression of every

---

[88] *Jenny Dale,* w. S.W. Hazeltine, m. J.C. Bowker (Boston: Ditson 1854).

human life, delineating its distinctive traits and capacities. When we listen to song after song from the antebellum years, we discover in their sum total a mythical representation "of natural conflicts, of human desire frustrated by non-human powers, hostile oppression, or contrary desires." Told is the story "of birth, passion, and defeat by death which is man's common fate." In an important sense, the "ultimate end is not wishful distortion, but serious envisagement of . . . fundamental truths; moral orientation, not escape."[89] I do not intend to claim that these things were said deliberately or consistently in the song literature. I do maintain that beneath the sentimental veneer is a solid symbolic system that we must study so that we can reach conclusions about the age.

Admittedly, the scale is unheroic and reduced to a dimension that the common imagination could encompass. Though in oblique and fragmentary fashion, a vision does appear in which our alter ego goes about questing for meaning in a strange world in order to arrive at spiritual knowledge. This counterpart of the self is endowed with decency and worth, a capacity for inexhaustible development, and a willingness to honor the rights of all free men.

In patriotic songs, the self so endowed can be interpreted as the image of democratic man ready to battle for liberty and to uphold that unique national union of unfettered spirits, the United States. Here the symbols of democracy divide into at least four main types: (1) abstractions like the terms *freedom* and *liberty;* (2) visual substitutes for complex ideas, like the flag and the log cabin; (3) personifications like George Washington and Andrew Jackson; and (4) happenings and places, like the Battle of New Orleans and Bunker Hill. If someone pointed to the political dissensions of the times and the anomalies in freedom between white and non white, Americans would have replied that they espoused an ideal for future realization in the only country in the world that permitted its eventuation. In contrast to Europeans, whom Americans' prejudiced eyes saw as completely oppressed by tyranny, here in this country whites for now, and all races eventually, could find a way to fulfill their destinies.

[89]Langer, *Philosophy* 143. See also Ina Corinne Brown, *Understanding Other Cultures* (Englewood Cliffs, N.J.: Prentice-Hall 1963) 133.

Under these resolute words hid dismay over the internal political and economic struggles between South and North, and between West and Northeast, the hatred exchanged by advocates for a truly classless society and those for a republic guided by men of ability and merit, and the threat of further ingressions on New World territories by European powers. All-important guides for free men became the American flag and the Union. Taken to heart was the warning contained in George Morris's lyric to *The Flag of Our Union:*

> A song for our banner! The watchword recall
>   Which gave the Republic her station:
> "United we stand, divided we fall!"
>   It made and preserves us a nation.

Set to music by William Bradbury, it was sung up and down the country during the 1850s, by the Continental Vocalists and other American vocal groups.

Throughout these years, which witnessed intense debate over the nature of American democracy, national songs voiced an assemblage of concepts in which imminent disunion was countered with a faith in nationhood that verged on a civic religion. The pro-South composer John Hewitt put aside sectionalism in his composition *Our Native Land,* to call on all patriots to defeat treason and speak up "for God, for Fame and Liberty,/For Union and our Native Land!" In tones edged with hysteria, he pleads:

> Our Country dear—Our Country dear!
>   Shall Faction spurn thy holy laws?
> Shall Freedom's sword and Freedom's spear
>   Be wielded in disunion's cause?
> Thy fairy fields, shall they be strew'd
>   With brothers slain by brother's hand?[90]

Ominous, however, is the absence of any gesture toward accommodation. Is "Treason's hand," we must speculate, raised by a Northerner ready to force his views on the South?

This is the same Hewitt whose other songs breathe a Walter Scottian atmosphere of gallant and noble warriors urgent for fame and

---

[90] *Our Native Land,* w. and m. John H. Hewitt (Baltimore: Willig 1833).

honor on the battlefield. In *The Minstrel's Returned from the War,* a "minstrel" who can come away from war "with spirits as buoyant as air," to the "sweet lady, dear lady" he loves, can as blithely depart again when "fame" calls him "to the field" where he will die "true to love and to duty!" In Hewitt's *The Knight of the Raven Black Plume,* a nobleman tells his lady:

> I come from the field of the slain,
>   The meed of the tournament's mine;
> Yet, never a smile could I gain,
>   So dear to my bosom as thine!"
> The Warder then open'd the gate,
>   And the halls with high revelry rang;
> For long did the fond lovers prate,
>   While the minstrels in joyous notes sang.[91]

The ability to smile after killing humans in a tournament and to dismiss lightly any burden of conscience with trifling lover's chatter indicates a callousness difficult to condone, however romanticized the theme may be. What is more significant is that, while a certain vogue for Hewitt's songs occurred around the late 1820s and early '30s, a strong following for his music soon ceased to exist, especially outside the South. (He himself admits in his autobiography that he eventually discontinued publishing anything at all.)[92] Knights and aristocratic ladies were not from democratic ranks; fame and glory won in meaningless battle held no symbolic significance for ordinary men and women.

Americans outside of the South were as ready as Hewitt to exclaim: "We know no South, we know no North/Our Union right or

[91] *The Minstrel's Returned from the War,* w. and m. John H. Hewitt (New York: James Hewitt c. 1827); *The Knight of the Raven Black Plume* (New York: James Hewitt c. 1832).

[92] John H. Hewitt, *Shadows On the Wall* (Baltimore: Turnbull 1877) 66. Hewitt claims the cessation in publication was owing to his inability to abide greedy publishers, who allowed him little profit. Yet, while studying hundreds of private music collections from before 1860, I noticed the precipitous decline of the presence of Hewitt's works, commencing as early as the mid-1830s. Apparently the public had discontinued purchasing, and professional singers performing, the music.

wrong." But they were thinking more of proslavery secessionists when they sang of treason:

> The temple our brave Fathers made,
> The Wonder of the World,
> Shall they behold their sons dismay'd
> When treason's flag's unfurled?
> Oh, never, by the glorious stars
> Which on our banner throng.[93]

They found little in soldiering that merited lofty admiration. A satirical James Russell Lowell writes, in *The Biglow Papers:* "General C. he goes fer war;/He don't vally princerple more'n an old cud;/Wut did God make us raytional creeturs fer,/But glory an' gunpowder, plunder an' blood?"[94]

Again and again contemporary native observers, and some foreign observers, speak with approval of the American's distrust of the military and the absence of professional standing armies, in contrast to Europe's largely nondemocratic countries, where huge military establishments were the rule. Samuel Griswold Goodrich states, in *Manners and Customs,* published in Boston in 1845: "Such a thing [large armies] would not be endured here. The few soldiers with us are confined to regular garrisons. The bristling of the bayonet, as signal to the people of their servitude and the necessity of their obedience, is revolting to every sentiment of an American bosom."[95]

No nonsense about honor and glory colors the thinking of the waiting woman in *The Absent Soldier.* She wants to rush to the battlefield and, ignoring "the roll of the drum and the shrill bugle," seek out her lover if he "yet lives," in order to "invite him to come and

---

[93]*Our Union Right or Wrong,* w. S.S. Steel, m. Frederick Buckley, in *The Gentle Annie Melodist* (New York: Firth, Pond 1858) 34.

[94]Lowell, *Biglow,* Vol. IX of The Writings of James Russell Lowell (Boston: Houghton Mifflin, 1894) 66.

[95]See also Harriet Martineau, *Society in America,* 3 vols. (London: Saunders & Otley 1837) I, 11; James Fenimore Cooper, *Notions of The Americans* (1828), reprint (New York: Ungar 1963) I, 234; Cooper, *American Democrat,* 55; Lowell, *Letters, Vol. I,* 132.

fly from rude war and alarms."[96] The lyric of another song, *The Capture of Monterey*, stresses, neither the exhilarating excitement of battle nor an act of heroism but, rather, the tragedy of the many buried on the gory plain where they had fought and died.[97]

An extremely negative view of the military is presented in *The Fireman's Song*, when the fireman explains:

> The soldier but fights, his own race to despoil,
> We triumph, o'er double his danger, his toil,
> To save our own homes from that pitiless foe,
> Who laughs at destruction, exults at our woe.[98]

The fireman, not the soldier, is the symbol endowed with desirable attributes. American song composers spurned well-worn British themes like the joys of "the bowl'd sojer boy," the favorite of all the handsome ladies (he leaves his women "in despair" when he valiantly marches forth, certain that "the world is all before us"); or like the irresistibly "dashing white sergeant" to whom no lovely girl can say "no."[99] Bold soldiers and dashing sergeants had little of the gallant about them as far as most American writers of popular song were concerned. Foreign to their compositions are ladies for whom "tales of valor" seem emotional manna and legitimized gunmen who think theirs "is a noble trade" and, contradictorily, a surefire route to winning untold riches.[100] While Americans might feel empathy for an aristocratic warrior who fought off the invaders of his native land, they would hesitate to let him proclaim: "My birth is noble, unstained my crest, as is thine own." Whose birth? The common citizen's? Nor would they condone the sailor who decides to

---

[96] *The Absent Soldier*, w. William Lewers, m. arr. S.O. Dyer (New York: Holt 1847).

[97] *The Capture of Monterey*, w. Ned Buntline, m. Isaac B. Woodbury (Boston: Prentiss & Clark 1847).

[98] *The Fireman's Song*, w. and m. arr. John Smith (Boston: Parker & Ditson 1836).

[99] *The Bowl'd Sojer Boy*, w. and m. Samuel Lover (Boston: Ditson c. 1850); *The Dashing White Sargeant*, m. Henry R. Bishop (Boston: Graupner c. 1826). Both had been previously published in London.

[100] *Cheer Up My Own Jeannette*, w. Charles Jefferys, m. Charles W. Glover (New York: Vanderbeck c. 1850); published earlier in London.

fight for "the star of Empire."[101]

Empire, indeed! Parasitical despots were the ones seeking empire and domination over others. The American sailor would fight not against the helpless, but against those who infringed his liberty— which, historically, included the British navy, because of its high-handed impressment of American tars. The citizens of the United States in those days desired the dethronement of all kings. They celebrated Louis Philippe's fall in France, sympathized with the Greeks in their revolt against the Turks, and gave sanctuary to revolutionists like the Hungarian Louis Kossuth and the Italian Giuseppi Garibaldi.[102] As with most nations, America never admitted to its own yen for empire, exemplified in the Mexican-American War and the annexation of Texas. Yet many Northerners would have exculpated themselves, calling the venture more an affair of the South. Some, like Abraham Lincoln, did openly question the morality of the action. Of course Southern propagandists depicted it as a struggle against a cruel, even sadistic, and arbitrary overlordship, thus justifying American military intervention.

Capturing the attitude toward nation, *The Hunters of Kentucky*, a song born of the War of 1812 and the Battle of New Orleans, in particular, flatly states: "We are a hardy free-born race . . . despising toil and danger." No man weakens "to fear a stranger." "If a daring foe annoys," then "we'll show him that" we "are alligator horses!"[103] Songs of this type also sharpened the sense of mutual loyalty and of accomplishment in confronting danger and subduing faintheartedness cofraternally.

Vis-à-vis other nations, Americans regarded themselves not so much as aggressors as democracy's defenders in spite of a hostile world. Against the machinations of malevolent foreigners, they either united or underwent separate conquest. Accordingly, in one

---

[101] *Cheer! Boys, Cheer!* w. Charles Mackey, m. Henry Russell (New York: Hall c. 1850).

[102] Nye, *Society* 13–14.

[103] *The Hunters of Kentucky*, w. S. Woodworth, arr. William Blondell, as sung by Mr. Petrie (Philadelphia: Willig c. 1824). The specific references are to "Kentucky boys," the embodiments of the new Americans.

song, *The Union Hymn,* Americans were advised, like their fore-fathers, neither to despond nor to despair when threatened by tyrants, but to sally forth boldly, solemnly, and conjointly to defend the freedom they valued: "Oh! sacred union! marriage tie of heaven,/ Who dare divorce what God himself has joined?/ . . . Together! together! a band of brothers all/Together will we stand or fall."[104] Covetous of empire, of foreign riches? Nonsense! Americans, after all, "didn't care a pin for wealth or booty."[105] Such was the myth Americans created about themselves.

They identified, in their songs, with "Columbia's" proud sons, with the "patriotic freemen" fighting and dying with Lawrence on the U.S. Frigate Chesapeake against the British foe, and with all Yankee crews at the front of the nation's defense.[106]

As if prompted by the U.S. Constitution, a recognition of human weakness and a wariness of political figures peeks through the song verses. The demos might become the mark for a demagogue; rabble-rousing might displace an allegiance to rule by law and justice. Therefore, a nation under law was thrust up as a concept of overriding importance. The song *Whilst Happy in My Native Land* warned citizens never to barter away their country's liberties. Every person of whatever background must maintain the "noble mind" that "is not at all by poverty degraded." Advanced is the precept:

> Though small the power which fortune grants,
> And few the gifts she sends us,
> The lordly hireling often wants
> That freedom which defends us;
> By law secured from lawless strife,
> Our house is our castellum.[107]

---

[104] *The Union Hymn,* composed by George J. Webb, in *The American National Song Book* (Boston: Mussey 1842) 72. Much the same message is contained in *Columbia, The Land of the Brave,* w. and m. David T. Shaw (Philadelphia: Willig 1843).

[105] *The Tea Tax,* w. Gentleman of Boston, m. arr. T. Comer (Boston: Bradlee c. 1830).

[106] *The Death of Lawrence,* w. T.W. Tucker, m. Leonard Marshall (Boston: Keith 1847); *A Yankee Ship and a Yankee Crew,* w. J.S. Jones, melody C.M. King, arr. T. Comer (Boston: Parker & Ditson 1837).

[107] *Whilst Happy In My Native Land,* in *The Sailor's Song Book* (Boston: Kidder & Wright 1842), p. 64. Also see Ralph H. Gabriel, *American Values* (Westport, Conn.: Greenwood 1974) 24–25.

At a time of peril, George Washington "came to guard young Freedom's paradise" and proved himself "the prophet of the free,"[108] not a leader desirous of personal advantage. After his example, so also must every American guard "Freedom's pile . . . eternal vigil keeping,"[109] with advantage devolving to all democrats.

A conviction of national mission, of unstoppable destiny courses through contemporary speeches, writings, and vocal music. Lowell, for one, invoked the image of our "irretrievable Destiny," which, he claims, neither Calhoun nor the slave states can threaten. Emerson lectured the Mercantile Library Association on "the expansive and humane spirit" of the United States, "the country of the Future." John L. O'Sullivan, the Jacksonian editor, hyperbolized upon a United States "destined to manifest to mankind the excellence of divine principles, to establish on earth the noblest temple . . . governed by God's natural and moral law of equality, the law of brotherhood."[110]

Among the like-opinioned songs, *The American Star* exalted our nationhood: "To us the high boon by the gods has been granted,/To speed the glad tidings of liberty far." Abandoning all pretense of reticence, *When Freedom on the Battle Storm* called on Americans to "Rule, rule the sea, possess the globe." With missionary zeal, it exhorted:

> Go tell the world, a world is born,
> Another orb gives light,
> Another sun illumes the morn,
> Another star the night;
> Be just, be brave, and let thy name
> Henceforth Columbia be:
> Wear, wear the oaken wreath of fame,
> The wreath of liberty.[111]

---

[108]*Birthday of Washington,* w. G.D. Prentice of Louisville, m. W. Nixon of Cincinnati (New York: Dubois & Bacon c. 1837).

[109]*Battle of Bunker Hill,* w. and m. H.T. Tuckerman (Boston: Ashton 1843). The composition was first sung on 17 July 1843 at an anniversary festival.

[110]Lowell, *Biglow* 90; Emerson, *Essays* 423–30; Nye, *Society* 13.

[111]*The American Star,* in *The Sailor's Song Book* 99; *When Freedom on the Battle Storm,* w. Boston Bard [Robert S. Coffin], m. Gentleman of New York (New York: Sage c. 1823).

Alongside musical compositions mythicizing our singular democratic nation and citizenry were others delineating the archetypal patterns of life that were experienced privately by every human. Turning from examining democratic man in macrocosm, these songs studied him in microcosm. Seemingly without conscious direction, intuitive perceptions underwent transmutation into symbolic narrations. These were reiterated in deliberate fashion and in accordance with a prevailing mode of usage.[112] Thus, the same few ideas received emphasis in countless works. At the same time, certain consistently employed details tended to collect about these ideas, serving to enhance the forcefulness of the expression and to prevent any misunderstanding.

When the protagonist feels happy, he looks on a pleasant scene: streams "murmur," birds "gaily sing," and a "sweet, gentle Nell" floats lightly through the "green vale." When the protagonist sorrows, he views desolation: skies are "dark and threatening," "tortured cries" come over the restless waves, and a "Nell so pale and silent" is borne through "withered fields" to her tomb. Susanne Langer warns: "To regard the presence of borrowed phrases, or indeed of *any* materials however shopworn [as some of the above certainly are], in itself as a criterion of badness is dangerous. Materials are neither good nor bad, strong nor weak. Judgment, therefore, must be guided by the virtual results, the artist's success or failure, which is intuitively known or not at all."[113]

A great many of the symbols contained in popular songs appear Janus-faced, looking on both the joyous and the sad happenings in one's existence. The "clear brook" that happily babbles when "rosy-cheeked Kitty Clyde" rambles beside it, also is the "pallid little stream" close to the grave of "blue-eye'd Nell."[114] The bright flowers that capture the fresh purity of Annie Lisle are also the faded blossoms depicting the ephemeral survival and premature death of

---

[112]See the discussion of these changes as ritualistic concepts, in Langer, *Philosophy* 39–40, 128.

[113]Langer, *Feeling* 406–07.

[114]*Kitty Clyde,* w. and m. L.V.H. Crosby (New York: Firth, Pond 1853); *Darling Little Blue Eyed Nell,* w. B.E. Woolf, m. Frederick Buckley (New York: Firth, Pond 1859).

innocent Lilly Dale.[115] The cheery bells celebrating the village maiden's wedding also chime "sad and slow" in "a requiem soft and low" when "her brow with grief is shaded."[116]

The tree (oak, willow, cypress, or yew) is an especially potent symbol of the eternal and patient life-force. Its spreading leafy boughs protect and comfort as a person stumbles through the world—sheltering the child, screening young sweethearts, shading the traveler, and standing guard over the dead.[117] When an anguished lover exclaims: "I'll hide the maid in a cypress tree/When the footsteps of death draw near," he reveals his faith in the tree's promise to succour the sojourner on earth. The incredible popularity and furor over the Morris-Russell song *Woodman! Spare that Tree!* attests to the weightiness of the image. Here, an oak that has sheltered generation after generation of one family awaits the axe. But the wood chopper's hand is stayed at the last moment with a warning shout:

> Woodman spare that tree!
>   Touch not a single bough,
> In youth it shelter'd me,
>   And I'll protect it now.
>
>   . . . . .
>
> My heart-strings round thee cling,
>   Close as thy bark, old friend!
> Here shall the wild bird sing,
>   And still thy branches bend.
> Old tree! the storm still brave!
>   And woodman, leave the spot;
> While I've a hand to save,
>   Thy axe shall harm it not.[118]

---

[115]*Annie Lisle,* w. and m. H.S. Thompson (Boston: Ditson 1860); *Lilly Dale,* w. and m. H.S. Thompson (Boston: Ditson 1852).

[116]*The Village Maiden,* w. and m. Stephen C. Foster (New York: Firth, Pond 1855).

[117]The rich symbolization of the tree is clearly set forth in *Bell Brandon.* Also see Langer, *Feeling* 227.

[118]*Woodman! Spare that Tree!,* w. George P. Morris, m. Henry Russell (New York: Firth & Hall 1837).

Another cogent device is the dew-tear biformity. The kinship of bedewed flower and wetted cheek appears when a weeping mourner sighs for the love of his youth: "Thy mem'ry be to me/What the dew is to the rose/It shall come as gratefully/In the hour of my repose." The nourishment of tears is likened to that of dew and rain when a grieving husband plants a willow-tree over his wife's grave and states: "I bathed its roots with many a tear/That it might shelter me." Moisture from clouds, atmosphere, or eyes can be like a life-supporting nectar, or a sacrificial offering in remembrance of one being by another; or it can be an outward sign of the spiritual union and flow of feeling between two individuals, or any combination of the three.

Other frequent bifurcated images include those of sleep and death, light and dark, the hearth's warmth and the conflagration's destructive heart. Whatever the benign symbol, we can be certain its *Doppelgänger* lies close.

Each symbol has a complex of connotations. Like a many-toned chord orchestrated variously by a composer, now some meanings are stressed, now others. But always, all the implications of the image vibrate simultaneously in the listener's mind and feelings.

THE GRAND DESIGN

Walter Lippman has said that a fiction will be taken for truth if it is badly needed, and that it can influence behavior to an undeterminable extent.[119] The symbology in serious popular song of the mid-nineteenth century was such a fiction.[120] It did not try to portray earthlings warts and all. Rather, it attempted to hold the Ideal before us, to demonstrate the possible consequences of diverging from that Ideal—however necessary or forced the divergence—and to suggest ways of returning to the Ideal.

---

[119]Walter Lippmann, *Public Opinion* (New York: Harcourt, Brace 1922) 19–21.

[120]Richard Chase, *Quest for Myth* (Baton Rouge: Louisiana State University Press 1949) 111, states: "We live in the same world as the savages. Our deepest experience, needs, and aspirations are the same, as surely as the crucial biological and psychic transitions occur in the life of every human being and force culture to take account of them in aesthetic forms."

Implicit in this delineation was a religious ambiance. Assuredly the supreme symbol of the Ideal was God. He figures in song after song, whether named or understood. The percentage of the public who were church members had doubled between 1800 and 1850. The religious read the Bible closely and regarded it as a symbol of the family's link to divinity. Its pages guarded the family's record of births, marriages, and deaths over several generations; its wisdom could guide the troubled through every dilemma. In addition to the written Word, otherworldly manifestations might occur to the quick and ready and also bring revelation; or so Americans were inclined to believe. By mid-century a rampant spiritualism, personified in the Fox sisters, had pervaded much of the country.[121] Many songs took on an imagery influenced by the Bible and the spiritual world.

These were decades when hymns, especially those of Lowell Mason, became people's songs: *Nearer My God to Thee, From Greenland's Icy Mountains, My Faith Looks Up to Thee;* and when some popular songs became almost indistinguishable from hymns. Certain propositions about man's relation to God, the givens in most serious songs, now and again are made explicit. A few compositions openly state that God can create or destroy, upraise the humble or cast down the arrogant.[122] These two aspects of divinity are portrayed in the song *He Doeth All Things Well,* where a little sister is adored while God is forgotten:

> Years fled—that little sister then, was dear as life to me,
>> And awoke, in my unconscious heart, a wild idolatry,
> I worshipped at an earthly shrine, lured by some magic spell,
>> Forgetful of the praise of Him "who doeth all things well."

Beautiful and pure though she is, "the Destroyer" kills the child.

> I remember well my sorrow, as I stood beside her bed,
>> And my deep and heartfelt anguish when they told me *she was dead;*
> And oh! that cup of bitterness—*let not my heart rebel;*
>> God gave—He took—He will restore—*"He doeth all things well."*[123]

[121]Douglas, *Feminization* 24; [Mitchell], *Dream Life,* by Ik Marvel (New York: Scribner 1854) 99; Nye, *Society* 315; Brooks, *Flowering* 61.

[122]Gabriel, *American Values* 62; Stewart, *American Literature* 59.

[123]*He Doeth All Things Well,* w. F.M.E., m. Isaac B. Woodbury (Boston: Reed 1844).

The brother must learn to adore God alone, without question—this is the song's important lesson.

Nor is the admonition an isolated one. It recurs in *The Mother's Vow*, among other songs. The subject is a mother begging God to save the dying child she loves completely. She vows:

> Oh God, if in this heart enshrined—
>   The object of each thought,—
> I've made thy gift [her child] an idol there,
>   The Giver quite forgot;—
> Forgive the sin—Oh spare my child!—
>   Henceforth my aim shall be
> To take this idol from its throne,
>   And give my heart to Thee.

God relents. Her child revives. But the song ends on a question:

> *But O, remembered she the vow*
> *She made to God above?*[124]

The course of spiritual growth continued throughout life and involved a person's persuasion to adhere to Christian principles. While any individual lived, he should never be considered unalterably lost to sin. Any sin, which fettered the soul with its craving for mundane things, would dissolve when a person grew more aware of his God, the comforter and forgiver.[125] True and lasting happiness arrived when one could pray without reservation, as in the song *To Jesus the Crown of My Hope:*

> Dissolve Thou the bands that detain
>   My soul from her portion in Thee,
> Oh strike off the adamant chain,
>   And make me eternally free.
> Then that happy era begins
>   When arrayed in Thy glory I shine
> And no longer pain with my sins,
>   The bosom on which I recline.[126]

---

[124] *The Mother's Vow*, w. E. Bradford, m. H. Waters (Boston: Ordway 1848).
[125] See Ahlstrom, *Religious History* 611; Longfellow, *Letters* I, 97–98.
[126] *To Jesus the Crown of My Hope*, m. Oliver Shaw (Providence: Shaw 1834).

The God–man viewpoint just exposed is a vital warp in all serious songs. It threads through a complex mythology that explores man's passage through life in ritualistic terms; a mythology never entirely revealed in one work but having a cumulative impact when singers progressed from one composition to another. The consistency in the reappearance of the same limited number of situations argues for their significance in American thinking.

Emerson was convinced his age had a mythology. He maintained that any "true symbol of our human life is a perpetual series of transits," for "everything teaches transition, transference, metamorphosis."[127] What he had in mind was his society's way of picturing a human's movement from one state to another: birth, childhood, youth, maturity, old age, and death.

The series of transits has had a full exposition in Arnold van Gennep's *Les Rites de Passage* (Paris: Nourry, 1909). Gennep establishes that the human "rites of passage" are marked out in three distinct stages: (1) of a person's stable young life and his eventual separation from it; (2) of a betwixt-and-between existence where one knows neither who he is nor where he belongs; and (3) of the return to stability and the harmonious readjustment to a society, which now recognizes his previous efforts and honors his accomplishments. The reconciliation of Gennep's ideas to the symbolic life of Americans has been attempted by W. Lloyd Warner, among others.[128]

Several writers, like Richard Chase and Daniel Hoffman, give a somewhat different emphasis to the transitions. They claim that the overriding myth in American fiction concerns man's nature before the Fall, his separation from innocence, his initiation into life and the possible defeat of all his hopes, and finally his symbolic death and rebirth.[129]

When we turn to the evidence in the American popular songs composed between 1830 and 1860, we find delineated an unmistakable progression in the human condition. Going from birth to death, the way stations may be designated as the life of innocence, the de-

---

[127]Emerson, *Journals* X, 76, 109–10, 146.
[128]Warner, *The Living* 303.
[129]See, for example, Hoffman, *Form and Fable* xi, 10.

parture from innocence, the trial of the life in experience, and death and reconciliation. The great majority of the serious songs group themselves into these four divisions. In the chapters that follow, I propose, first, to examine the American attitudes manifested in these compositions; next, to study the antithetical statement made by comic songs; and last, to consider the music to both serious and comic works for symbolical meanings beyond the context of the sound *per se*.

CHAPTER 2

Sojourning in Paradise

The American setting for humankind's spiritual youthhood was in a prelapsarian arcadia. This Eden of popular song, the fabulous creation of nineteenth-century minds, existed usually in a time gone by, imagined as surrounded by the flawed time present. It was a vision revealed in elusive glimpses, never as something that one could believe had once been palpably there. Significantly, this rural paradise frequently appeared in a dream—the singer, as it were, questing the unconscious for a particular archetypal symbolization to assist his coming to terms with what he has become.[1] The greater the perceived external and inner evils, the greater was the need for the dream. Arcadia became song's subject more and more frequently as the years of civil war approached.

A beautiful countryside gave habitation to an ideal society, which nineteenth-century Americans like Emerson longed to join but found "always to be only a dream, a song, a . . . vision of living." The very few "heroes" who miraculously managed to bridge the

---

[1] Carl Jung writes, in "Approaching the Unconscious," in Jung *et al., Man and His Symbols* (New York: Dell 1968) 74-75, that man has "a hallowed archetypal dream" of paradise, where everything is provided for everyone, and where there is justice and wisdom. "The sad truth is that man's real life consists of a complex of inexorable opposites—day and night, birth and death, happiness and misery, good and evil. We are not even sure that one will prevail against the other, that good will overcome evil, or joy defeat pain. Life is a battleground. It always has been, and always will be."

gap between the ideal and their lives became "a celestial sign to all succeeding souls as they journied through nature."[2] On the other hand, the multitude attempted to achieve the ideal but confronted an impossible obstacle, the actual world. For brief moments only, members of the crowd looked on a musical landscape of consummate delight but always returned to that self which was a collection of unintegrated perceptions following one upon the other. The ordinary person resembled the diffident Emily Dickinson, who wrote: "I think of the perfect happiness I experienced while I felt I was an heir to heaven as of a delightful dream, out of which the Evil One bid me wake and again return to the world and its pleasures."[3]

Edgar Allan Poe, in "The Landscape Garden" (tells), of "four unvarying laws, or rather elementary principles, of Bliss." They comprise healthy, unfettered movement in the open countryside, love of woman, absence of ambition, and unceasing pursuit of objects endowed with the highest spirituality.[4] All four of Poe's modes of conduct help give coherence to the imaginative region described in the song lyrics. Bliss, in the songs, is also thought of as an outcrop of true artlessness. Neither guilt nor sin mars the scene. Hearts remain pure; minds guileless; manners easy and natural. The "I" of the lyric joins a loving and caring community, where all things and all people are intersupportive.[5] The scene that materializes remains serene, pleasing, and salutary; its parts combine to soothe and revive the heart's oppressed core.

---

[2] Ralph Waldo Emerson, *The Journals and Miscellaneous Notebooks,* XI Vols. (Cambridge, Mass.: Bellknapp Press 1969-1975) X, ed. Merton M. Sealts, Jr. (1973), 10.

[3] Emily Dickinson, *Letters,* 2 vols., ed. Thomas H. Johnson (Cambridge, Mass.: Belknap Press 1965) I, 30.

[4] Edgar Allan Poe, "The Landscape Garden" in *Works,* (New York: Redfield 1856) IV, 337.

[5] Willard Gaylin, *Feelings* (New York: Harper & Row 1979) 54–55, writes that this desire for a sense of community is "a biological necessity" for human survival. "The human being is human because of the nurture of other human beings, and absent this, will not survive."

THE DREAM OF INNOCENCE

In no way does any sort of wilderness intrude on this paradise-garden. On the contrary, song lyrics usually portray uncultivated and uncontrolled nature as a malignant realm of destructive storms, engulfing seas, and obdurate forests. Without remorse, a hostile environment visits cold, heat, thirst, starvation, and violence upon the unwary and defenseless. Those men and women who continually claw their way through this ferocious hinterland and fail to transcend its brutalizing impact are in danger of turning into passion-ridden, depraved monsters of a type frequently seen in America's western wilds.[6] Nowhere is there a trace of the noble children of noncivilized nature that James Fenimore Copper wrote about in his Leatherstocking tales. The wilderness is a place best avoided. It is no wonder that in the song *Down in Alabam* the relieved protagonist joyously sings out "aint I glad I got out de wilderness," and away from "de wild goose nation," when he returns to his plantation home, his roaming days over.[7]

The first of the "principles of Bliss" is invariably portrayed in song as activity conducted in a gardenized parkland, a fertile spot sheltered from the life-threatening wilderness. The singer could leave "strife and ambition" behind for as long as the song lasted, steal away for an instant's "healthful regrowth into the darling Past," and reexperience "Spring's young balmy time/Where ev'ry blossom seems a bride."[8]

Although homes, churches, and plowed fields—the handiwork of

---

[6]Harriet Martineau *Society in America,* 3 vols. (London: Saunders & Otley 1837) I, 28; Henry Nash Smith, *Virgin Land: The American West as Symbol and Myth* (Cambridge, Mass.: Harvard University Press 1950) 215–18; David Grimsted, "Melodrama as Echo of the Historically Voiceless," in Tamara K. Hareven ed., *Anonymous Americans* (Englewood Cliffs, N.J.: Prentice-Hall 1971) 86.

[7]*Down in Alabam,* w. and m. J. Warner, arr. Walter Meadows (New York: Hall 1858).

[8][Donald G. Mitchell], *Dream Life,* by Ik Marvel (New York: Scribner, 1854) 115. The two lines of verse are from the song *Agnes May,* w. Anson C. Chester, m. Henry Tucker (New York: Firth, Pond 1853).

humans—are visible in the musical landscape, their appearance in the graceful and congenial scene is seen as proof of God's concern for the living and as an earthly stage in human existence meant to betoken God's promise of an immortal spiritual state after death. All thing considered, the lover of song was also a Bible-reading lover of God. Home, church, and greening furrow symbolized human conduct in complete harmony with God and expressive of God's intimate connection with terrestrial things. Ostensibly the result of man's efforts, all three required a divine infusion to make them viable. Thus, an unpublished version of Dan Emmett's *Dixie* (a name given to one arcadian manifestation) had read:

> Dis worl' was made in jis six days
> An' finished up in various ways—
>   Look away! look away! look away!
>   Dixieland.
> Dey den made Dixie trim and nice
> But Adam called it Paradise—
>   Look away! look away! look away!
>   Dixieland.[9]

It is fascinating to discover how many songs locate felicity's domain in the American southland. Even Abolitionist composers like Benjamin Hanby saw nothing incongruous in writing a composition condemning slavery and the horror of having a wife, forcibly separated from her husband, dragged in chains "to Georgia for to wear her life away/As she toils in the cotton and the cane," and at the same time describing the location of her congenial home as follows:

> There's a low green valley on the old Kentucky shore,
>   There I've whiled many happy hours away,
> A sitting and a singing by the little cottage door
>   Where lived my darling Nelly Gray.

---

[9]Constance Rourke, *American Humor* (Garden City, N.Y.: Doubleday, 1953) 77; see also H. Marion Stephens, *Home Scenes and Home Sounds* (Boston: Fetridge 1854) 140; Gordon Milne, *George William Curtis and the Genteel Tradition* (Bloomington: Indiana University Press 1956) 21. The unpublished stanza of *"Dixie"* is printed in Hans Nathan, *Dan Emmett and The Rise of Early Negro Minstrelsy* (Norman: University of Oklahoma Press, 1962), 254.

Her joyous existence along the "old Kentucky shore" ended, Nelly Gray regains it only when she enters heaven.[10]

The determination to locate arcadian territory on some "shore," whether the reference is appropriate or not (and singing of a "Kentucky shore" is definitely mystifying), affects a number of compositions. Yet, it makes symbolic sense. Eden becomes, not universal, but contained within boundaries. It becomes a place where one disembarks and sojourns for only a limited time. A static shore reposes beside restless waters. The contingent body of water, unfixed and unfamiliar, stays in readiness to bear a person away after completion of the first stage in the human passage through life. In another sense, "shore" conveys the idea of underpinning and support, for one important characteristic of the paradisial concept is that it will continue to sustain the individual through all of life's subsequent stages. Finally, the shore exists to permit a person to eventually board ship and journey toward another "distant shore" that terminates life's journey with death and subsequent arrival at the transcendent domain of God.

Why the South as the "home" of man's desire? First, the South was what remained of the American past that was still unchanged by modern innovation. It continued rural, while the North was rapidly becoming industrialized and urbanized. Second, its climate was milder and its earth richer, compared with the North's more frigid winters and thin, rocky soils. Then again, the normal place of residence for blacks—the chief characters of the extremely successful minstrel songs—was the Southern farmland, less the Northern city. Therefore, when the black's "home" was depicted in song, perforce it was located below the northeastern states. Although singers knew full well what the real South stood for (they certainly were not flocking to live there), they executed an imaginative sleight-of-hand to transmute the actuality into an idealized pastoral country denominated variously as old Virginny, old Kentucky, Dixie, and whatnot.

"Way down upon de Swanee ribber/Far, far away" is the focus of Foster's longing. " 'Twas in a southern grove I dwelt/No sorrow then I knew" sings and unhappy reminiscer. "In soft repose I'll

---

[10] *Darling Nelly Gray*, w. and m. Benjamin R. Hanby (Boston: Ditson 1856).

sleep/And dream for ebermore/Dat you've carried me back to Old Virginny/To Old Virginny's shore," whispers an enfeebled oldster. In "Dixie's land," "old times dar am not forgotten" maintains an otherwise bumptious comic.[11]

Songs other than the minstrel compositions, however, normally prefer to locate their dreamworld away from the American southland; in quiet valleys by gentle streams, as in "the vale of the Mohawk" that is lauded in *Bonny Eloise;* less often at a seashore, as in *O Give Me a Home By the Sea.* Occasionally, the singer o'erleaps the temperate clime and describes an improbably fecund jungle-garden complete with waving palms and scented orange blossoms, as in *The Captive's Lament.*[12]

Wherever the locale, its landscape normally includes a modest church, one-room schoolhouse, and rustic mill in intimate relationship to the singer. They are proposed as optimal and objectified signs of worship, learning, and work. They stand for what should be, or what might have been, but that no longer is found in people's lives. The rural church is not your fashionable and imposing urban edifice, but one erected by humble villagers of yore and dear to their descendants, who continue strong in their faith.[13] The schoolhouse rejects the impersonality found in the city school of multiple classrooms and faceless educators. The mill has nothing in common with the Lowell factory complex:

> Oh! don't you remember the wood, Ben Bolt,
> Near the green sunny slope of the hill,

[11]*Old Folks at Home,* w. and m. Stephen C. Foster (New York: Firth, Pond 1851): *The Young Folks at Home,* w. Frank Spencer, m. Hattie Livingston (New York: Gould & Berry 1852); *Carry Me Back to Old Virginia,* as arr. and sung by E.P. Christy (New York: Jacques & Bros. 1847); *Dixie's Land,* w. and m. Dan D. Emmett (Boston: Ditson 1860), respectively.

[12]*Bonnie Eloise,* w. George W. Elliott, m. J.R. Thomas (New York: Hall 1858); *O Give Me a Home By the Sea,* w. and m. E.A. Hosmer (Boston: Reed 1853); *The Captive's Lament,* w. by a member of the Massachusetts Female Emancipation Society, m. S.C. Fessenden (Boston: Ditson 1844), respectively.

[13]*The Church of Our Fathers,* w. Robert Story, m. Robert Guylott (Boston: Bradlee 1847); *The Church Within the Wood,* w. and m. George F. Root (Boston: Richardson 1855).

Where oft we have sung 'neath its wide spreading shade,
  And kept time to the click of the mill.

. . . . .

Oh! don't you remember the school, Ben Bolt,
  And the Master so kind and so true,
And the little nook by the clear running brook,
  Where we gather'd flow'rs as they grew.[14]

Another song tells us the lovely byway that harbors these buildings is:

A nook in the forest—a sweet retreat,
  From the tumult of men in the noisy street,
From the city's trade—the hum of the crowd,
  As they wended forth with their voices loud.[15]

The usual scene sparkles in sunny daylight; the season is spring or summer. Waters flash, flowers radiate color, and birds carol brilliantly. The yeoman tills his field, the oldster rests at his doorsill, the child plays, and the maiden trips weightlessly through an inviting woodland. In some songs the child's day unfolds differently. He hears the schoolmaster's handbell call in order to teach him wisdom; the mother's voice, to teach morality; the church bell's summons, to teach love of God. Doubt and protest never intrude to blemish the picture.

Evening in arcadia also presents an image of peace, harmony, and integration with nature. Darkness is absent, because if night is not to betoken death and the underworld, it must introduce light. Emerson once wrote of the month of July: "Night . . . in this enchanting Season is not night but a miscellany of lights. The journeying twilight, the half-moon, the kindling Venus, the beaming Jove."[16] A

---

[14]*Ben Bolt,* m. Nelson Kneass, adapted from an old German melody (Louisville: Peters 1848).

[15]*Oh Give Me a Home 'Neath the Old Oak Tree,* m. Isaac B. Woodbury (New York: Gordon 1855).

[16]Emerson, *Journals,* VII, ed. A.W. Plumstead and Harrison Hayford (1969), 230.

typical song begins: "In the sky the bright stars glittered/On the grass the moonlight shone."[17]

A fulfilled couple may sometimes be discerned in the twilight: "Ben Fisher had finished his hard days work/And sat at his cottage door,/His good wife Kate sat by his side./And the moonlight danced on the floor."[18] More often, a loving youth and maid wander through a hushed glade:

> Oh! Come along wid me, love, come wid me,
>   de stars am shining bright,
> While de silver moon am gilden ebry tree
>   Wid her galvanicumizing light.[19]

Most often, a suitor whispers up to his sleeping beloved to leave off dreaming and descend to enjoy the lovely quietude below:

> 'Tis midnight hour, the moon shines bright,
>   The dew drops blaze beneath her ray,
> The twinkling stars their trembling light
>   Like beauty's eyes display;
> Then sleep no more tho' round thy heart
>   Some tender dream may idly play,
> For midnight song with magic art
>   Shall chase that dream away.
>
> 'Tis midnight hour, from flow'r to flow'r
>   The wayward zephyr floats along,
> Or lingers in the shaded bow'r
>   To hear the night bird's song.
> Then sleep no more . . .[20]

LOVE

Love, the second of Poe's "principles of Bliss," is fundamental to popular song. Its nurturing and direction toward a proper goal ap-

---

[17] *When I Saw Sweet Nelly Home,* m. P.S. Gilmore (Boston: Reed 1856).

[18] *Ben Fisher,* w. Francis D. Gage, m. L.V.H. Crosby (Boston: Ditson 1853).

[19] *Come Along Wid Me,* m. H. Avery (Philadelphia: Couenhaven 1853).

[20] *'Tis Midnight Hour,* m. by an Amateur (Boston: Reed 1843).

pears as a paramount consideration in the realm of innocence, if a human expects to succeed to the knowledge of virtue, verity, and beauty. Lurking at the same time in the mind of the singer is the cognizance that love, however happy its beginnings, also signals that man's destiny is to die. In holding another dear, an individual feels first the loved one's happiness; next, the loved one's heartaches and frustrations; and later, the necessity for the loved one's death. While only the happiness exists in arcadia, every man's further journeying through life leads to a deepening of the experience, until love tempered in pain and crisis becomes the steel stiffening the will to withstand all adversities, and the incandescence to illumine truth in all its dimensions. But first, like a babe new from the womb, love is born in innocence of the future.[21]

In popular song, love comprised neither self-indulgent sexual desire, nor an urge for procreative coupling, but a tender affection for, and a watchful cherishing of, one person by another. In addition, song lyrics make clear that love signified close companionship and solicitous concern for another's well-being. It meant an emotional dedication that forced an individual to come out of his shell in order to become one with something greater than himself.[22] Lastly, to nineteenth-century Americans, love was "the ultimate [Christian] image that is able to unite all men . . . [and] the answer to the emotional disturbance and aggressiveness of" their age.[23]

A paragraph from a letter George William Curtis wrote to his wife, in 1860, shows how another of Poe's principles—the absence of ambition and its attendant aggressiveness—can come through love: "I suppose no man who loves as truly as I do you and who knows himself loved as I feel I am is very much troubled by external ambition. Love is a spur to action certainly, but not to selfish action, which is the law of ambition. A man can be ruled by only one central

[21]See Rollo May, *Love and Will* (New York: Norton 1969) 100–02; Lewis Mumford, *The Conduct of Life* (New York: Harcourt Brace Jovanovich 1970) 66–67; Clemens E. Benda, *The Image of Love* (New York: Free Press of Glencoe 1961) 5.

[22]For a discussion of the different types of love, see May, *Love* 37; Ernest Becker, *The Denial of Death* (New York, Free Press 1973) 152; Eric Fromm, *The Art of Loving* (New York: Harper & Bros. 1956) 18, 26, 33–34.

[23]Benda, *Image of Love* 2.

passion . . . and mine, thank Heaven! is love, not ambition."[24]

The love portrayed in American popular songs is always human-centered and through humans, God-centered. Never, for example, is nature loved romantically for itself alone, as it is in some contemporary British songs. Charles Horn's *The Breaking of Day*, published for the London public and reprinted in America around 1835, sings nature's praises without reference to affection for another human:

> The sun is in the mountain,
>> His beam lies on the sea,
> And far and near is echo'd loud,
>> The sky lark's melody.
> The Hind plods o'er the dewy field,
>> And hails the rising ray,
> As he feels while he steals,
>> The breaking of the day.

Note the contrast with Foster's *Dolly Day*, where nature must take second place to humans:

> I like to see de clover
>> Dat grows about de lane,
> I like to see de 'bacco plant,
>> I like de sugar cane.
> But on de old plantation
>> Der's nothing half so gay,
> Der's nothing dat I love so much
>> As my sweet Dolly Day.[25]

When morning breaks, in American song, as it does in Woodbury's *Dream No Longer, Maiden Fair*, flowers shine with dewy droplets, "spicy groves" fill with bird song, breezes carry the fragrance of blooming roses, and "sweetly humming" bees flit from blossom to blossom. The composer, however, does not leave it at that. He has purposely delineated a day fit for young innocence to awaken into. The protagonist summons his beloved to awaken. Only because she

---

[24]Milne, *Curtis* 107.

[25]*Dolly Day*, w. and m. Stephen C. Foster (Baltimore: Benteen 1850).

exists and he cares about her can he say: "Love and joy are in the scene."[26]

Passion as vehement overmastering emotion participated in no portion of the love so described. To the American public such intense feeling was an external influence exerting a power alien to one's true nature. Possession, not commitment, was its consequence. No spiritual union or achievement of transcendent selfhood resulted from its gratification. It desired to take from another, without thought of joint sharing. Like people of all ages, the men and women of these decades did feel and act to satisfy powerful sexual drives. But their conventions precluded singing about them in serious ballads and most comic ditties, and never with reference to a visionary arcadia, where no symbolic necessity existed for passion's depiction.[27]

Love, of course, did result in marriage and the begetting of children. James Fenimore Cooper, for one, was proud that "love, in this country, nineteen times in twenty, leads to matrimony"; that unlike Europe, here "pure heartfelt affection," not negotiation, joined two people together. Only a British song like *A Daughter's Love* would have a girl reject every suitor and fear to feel anything " 'till a parent's choice approve the object I must yet adore." Obedience first is a motto absent from American lyrics.

Nevertheless, Cooper was exercising a bit of hyperbole. He and other Americans knew that if marriages veered from the rocks of passion or loveless arrangement, they might still go aground in the shoals of mere infatuation. They recognized that after mere physical attraction had had its day and had melted away, which it inevitably did, every marriage had to pass "the riper judgment of manhood." Every husband had to learn to receive a woman's affections as a gift,

---

[26]*Dream No Longer Maiden Fair*, m. Isaac B. Woodbury (New York: Hall 1849).

[27]For more on the effects of passion, see [Mitchell], *Dream Life* 186–90; Sydney E. Ahlstrom, *A Religious History of the American People* (New Haven, Conn.: Yale University Press 1972) 485; Benda, *Image of Love* 16–19; Havelock Ellis, *More Essays of Love and Virtue* (Garden City, N.Y.: Doubleday, Doran 1931) 2–3. William W. Sanger, *The History of Prostitution* (New York: Harper 1858) 75, writes about sexual appetite in nineteenth-century America. Despite a reluctance to admit publicly to such desire, New York City's prostitutes interviewed by Sanger gave "inclination" as a main reason for becoming prostitutes.

"the sweet retired dalliance of a wife's chaste embrace, and not as the gages of a harlot's constant inconstancy."[28] On occasion a song is discovered that makes a distinction between lasting love and superficial infatuation. Stephen Foster's *A Penny for Your Thoughts* hints at sexual attraction, when a penny is offered for the "little, wicked darts" that "are sporting with" a lover's "brain." Bluntly Foster warns that this sort of affection is insubstantial: "Do you think that you will love her/When all those burning dreams have flitted from your heart?" As if to prove the impermanency of such ties, the object of the suitor's attentions soon gives her affection, about which she has thought little and felt less, to another. Foster's conclusion is: "Fair maids [like this one], though full of vows, are fickle and untrue."[29]

Inconstancy as here described can have no place within an idealized paradise. All love is deep, all hearts are true in arcadia. Lovers exhibit the utmost devotion toward each other, married couples have already lived through the testing period and stripped their relationship of its dross, and parents and children thrive on mutual goodwill. Not an individual is found in American song who, like the Adonis in the British composition *Even As the Sun*, willingly admits that "hunting he loved but love he laugh'd to scorn," or like the eulogist in another British composition, *Beauty's Queen*, ardently worships beauty in a woman for beauty's sake alone, and without moral or religious justification.[30]

Although innocents have few premonitions of later suffering, and arcadian love paints the world "springtime fresh," the singer is often a saddened male looking back on days long gone, when he "fondly

---

[28]Respectively, James Fenimore Cooper, *Notions of the Americans*, (1828), reprint (New York: Ungar, 1963) I, 196; *A Daughter's Love*, w. W.T. Moncrieff, m. J. Cooke (New York: Mesier c 1830); [Mitchell], *Dream Life* 194; James Russell Lowell, *Letters, Vol. I,* in Vol. XIV of *The Complete Writings of James Russell Lowell*, (New York: AMS 1966) 101. See also William A. Alcott, *The Young Wife* (Boston: Light 1837), 69–70.

[29]*A Penny for Your Thoughts*, w. and m. Stephen C. Foster (Boston: Ditson 1861).

[30]*Even As the Sun*, m. Charles E. Horn (New York: Mesier c. 1830); *Beauty's Queen*, w. Edmund Smith, m. John A. Barnett (New York: Atwill c. 1837).

[31]*Blue-Eyed Jeannie*, w. and m. J.R. Thomas (Boston: Tolman 1856).

deemed that life was one long summer-time of love."[31] He urges the young to "Love now! ere the heart feel a sorrow;/Or the bright sunny moments are flown;/Love now! for the dawn of the morrow/May find thee unloved and alone."[32] Interestingly, the above song, *Love Now!*, which had wide American currency, was in rebuttal to the British song *Love Not!*, which found love painful and best avoided, since nothing is lasting and every living thing dies.

Americans rarely associated love with constant happiness. Paradisial life was but a primary stage in existence. Song viewed innocent affection from a vantage point later in time, after men and women, like H. Marion Stephens, had learned that "earth is all around us" and "in time the few dear ones of *my* love will be claimed, as others have been. Those who love most suffer most; why should I be exempt?" Note, she does not say "love not."[33] She might, however, have injected the strong Christian belief that, yes, people dwell a short period on earth; but love will continue and loved ones will be born again into immortality. As the song *Yes! Tis True that Thy Kate Now Is Sleeping* states of the dead: "For by day and by night she is near thee,/Tho' she rests now in peace beneath the sod,/ . . . For a love that can not fade or perish,/Watcheth all thy pathway o'er."[34] In such works love becomes the vital impulse, the cardinal force in the struggle against death.[35] One loves not for pleasure, not voluntarily; one loves because he must.

The unfeeling human stands helpless, isolated, and anxious. He needs and searches for love. His unease showing, the singer in Foster's *Molly! Do You Love Me?* pleads:

> Though the tender blossoms
> Need the summer light,
> Let our hearts, united,
> Brave affliction's blight.

---

[32] *Love Now*, w. "Dr. L.", m. R.C. Clarkson (Philadelphia: Ferrett c. 1844).

[33] Stephens, *Home* 157.

[34] *Yes! 'Tis True that Thy Kate Now Is Sleeping*, m. Charles Jarvis (Philadelphia: Gould 1853).

[35] On this subject, see May, *Love* 86; Fromm, *Art of Loving* 8; Jacques Choron, *Modern Man and Mortality* (New York: Macmillan 1964) 157.

Repeatedly, he asks:

> Molly! do you love me?
> Tell me, tell me true![36]

The more we examine the songs, the more we realize that in them love is made to pervade every moment of human existence. In one composition an adored voice permeates the air and vibrates in a man's ear as he sallies forth into the world: "Nelly Bly hab a voice like de turtle dove,/I hears it in de meadow and I hears it in de grove." In another, tender feeling turns into a powerful specific against pain: "Love's bewitching in the moonlight,/Care and trouble now be gone." In still another, affection serves as an earthly guide, for through the medium of love, the dead "not present in spirit yet were near,/And as we toiled and struggled,/Did whisper in our ear."[37]

In conclusion, love first shines forth in innocent Eden-tie; then it "cheers and blesses" even through "Life's declining moments;" and last, it becomes man's sole companion into immortality.[38]

WOMAN

Woman is love animated. Speaking for his generation, Oliver Wendell Holmes wanted her "as true as Death" and "moulded in the rose-red clay of Love, before the breath of life made a moving mortal of her."[39] The more song lyrics are read through, the more they convince the reader that the woman they depict represents man's

---

[36]*Molly! Do You Love Me?* w. and m. Stephen C. Foster (Baltimore: Benteen 1850).

[37]*Nelly Bly,* w. and m. Stephen C. Foster (New York: Firth, Pond 1850); *Silver Midnight Winds,* w. and m. John P. Ordway (Boston: Ordway 1858); *'Tis Sweet to Be Remembered,* w. John S. Adams, m. George O. Farmer (Boston: Ditson 1849).

[38]*When I Saw Sweet Nellie Home,* m. John Fletcher (New York: Pond 1859). Another popular song based on the same lyric was composed by P.S. Gilmore (see note 17).

[39]Oliver Wendell Holmes, *The Autocrat of the Breakfast-Table* (1858), reprinted in Vol. I of *Works,* 14 vols. (Boston: Houghton Mifflin 1891–1892), 270.

steadfast psychic core given archetypal form. She is the *anima* that Jung describes, the feminine principle, as opposed to the *animus,* the masculine principle. She represents the true inner self concealed by the *persona,* the outer surface of personality.[40] She illustrates Emerson's claim, in the 1840s, that Man-Woman is in every person as action-idea. She is described over a hundred years later by the psychiatrist M.L. von Franz, in terms of the feminine personification of man's inmost being, which contains the "psychological tendencies in a man's psyche, such as vague feelings and moods, prophetic hunches, receptiveness to the irrational capacity for personal love, feeling for nature, and—last but not least—his relation to the unconscious." She is a mediator between "ego" and "self," and a guide to the human inner world.[41]

It is significant that song depicts woman, whether virginal maiden or saintly mother, as the bearer of God's word to humankind. In earlier decades, American Protestantism had attempted to substitute a more masculine, active concept of divinity to replace the soft-toned worship of Catholicism's Virgin Mary. Now it found itself giving way to the cult of an incognito Virgin Mary, which was swiftly materializing in the New World. She became the spiritual and moral ideal against which to measure the rightness or wrongness of every action. Though quiet, gentle, and unobtrusive, she had the overwhelming persuasiveness and power that only purity, goodness, and a limitless capacity for unselfish affection could bestow. We find her in Stephen Foster's *Little Ella,* where he tells of an "earthly cherub coming nearest to my dreams of forms divine"; she offers a "bright presence" that "solace brings," and "her spontaneous love restrains me from a thousand selfish things." The obscure recesses of conscience are though to be illumined by her. The composer John Ordway states in a song lyric that "like the queen of night," she comes to bless and "fill darkest space with loveliness."[42]

[40]Jung, "Approaching," in Jung *et al. Man* 17.

[41]Emerson, *Journals* VIII, ed. William H. Gilman and J.E. Parsons (1970), 356; XI, ed. A.M. Plumstead and William H. Gilman (1975), 53; M.L. von Franz, "The Process of Individuation," in Jung *et al., Man* 186–87, 195.

[42]*Little Ella,* w. and m. Stephen C. Foster (New York: Firth, Pond 1853); *Twinkling Stars Are Laughing, Love,* w. and m. John P. Ordway (Boston: Ordway 1855).

Because the American male wanted and needed to believe fervently in women as representatives of human virtue, not surprisingly for the society of the time more than a few women did try to conduct themselves in accord with this belief. Humans in every age are taught to play roles, to put on public faces that, amazingly enough, often change into an outward enactment of what they wish to become within themselves. This was no less true of nineteenth-century Americans. Possibly American women of mid-century put what they perceived to be societal needs above their own personal needs. For whatever the reason, they also desired to please their men. They had little desire to be taken as flinty characters who refused to be tricked into what a later age would interpret as a demeaning status. Seeing the shambles that threatened their communities, they knew that someone had to appear morally firm in order to recement human relationships. And that someone might as well be they. Even the militant women's liberationists of the times saw the female as superior to the male in virtue, steadfastness, and the capacity to love—and as bringers of rule to the hopeless spiritual tangles men got themselves into.

We can discover nineteenth-century women studying the Bible, singing uplifting songs, elevating suitors and husbands to feelings of moral purpose and responsibility toward others, and generating criteria of refinement or checking incivility and lawlessness. Dazzled by what he thought was the abundant goodness of many of the American women he knew, Cooper decided they were special designs of nature meant to serve as "repositories of the better principles." One foreign commentator on the American nation agreed with Cooper. In Alexis de Tocqueville's description of *Democracy in America,* this French writer asserts that an American source of inherent power was the high moral standard of women. Yet, he also observed, unlike her European counterpart, the American girl before marriage had learned to think for herself and was allowed to speak freely. Nothing was concealed from her. She viewed her society without illusion or fear. She learned self-reliance and confidence at an early age. When such an upbringing was united to high ideals, then women grew into an active force whose influence was evident in every phase of man's life. Furthermore, they had the capacity to cope with any emergency that might arise.[43]

A seriocomic monologue by William Levison, published in his *Black Diamond* of 1857, gives us some notion of woman's various manifestations in antebellum popular literature:

> Let us be born as young, as ugly and as helpless as we plese, a woman's arms am open to recebe us. She it am who gubs us our fuss dose ob castor oil, and puts cloze 'pon our helplessly naked lims, and cubbers up our foots and toeses in long flannel petticoats, and it am she who, as we grow up, fills our dinner basket wid doenuts and apples as we start to skool, and licks us when we tare our trowsers. It am she who in our manhood makes de moon brighter and bigger, and de stars to twinkle in de ferminence wid de splendid glory (for take woman out ob de world, and night would lose de moss ob its beauty). It am she who robs trouble ob haff its sting, when de trouble ain't 'bout anudder woman. It am she who teaches us wortue and goodness fru life, providin she ain't bankrupt in boff ob dem herself. It am she who makes de sweetmeets and home-made kakes. It am she who watches in de sick room, and gubs you de calomal and jollop, and rubug and curren jelly—and it am she who sticks to you in de lass hour ob life, and consoles de troubled spirit as long as it clings to dis mortal body. Who kan help lubin women?[44]

What is the maid of every man's dream like? First, she is not city-born or city-tainted, but of humble rural origin and upbringing. Her age is around a marriageable sixteen years. Lacking wealth and position, she asks neither one or the other of a suitor. A man's charac-

---

[43]Robert Lacour-Gayet, *Everyday Life in the United States Before the Civil War, 1830–1860,* trans. Mary Ilford (New York: Ungar 1969) 66; Walter Blair, *Horse Sense in American Humor* (New York: Russell & Russell 1962) 87; Henry Bamford Parkes, *The American Experience* (New York: Vintage 1959) 179; Cooper, *Notions* I, 105; Alexis de Tocqueville, *Democracy in America* 2 vols. (1835–1840), the Henry Reeve text, rev. Francis Brow, ed. Phillips Bradley (New York: Knopf 1945) II, 208–09.

[44]William Levison, *Black Diamonds* (1857), reprint (Upper Saddle, N.J.: Literature House 1969) 302–03.

ter, not his status or financial expectations, assures her affections. Therefore, in *Song of the Little Heart* she is made to refuse the hand of a wealthy and titled man, who perforce may be tainted in his morals, conceited, and undemocratic, in favor of a youth rich only in the honesty of his speech and the integrity of his behavior.[45] She is the innocent girl in *Jenny Lane,* whose idyllic existence knows no suffering and inflicts no pain.[46] She is simple without being dim-witted, sensitively diffident without artificiality, beautiful without vainglory.[47]

In *Bonny Blue Eyes,* a lover sees truth, love, intellect, hope, and Heaven mirrored in her eyes. In another song, *Annie Law,* he sees her standing without "a fleck or flaw, a diamond in love's diadem," and revealing a loveliness consonant with the fauna and flora of Eden. Then he suggests:

> My days would be so pleasant
> Though my roof were thatched with straw,
> A king would be a peasant
> For my cot and Annie Law.[48]

This feminine vision, "half of earth and more than half of Heaven,"[49] could be offered nothing save a pure and respectful life, one cleansed of sensual blemish. Only then could come the bliss of her acceptance: "Her soft notes of melody around me sweetly fall;/Her eye, full of love, is now beaming on my soul;/The sound of that gentle voice, the glance of that eye,/Surround me with rapture . . ."[50]

[45]*Song of the Little Heart,* m. O.R. Barrows (Boston: Ditson, 1856). See also [Mitchell], *Dream Life* 228, 332; Emerson, *Journals* VIII, 381; Lacour-Gayet, *Everyday Life* 67, writes that girls married at about sixteen years of age, and some girls in the South married at thirteen and fourteen.

[46]*Jenny Lane,* w. and melody R. Bishop Buckley, arr. J.P. Ordway (Boston: Wade 1850).

[47]Cooper, *Notions* I, 25; Martineau, *Society* III, 171–72.

[48]*Bonny Blue Eyes,* w. Joana Tyler of Leominster, Mass., m. arr. J. Gibson (Boston: Ditson 1849); *Annie Law,* w. W.W. Fosdick, m. J.R. Thomas (New York: Firth, Pond 1857).

[49]Lowell's comment on his future wife, Maria White, is in *Letters, Vol. I,* 71; Longfellow made a similar comment on his own future wife, Mary Potter, in his *Letters* I, 348.

[50]*Fairy-Belle,* w. and m. Stephen C. Foster (New York: Firth, Pond 1859); see

A large group of popular songs, however, describe the beloved as temporarily unheeding. She is metamorphosed into an ages-old ideal conception, the sleeping beauty. Her active suitor waits outside in darkness or the first light of dawn and calls to her, while above her passive, sleep-laden "life flows calmly like a summer sea."[51] He is a moth attracted by the glow of goodness humanized; she, a gossamer glory to be reverenced from a psychical distance. Her dream state allows her to float through limitless time and space, in tranquil vision quest. At times the feminine sleeper grazes the edges of death and briefly looks on the hereafter.

He whispers in awe from the shadows:

> Linger in blissful repose,
>   Free from all sorrowing care, love,
> While round thee melody flows,
>   Wafted on pinions of air, love.
> Let not thy visions depart,
>   Lured by the stars that are beaming,
> Music will flow from my heart
>   While thy sweet spirit is dreaming,
> Dreaming, dreaming, unfettered by the day,
>   In melody, in melody I'll breathe my soul away.[52]

He knows that "sweetly she sleeps"; yet he would have her awaken, for he longs for her companionship and can feel whole only with her beside him.[53]

His completeness is assured when she fulfills her destiny as wife and mother. "What is home without a mother?" goes the song by

---

also *Aleen, the Pearl of the Juna,* m. George F. Root (Boston: Russell & Tolman 1858).

[51] *Slumber, Gentle Lady,* m. Towner Root (Boston: Reed 1845).

[52] *Linger in Blissful Repose,* w. and m. Stephen C. Foster (New York: Firth, Pond 1858).

[53] *Sweetly She Sleeps, My Alice Fair,* w. and m. Stephen C. Foster (New York: Firth, Pond 1851); *Wake! Dinah, Wake!* w. and melody S.C. Howard, arr. J.P. Ordway (Boston: Ordway 1854); *Dream No Longer, Maiden Fair,* m. I.B. Woodbury (New York: Hall 1849).

Septimus Winner,[54] and what indeed? As beloved is essential to suitor, so is she essential to husband and child.

Love heretofore discussed was a young, exclusive condition, an indispensable substance that must be sought out and possessed by every human. Love seemed a monopoly on feeling, something that excluded others beyond the magic circle of two. Under these circumstances love remained private and enclosed, the person speaking sometimes apprehensive about its possible loss. He saw it as fragile. He felt that it could flit away into the joyless shadows of night if the beloved died—which she does, in many songs.

Love as it is now discussed is an older, inclusive emotion, a comprehensive state embracing all objects that fall naturally within its purview. It has acquired a mature strength, which it donates freely to others; a wisdom, which it teaches to children. Now it appears as a gift to be universally bestowed, never diminished in the giving, and never threatening to pass from view.

The mother pictured in the songs loves her child absolutely, because he exists, and not merely because of his physical beauty, mental acumen, or spiritual development. A woman kind and caring, a refuge from pain, and an interceder before God is Woodbury's portrait in *There's Music in a Mother's Voice*.[55] Other compositions have her resemble a great earth mother, a God-delegated giver and nourisher of life. Her realm is the home; her responsibility, the children. She inducts the young into the paths of right behavior. To give one example, in John Baker's *My Trundle Bed*, we find an adult rummaging through the attic. When he comes upon his childhood bed, he naturally recalls his mother:

> So I drew it from the recess
>   Where it had remain'd so long,
> Hearing all the while the music
>   Of my mother's voice in song;
> As she sung in sweetest accents,

---

[54] *What Is Home Without a Mother,* m. Septimus Winner (Philadelphia: Lee & Walker 1854).

[55] *There's Music In a Mother's Voice,* m. Isaac B. Woodbury (Boston: Ditson 1847). On mother-child love, see Fromm, *Art of Loving* 41–42.

What I since have often read—
"Hush my dear, lie still and slumber,
Holy angels guard they bed."

Then it was with hands so gently
Placed upon my infant head,
That she taught my lips to utter
Carefully the words she said;
Never can they be forgotten,
Deep are they in mem'ry riven—
"Hallowed be thy name, O, Father!
Father! thou who art in heaven."

This she taught me, then she told me
Of its import, great and deep,
After which I learned to utter
"Now I lay me down to sleep."
Then it was with hands uplifted,
And in accents soft and mild,
That my mother asked—"Our Father!
Father! do thou bless my child."

Despite its obvious sentimentality, the song speaks to us across the
decades of the contemporary anxiety to strengthen home life and to
encourage moral teaching as bulwarks against the insidious hurly-
burly of the outside world.

CHILDREN AND THE HOME

Childhood meant compliance, a period when the unformed and re-
ceptive mind might readily yield to direction. The guidance given
the young, it was believed, would remain of lasting value throughout
adulthood. T.S. Arthur writes, in *The Mother's Rule* (1856), that a
mother's "real object of education is to give children resources that
will endure as long as life endures, habits that will ameliorate, not

[56]Quoted in Bernard Wishy, *The Child and the Republic* (Philadelphia: University
of Pennsylvania Press 1968) 298.

83

destroy; occupations that will render sickness tolerable, solitude pleasant, age venerable, life more dignified and useful, and death less terrible."[56] The obedience that fear exacts was abhorred; the sense of duty that love gently draws forth was praised. If the child could learn an outgoing behavior enjoined by awareness of rightness, later in life he would demonstrate a feeling of linkage and social indebtedness, which were essential for integrating both home and community.

Coercing the young American to grow up conforming to some detailed plan of childrearing denied him flexibility. Flexibility was necessary for fielding extemporaneously the many problems that one was likely to encounter in the mercurial society of mid-century. General principles of conduct learned in affectionate trust were a better preparation. Therefore, the compleat mother of arcadia did "speak gently," for she knew "it is better far to rule by love than fear."[57]

As for arcadian childhood, it signalized days when the adult was "but a laughing boy," when his "young heart could beat to praise/ And every pulse respond to joy;/When every word was of the heart/ When every feeling was sincere."[58]

One person in song looks back and sees "young folks" as able to "cast aside de cares ob life." "How happy dey all seem," he says; "Wid all dey lub on earf around/(Looks bright as am a dream)." In like fashion, Mrs. Parton, writing in the guise of Fanny Fern, speaks enviously of the "perfect happiness, the perfect faith in all future tomorrows" felt by boys and girls shielded from "awful reality." This belief in the promise of the years to come, she claims, is an additional aid to education. No interfering "fear of the waking hour" or apprehension "of pain and care" deflects the learner.[59]

An equality of innocence unites all the children of song. Their

[57]*Speak Gently,* m. Joseph Bird (Boston: Bradlee 1846). See also Philip Greven, *The Protestant Temperament* (New York: Knopf 1977) 151, 162, 178; Oscar and Mary Handlin, *Facing Life* (Boston: Little, Brown 1971) 81; Wishy, *Child* 32–33.

[58]*My Boyhood Days,* m. John C. Baker (Boston: Ditson 1849).

[59]The first song quoted is *Young Folks from Home,* w. and m. H. Craven Griffiths (New York: Gould 1852); the Parton quotation is from *Folly As It Flies* 42–43; the second song quoted is *The Midnight Dream,* w. "Estelle", m. C. Rubin (Baltimore: Benteen 1847).

world appears beautiful, even heavenly. They conduct sinless lives incorrupted by the concerns of earth. They seem tender creatures with winning ways, new Adams who have yet to bite the fruit of knowledge. Andrew McDowall, in his composition *Years Ago,* states bluntly that every child is born "free of sin and care." Because undefiled, a child dreams easily of heaven, of angels who unbidden come to him and conduct him on visits with members of the celestial hierarchy—so musical works like *The Child's Wish* and *The Child's Dream* tell us. Child and deity are almost one in Foster's *Little Ella:*

> Little Ella, fairest, dearest,
>> Unto me and unto mine,
> Earthly cherub coming nearest
>> To my dreams of form divine.

Obviously, Foster has fashioned Ella into a figure who is more than mortal, and who exhibits some awesomness associated with ethereality.[60]

By mid-century many Americans, apparently, had difficulty blaming themselves entirely for the corruption they perceived within their own persons. They preferred, as we can see in their songs, to attribute a little responsibility for the falling away to externals—the environment, society, circumstances. It was a comfort to believe that one entered this world pure. If one was born in sin or predetermined for heaven or hell, then hope diminished. If one was born undefiled, then however tainting were the earthly years, one might more comfortably think to cleanse one's spirit and eventually present a pristine soul to God. The faultless maiden, the irreproachable mother, and the lamblike child of song show how far from the stern Calvinism of the previous century Americans had come.

When we consider the concept of home and family, again we find the pose of looking back from a troubled present common to many mid-nineteenth-century songs. The "I" who sings strikes us as agitated, uncertain of himself; he broods on the threatening contempo-

---

[60] *Years Ago,* w. and m. Andrew J. McDowall (New York: Riley 1842); *The Child's Wish,* m. H.D. Munson (Boston: Ditson 1851); *The Child's Dream,* m. Bernard Covert (Boston: Wade 1848); *Little Ella,* w. and m. Stephen C. Foster (New York: Firth, Pond 1853).

rary scene with feelings of apprehension and helplessness. His lonely isolation hints at a growing incapacity for handling further experiences, which renders meaningful communication with others increasingly difficult. Within this context of anxiety occurs the dreamy recollection of home.

Home is projected, first as a microcosmic envelope surrounding the people one loves. It is a physical milieu having mental and moral influence, and it is linked to arcadia, which is a macrocosmic envelope distinguishing an entire region where simple happiness, rustic uprightness, and continuous tranquility prevail, so that arcadia, and home within arcadia, are thus set apart from the world at large. Home signifies a private, personal dwelling, one devoid of strangers, untouched by modern institutions, and unregulated by any external organization. In song after song it promises shelter for the distressed, asylum for the destitute or disgraced. How the singer longs to enter this sacred and inviolable sanctuary, from which he cannot be forcibly extracted without the commission of sacrilege. Here he can find deliberance from torment; here he can survive.

Listen to Donald Mitchell, in *Dream Life,* when he writes that the boyhood home gives a sense of "protecting power that no castle walls can give to your maturer years. Aye, your heart clings in boyhood to the roof-tree of the old family garret, with a grateful affection, and an earnest confidence, that the after years—whatever may be their successes, or their honors—can never recreate. Under the roof-tree of his home, the boy feels SAFE: and where, in the whole realm of life, with its bitter toils, and its bitter temptations, will he feel *safe* again?"

An unpretentious cottage encloses a harmonious family group whose members accept mutual obligation. Parents and children behave openly, forbearingly, and warmly toward each other. The days pass in pleasant conviviality with intimates of every age. "Home, home, I love thee!" sings the dreamer of the past, becoming emotionally overwhelmed by this picture of "love and purity."[61]

An orgy of yearning for the old family hearth began in the early

---

[61]*Home, Home, I Love Thee,* w. and m. Joseph W. Turner (Boston: Ditson 1851). See also Tuckerman, *Optimist* 110; Martineau *Society* III, 66; Handlin, *Facing Life* 73.

1820s, with the swift and unparalleled rise to popularity of *Home! Sweet Home!*, music by the Englishman Henry Bishop, lyric by the American John Howard Payne, an expatriate living in London. Hundreds of British and American home songs followed in its wake. Then, in 1851, came Stephen Foster's *Old Folks at Home*, and its extraordinary success incited the composition of thousands of additional musical variations on the subject. For the remainder of the century, millions of people roamed disconsolately amid fictional pleasures and palaces, thinking of the little home where the old folks stayed. They could find nothing to equal the joy contained in the lowly rural cot of their imagination.

A typical home song tells of "how sweet the rest that labor yields/ The humble and the poor,/Where sits the patr'arch of the fields/ Before his cottage door!" The song continues:

> The lark is singing in the sky,
>   The swallow in the eaves,
> And love is beaming in each eye,
>   Beneath the summer leaves.
> The air amid his fragrant bow'rs
>   Supplies unpurchas'd health,
> And hearts are bounding 'mid the flow'rs,
>   More dear to him than wealth!
> Peace, like the blessed sunlight plays,
>   Around his humble cot,
> And happy nights and cheerful days
>   Divide his lowly lot.[62]

On occasion the cottage stands near the ocean's shore. But the potential wildness of the ocean is ignored in favor of the serenity inherent in a pastoral image. Note, in the following, the gentle, civilized act of seashell collecting:

> Childhood's days now pass before me,
>   Forms and scenes of long ago,
> Like a dream they hover o'er me,
>   Calm and bright as ev'nings glow.

---

[62] *The Cottage Home*, w. and m. Isaac B. Woodbury (Boston: Ditson 1849).

Days that knew no shade of sorrow,
    When my young heart pure and free,
Joyful hail'd each coming morrow,
    In the cottage by the sea.

Fancy sees the rose-trees twining,
    Round the old and rustic door;
And below the white beach shining,
    Where I gather'd shells of yore,
Hears my mother's gentle warning,
    As she took me on her knee.
And I feel again life's morning,
    In the cottage by the sea.[63]

Since most songs that look back on the arcadian scene are describing the singer's boyhood, the marriage state is seen through the eyes of a son. Marriage from the viewpoint of husband and wife is rarely the subject of a back-of-beyond fantasy; far more often it is a subject of songs that describe a couple braving adversity together. A "home picture" of arcadian marriage fortunately is the main emphasis of *Ben Fisher* (1853). After "his hard day's work," Ben sits beside his loving wife Kate:

He loved at home with his wife to stay
    And they chatted merrily.
Right merrily they chatted on the while
    Her babe lay on her breast,
While a chubby rogue with a rosy smile,
    On his father's knee found rest.

Ben's farm "promised a glorious yield in the harvest time." His Kate continues to love him as before: " 'I tell you, Kate, what I think,' says he,/'We're the happiest folks in town!' " Kate replies that their "humble home has a light within," which money cannot buy, and "six healthy children, a merry heart, and a husband's love-lit eye." Overpowered by his emotions, Ben "leaned his head on her shoulders . . . took her hand in his, . . . [and] left on her lips a kiss."[64] Happy industry, in the fields for him, in the house for her, and the cheery gathering together in the evening of husband, wife,

[63] *The Cottage By the Sea,* m. J.R. Thomas (New York: Firth, Pond 1856).
[64] *Ben Fisher* (see note 18).

and children describes "one of the sweetest scenes of earthly felicity, and holiest associations of human nature; over which the monarch of heaven presides," to quote from Matthew Sorin's *The Domestic Circle*, published in Philadelphia, in 1840.[65] Much the same thing is said in J.H. McNaughton's song *When There's Love at Home* (Boston, 1859). Love in the home, McNaughton assures us, brings beauty, joy, peace, plenty, and perfect bliss.

The discussion of the arcadian vision closes as it began: on the means for achieving total happiness. Poe's earlier statement on this topic set forth the necessity for the pursuit of objects with the highest spirituality. These objects, as we have seen, were thought to be found preeminently in the home circle. When joined to love, to aspirations directed spiritward, and to wholesome activity, all of Poe's conditions for realizing blessedness were met. Whether this felicity had any possibility of permanency was another matter altogether.

THE DEPARTURE FROM PARADISE

The motifs expressed in popular song, whatever their symbolic implications, usually are abstracted from and reflect actual events. The ubiquity of the motif of departure from home shows the significance that this action had for nineteenth-century Americans. America was a nation on the move. Its people were like "gypsies—a mechanical and migratory race."[66] Everywhere, it seemed, young men were saying farewell to "their parents, never to return, as naturally and with as little emotion as young birds desert forever their native nest as soon as they are fledged."[67] Many of them migrated "westwards . . . leaving those who should be their wives to marry widowers of double their age."[68]

---

[65]Quoted in Carl Bode, *The Anatomy of American Popular Culture* (Berkeley: University of California Press 1959) 71.

[66]Oliver Wendell Holmes, *The Professor at the Breakfast-Table* (1859), reprinted as Vol. II of *Works* 246.

[67]Michel Chevalier, *Society, Manners, and Politics in the United States,* ed. John William Ward (Ithaca, N.Y.: Cornell University Press 1969) 398.

[68]Harriet Martineau, *Society in America,* (London: Saunders & Otley 1837) Vol. 111, p. 128.

If the new western lands were not their destination, they left to jostle with immigrants for urban employment and living space. Between 1830 and 1860, New York City grew from a population of around 200,000 to one over 800,000; St. Louis, from a population around 6,000 to one around 160,000. Even entire households were in motion. Between 1830 and 1840, when Boston had grown from 61,000 to 93,000 inhabitants, about 36,000 households had moved in and out of the city; between 1850 and 1860, when the population increased from 137,000 to 178,000 inhabitants, close to 100,000 households had moved in and out. Incessant restlessness characterized a democracy where common people wandered where and when they pleased, without restraint, and to an extent impossible in Europe.[69]

To be expected during these decades was the publication of thousands of popular works that contemplated departure from one's birthplace as an important stage in Americans's lives. Only slight manipulation was necessary to fashion the actual into a symbolic statement. Songs delineated a young man's leaving home as a separation from and a severance of ties with loved ones, as a setting out on a journey into the unknown, as marking a division in time between the blithe innocence of childhood and the troubled knowledge of maturity, and as a kind of dying—a total cessation of life as it had been.

Indians left when driven out by whites; black slaves, when sold, set free, or fleeing to the North; and American women, when married. No women were enticed from home or abducted by highwaymen, gypsy chieftains, or sultans—as they were in contemporary British works, like *The Captive's Song,* words by Mrs. Norton, music by John Blockley. Nor did lack of employment and food force men to leave, the theme of British songs like *The Irish Immigrant,* words by Lady Dufferin, music by George Barker. Home in American songs, remember, is a delightful place from which the young white male is rarely forced to leave owing to any specific set of conditions. Because

[69]Howard Chudacoff, *The Evolution of Urban Society* (Englewood Cliffs, N.J.: Prentice-Hall 1975) 46, 56; Deric Regin, Culture and the Crowd (Philadelphia: Chilton 1968) 10.

he left voluntarily, only to discover unhappiness, a man chastises himself, in *Recollections of Home:*

> Ah! why from my own native home did I part
>   With its mountains and vallies so dear to each heart;
> Ah! why did I leave the enjoyments of home
>   O'er the wide waste of waters a stranger to roam?[70]

He had been at liberty either to stay or depart and spontaneously had decided to leave.

Implicit in a lyric of this kind is the belief in some freedom to select between alternatives. To men who choose to abandon home, arcadia means a static, passive existence. Departure becomes a necessary action if it promises stimulating alternatives to stagnation and provides the dynamics for growth. The bond to home and loved ones must loosen so that the individual, without connection with anyone or anything, can learn further what it means to live and to be human. The song literature furnishes abundant examples of growth as a consequence of independence.

Unfortunately, the liberty to go forth introduces the possibility of sorrow and error, and the necessity to leave behind the safe and familiar for the unknown. Yet, heedless of consequences, some youths hasten to abandon what they have come to view as a "tame and dreary shore," a place where "our fettered souls . . . pine.[71]

Foreign to American song is the theme of *Blanche Alpen,* the composition of two Britishers, Charles Jeffreys and Stephen Glover. A man states that other lands may be beautiful, but he prefers to remain incurious and go nowhere, for "in sweet content my days are spent—then wherefore leave my home?" And later: "Love still retains some deathless chains that bind the heart to home."

---

[70] *Recollections of Home,* m. Asa B. Hutchinson, arr. E.L. White (Boston: Ditson 1846).

[71] *We Ride the Foaming Sea Once More,* w. and m. E.A. Hosmer (Boston: Reed 1855). On this aspect of departure, see Rollo May, *The Meaning of Anxiety* (New York: Norton 1950) 167. R.W.B. Lewis in, *The American Adam: Innocence, Tragedy and Tradition* (Chicago: University of Chicago Press 1955) 115, writes: "The valid rite of initiation for the individual in the new world is not an initiation into society, but, given the character of society, an initiation *away from it.*"

Note the contrast—"It is the order of Nature to grow," writes Emerson, "and every soul is by this intrinsic necessity ever quitting its whole system of things, its wife and home and laws and faith, as the shell fish crawls out of its own growth and slowly forms a new house." Departure in song indicates a quitting of Emerson's "whole system of things." Homebodies could have only limited personal encounters and participation in events, since for them these experiences must remain narrowly circumscribed. Inner growth threatened to become stunted.

Contemporary young men needed to know the world from observation, not just from books; so claimed the young Longfellow in a letter to his father. Surveying the twenty-six years he had already lived without leaving home, Henry Wadsworth Longfellow decided that, happy as these years had been, he wished to travel: "I was never fifty miles from Portland in all my life, which I think is rather a sorrowful circumstance in the annals of my history. When I hear others talking, as travellers are very apt to do, about what they have seen and heard abroad, I always regret my having never been from home more than I have hitherto." Whether an actual person, like Longfellow, or the fictional protagonist of literature, the young American male imagined himself an Adam-like individual sallying forth into a vast world that afforded rich variety in experiences favorable to self-discovery and suitable for self-testing.[72] "I ne'er had found the world within/Until I roamed the world throughout," is the burden of one popular song.

The new traveler's resolve is firmed by hope—that is to say, by ambition and the expectation of attaining one's aspirations. A strong drive for position, power, riches, or some idealized goal leaves in abeyance Poe's warning that ambition negates bliss. At nineteen years of age, Daniel Webster contemplated the ambition growing within him and the youths of his acquaintance. He claimed it was the lot of all young men to feel the desire to excel. Dependent on

---

[72]Emerson, *Journals* VIII, 203; X, 77; Longfellow, *Letters* I, 71; Lewis, *American Adam* 111; Daniel Hoffman, *Form and Fable in American Fiction* (New York: Oxford University Press 1965) xix.

[73]Irving H. Bartlett, *Daniel Webster* (New York: Norton 1978) 26.

whether it became the master or subordinate of virtue, ambition produced either an oppressive Caesar or a benign Washington. The problem for Webster was to have ambition always ruled by virtue. The possibility that happiness might hasten off does not occur to him.[73]

The obverse of the Adamic image is examined humorously in William Levison's *Black Diamonds* of 1857: Adam and Eve "must have slid on der backs, kase dey am kalled de fust backsliders. Dis, my frens, was de 'Fall ob Man,' 'luded to bekase dey was de fust man dat fell arter de kreashun; an dey woodent hab fell if dey had not wanted wat dey otn't to git. Wat a lesson dis teeches all ob us who am discontented wid our lot, and am grasping for tings beyond our reach. Here was Adam an Ebe, wid all paradise afore dem, an still dey war not satisfied; an jis so it am wid all human nature."[74]

The songs do not have God visibly drive young men out of arcadia, as Adam and Eve were driven out of Eden. Yet, in youth's portrayal, we detect a similar discontent, unquietness, and hunger for new experience. These feelings impel males to leave guaranteed felicity behind and go after an elusive chimera. Only with full maturity will men understand that they had "wanted wat dey otn't to get."

Some popular songs portray the first days ruled by youthful ambition as a "struggling, hoping, confident time," when masculine minds are "full of an aspiration which has not learned how hard the hills of life are to climb."[75] Notice how the departing young man, in the Ordway composition *Leaving Home,* states he is "a youth" whose "lot" it is to leave "home" and "dear ones." His goodbyes are cheered by "hope," which "stays all fears," both now and when he is "roaming far." And in the Fessenden song *We'll Bid Farewell,* the young man goes forth to seek "the priceless pearl of truth" that guides "the trusting heart of youth." He and others like him are buoyed by "uprising hopes" that "nerve us" for "life's toils."[76]

---

[74]Levison, *Black Diamonds* 53.

[75]Lowell, *Letters* I, 190.

[76]*Leaving Home,* w. and m. John P. Ordway (Boston: Ordway 1855); *We'll Bid Farewell,* w. A. Layton McKenney, m. L.G. Fessenden (New York: Waters 1854).

When referring to young men's heedless faith in their destiny, most songs also point out the grief of those left behind and the later disillusionment of those who fare into the world. The traveler, in Foster's *Comrades Fill No Glass for Me,* has left sorrowing parents to discover "blighted fortune, health, and fame." "When I was young, I felt the tide/Of aspiration undefiled," he tells his acquaintances. "But manhood's years have wronged the pride/My parents centered in their child." In another work, Avery's *Ah! Sing Again,* disenchantment underlies the words: "Sing of the past/When all the joyous dreams of youth now gone/Their brightest pictures cast/Around our hearts while bidding us speed on."[77]

The consistent message in the majority of songs mentioning departure is that however optimistic the youthful traveler may have been, he eventually learns ambition's reward is too likely to be ill fortune for him, sorrow for his parents, and torment for the beloved who awaits his return. A later, optimistic age would denominate such a conclusion as unduly pessimistic and an example of sentimental exultation in suffering. But the mid-nineteenth century lover of song would have rebutted that he was a realist. He demanded honesty about what he saw. Therefore his songs had to state that few achieve happiness and success; the great majority of strivers end their lives bankrupt in worldly goods and in spirit. Youth's expectations rarely match achievement. Yet optimism is high in the young, and goals beckon like the tops of comfortable hills, not like the peaks of formidable mountains. Young men in their thousands will fare daily from home, lacking knowledge of the world and requiring the correction of experience. This was the unalterable nature of things and therefore had to take its course. Obviously, what all of the above should indicate to us is that mankind in different ages is given the same human equation to add up. Every age adds it differently.

A few popular songs depicting departure from home abstain from overt symbolism and concern themselves mainly with actual conditions. They assert that in the mundane world, ambition's aim usually is the winning of a fortune. Possibly this goal owes something to

[77]*Comrades, Fill No Glass for Me,* w. and m. Stephen C. Foster (Baltimore: Miller & Beacham 1855); *Ah! Sing Again,* m. H. Avery (Boston: Ditson 1857).

94

an earlier Puritan attitude that wealth might prove its possessor to be one of God's elect. Assuredly, wealth can evidence earthly achievement. After all, what alternative remained to demonstrate that one had won success and deserved lasting honors in a democratic country that repudiated titles of nobility and swiftly and randomly voted up its plain citizens to the highest political offices and as swiftly and randomly voted them down?

It is as well to point out here that nowhere do these popular songs equate riches with moral achievement. They make clear that only a few young men have decided on money as a demonstration of success. Already noted is how the ideal woman never is swayed into pledging her troth to whomsoever, unless virtue of the highest order is present. With her money has no weight. We will see in the next chapter to what degree the identification of riches with arrival is a delusion of the young, which is dispelled after wider knowledge of life. Finally, it should be remarked that the issuance of popular songs whose theme is the acquiring of riches coincided mainly with the discovery of gold in California, in 1848, and the subsequent years of gold fever. Then it was that songs like *El Dorado* (words and music by Beman) came out:

> There is a wondrous land
>   Away beyond the mountains,
> Where glitt'ring golden sand
>   Rolls down in all the fountains. . . .
> Bus'ness, home and friends to me,
>   Dull and weary seem to be,
> There's no music to my ear
>   Sounds like California.
>
>   . . . . .
>
> Neighbor, crony, father, brother,
>   Sisters kind, and tender mother,
> All with me in one short hour,
>   All have lost their charm and power.[78]

---

[78] *El Dorado,* w. and m. S. Beman, *The Singer's Companion* 10.

Most departing gold-rushers appear musically as sensitive humans whose eyes readily fill with "the starting tear," at leaving sorrowing loved ones behind. But they also have formed a determination befitting the "brave and bold," to go off "to try our luck in search of gold/A brief adieu to all most dear."[79]

An occasional composition hints at more than avarice as the spur. For example, Jesse Hutchinson's *The California Gold-Diggers* seems to proceed on two levels. On one level, it describes men setting off after California's gold and ready to face all dangers in order to garner it. On another level, the work refers to a "journey afar to the promised land." To reach it, the traveler knows he must exchange the safety of home and love of parents and beloved for the pitiless "dark sea foam," for hunger relieved only by "the coarsest fare," and for nightly sleep on the disease-bearing "cold, damp ground," with wolves "howling 'round." God willing, he will at last arrive at "the distant shore" [Heaven?], where gold aplenty [truth?] rewards the mettlesome spirit.[80]

Clarification of departure as a symbolic act comes in a large body of compositions that forsake earthly matters in order to gaze inwardly. They purposely remain vague about any real-world conditions that have promoted the going away, and they hardly ever hint at the pilgrim's earthly destination. In these songs, to remain at home could result in a life limited to habitual activities in accord with fixed usage, however well-founded. A man under these conditions can turn into an uninformed innocent, a complacent human trifle whose existence has become of no account. Better to risk the dangers of the unknown, and expose one's being to the sweep of new experiences. Not until then can a person say he has truly lived and fully explored the possibilities of his nature.

"Who can blame men for seeking excitement?" Emerson asks. "Would you have them sleep in a dull eternity of equilibrium? Religion, love, ambition, money, war, brandy, some fierce antagonism

---

[79] *The Bag of Gold,* w. and melody E.W. Locke, arr. Nathan Barker (Dover, N.H.: Ingalls 1850). Stephen Foster's *Ring De Banjo* (New York: Firth, Pond 1851) is a minstrel song of departure that has an identical theme.

[80] *The California Gold Diggers,* w. Jesse Hutchinson, m. arr. Nathan Barker (Boston: Marsh 1849).

must break the round of perfect circulation or no spark, no joy, no event can be . . . In the country the lover of nature dreaming through the wood would never awake to thought if the scream of an eagle, the cries of a crow, or a curlew near his head did not break the continuity."[81] In chime with Emerson, the youth in the song *We Ride the Foaming Sea* exalts as he leaves the "tame" shore behind. His ship "dashes free" of the land where "fettered souls . . . pine," and confidently dares wild gales and mountainous seas. We get a sense that dangers are intended to bring out the man, to measure his intrepidity and resourcefulness under stress. Unfledged youth yearns to have events put him to the proof. Only through testing can character be defined, mind stimulated, and spirit solidified.[82]

The necessity for youth to leave arcadia takes precedence over all opposite considerations. Love, whatever its strength, cannot confute this imperative. The woman, in *Lorena,*[83] tries to hold her lover back but fails. She gives up when she realizes "a duty stern and pressing broke/The tie which linked my soul to thee." Departure owing to duty, in the several songs mentioning it, takes on the coloring of a moral obligation universally felt and prescribed because of its evident rightness. Mother and beloved let go with the greatest reluctance; fathers—possibly remembering their own past imperatives—let go more easily. The father in *Years Ago,* for example, urges his son to adventure forth and "join the free and brave."

Fathers, however, are scarcely mentioned at all in songs of departure. More often, resigned mothers say good-bye; most often, bereft beloveds acquiesce to their abandonment.

From one standpoint, the beloved personifies that love which breaches the walls separating one human from another. The attachment is one that the young man originally had supplicated for. But it is also a bond that denies him individuality and liberty. Love threat-

---

[81]Emerson, *Journals,* Vol. VII, ed. A.W. Plumstead and Harrison Hayford (1969) 272; see also Becker, *Denial of Death* 74.

[82]Lowell, *The Biglow Papers* (1848), Vol. IX of *The Writings of James Russell Lowell,* (Boston: Houghton Mifflin 1894) 90; William Cullen Bryant, in *Prose Writings,* 2 vols. ed. Parke Godwin (1884), reprint (New York: Russell & Russell 1964) II, 357; Berthoff, *Unsettled People* 217.

[83]*Lorena,* w. Rev. H.D.L. Webster, m. J.P. Webster (Chicago: Higgins 1857).

ens to become a tyrant interposing obstacles between a man and his inherent right to experience the further development of his own distinctive character. He must shake loose from domination, gracious as it may be.

Never mentioned in the songs, but certainly understood, was the need for escape from a situation where spiritual love was beginning to feel the first strong burst of young-male sexuality. Prevalent attitudes caused writers of serious songs to conceal physical passion. Its tenacious hold over young lovers was rarely suggested, although its extraordinary ability to rule arbitrarily over better judgment was well grasped. Sex's possible intrusion into the link of son to mother would have horrified most nineteenth-century minds. Nevertheless, an urgent fleshy appetite was inherent in first manhood. Not countenanced as an arcadian craving, most assuredly it contributed to the obligation to depart. Coming to terms with one's sexuality could take place only in the outer world of turbulent flux, never in the land of innocence. In addition, affection needed to be redefined and freshly perceived, not as a bondage, but as something freely exchanged between two equals. Only through the maturity that broad experience brought about could a person liberate himself from the protective love of parents, the static love of maidens, and the unreasoning love of youth. In short, the trials of the wider world brought feeling to ripeness.[84] "I love you" meant one thing at twenty years of age; "I love you" would mean something altogether different at sixty years of age.

Thus, a young man's destiny impelled him to leave arcadia. His unavoidable lot was that of a roamer moving unconstrainedly from new encounter to new encounter, at times purposefully, at times without specific direction. This compulsion to roam might be said to be the song writer's recognition of the active principle that underlies human personality, as surely as abiding at home represents the static principle. "Farewell, my Lilly dear," says Stephen Foster's optimistic youth, when he abandons his beloved "to roam the wide world."

[84]In this regard, see Benda, *Image of Love* 4–5; Fromm, *Art of Loving* 81; Joseph L. Henderson, "Ancient Myths and Modern Man," in Jung *et al., Man* 117–18.

Most compositions make clear that love will always be remembered; but the separation of lovers is likely to be "for years." The pilgrim voyages into a future where dear ones will be recalled not necessarily in felicity, but "in sorrow" and "in pain."[85]

In truth, the onset of sorrow, claim the song writers, is felt at the moment of departure. Carefully, they orchestrated the poignant minutes. The wayfarer gazes on dear, familiar faces, not knowing when he will see them again:

> The sun is in the west,
>   The stars are on the sea,
> Each kindly hand I've pres't,
>   And now, farewell to thee.
> The cup of parting done,
>   'Tis the darkest I can sip.
> I have pledg'd them ev'ry one
>   With my heart and with my lip.
> But I came to thee the last,
>   That together we might throw
> One look upon the past
>   In sadness ere I go.[86]

Then he finds himself alone. For a final moment he contemplates the home where he has felt secure:

> Farewell! old cottage;
>   You and I must part.
> I leave your faithful shelter
>   With a poor breaking heart.
> Farewell! old cottage.
>   Oft times from afar
> Yon window light hath served me,
>   As a loved guiding star,

[85]*Farewell, My Lilly Dear,* w. and m. Stephen C. Foster (New York: Firth, Pond 1851); *Come, I've Something Sweet to Sing for You,* m. John C. Andrews (New York: Firth, Pond 1848); *Jenny Grey,* w. Benjamin Jones, m. G.R. Poulton (Boston: Ditson 1855).

[86]*The Sun Is in the West,* m. A Lady Amateur [Mrs. C.E. Habicht], arr. Theo. T. Baker (Boston: Reed 1848).

> And cheered a heart that longed
>   To join the household mirth,
> Where happy faces thronged,
>   A hospitable hearth.[87]

The key phrases here are "faithful shelter," "guiding star," "happy faces," and "hospitable hearth." These are now behind him. What lies ahead, though still hidden in the future, is the opposite: falsity, joylessness, and inhospitality. Shelter will be impermanent, guidance absent, faces careworn, and hearths cold on the road stretching dimly before him. Nevertheless, he must start on his way.

Contrasting the unthinking youths who people a few songs, the everyday Adam in the typical departure song cuts himself off from paradise with no little apprehension. A brief repose was his portion. What then? Uneasily he reminds himself that God's mercy endures forever.

[87] *Farewell, Old Cottage,* w. and m. Stephen C. Foster (New York: Firth, Pond 1851).

CHAPTER 3

Confronting
Life and Death

Every society, at least until present times, has held to a definition of maturity that has included total acceptance of its moral values. Arrival into full membership meant an emergence from childhood's cocoon, years of fluttering from personal encounter to personal encounter, and a renaissance in which self-knowledge and societal lore became one.[1] Every society, too, has attempted to present a coherent symbolism, usually sacred in implication, that depicted the actions leading to this fusion.

The America of the 1840s and '50s was just such a society. This chapter is concerned with the symbolism that this society adopted to depict the world of personal encounter. To make its points forcefully, this symbolism was seen through the eyes of the melancholic, the tormented, and the unfulfilled. Nothing was left untouched by the probing finger of feeling. The psychological wounds inflicted by earthly living were laid open one by one.

For the reasons just given, popular works projected a perspective laden with the deep, grievous gloom of the disillusioned. They tended to depict arcadia, however happy the portrait, as the fabrication of a self-absorbed mind trying to soften an ever-present grief. Usually an aging protagonist casts his thoughts back over years lean in pleasure. Paradisial dream and hellish reality mix inextricably in his mind.

---

[1]For a detailed discussion of the meaning of maturity, see Daniel Hoffman, *Form and Fable in American Fiction* (New York: Oxford University Press 1965) 80.

Generally speaking, a serious song of this sort is an imaginative construct seeking insight into the evil and attendant suffering visited indiscriminately upon all humans. If superior to the average composition, it could befool its audience by conjuring up a fantasy that skillfully comingled verbal image with music, while giving the illusion of time in suspension. A worthwhile work left the music lover gratified, because it vividly limned some mode of experience deeply implanted within his and other people's psyches. Possibly the ideas a song expressed were less than imposing, even hackneyed. Yet the listener could feel he had been allowed a valuable peek into the inner nature of things.

These songs tell us that after departure from arcadia, the "I" becomes aware that he possesses an earthbound soul enchained by worldly interests and deficient in spirituality. During the course of time, a participation in a series of events has turned into a testing, an ordeal to purge the spirit of overweening pride and to bring the "I" into conformity with God's truth. Man turns into manikin when he learns to recognize the fragility of human life. In the words of William Cullen Bryant: "The earth, where she seems to spread a paradise for his abode, sends up death in exhalations from her bosom; and the heavens dart down lightenings to destroy him. The drought consumes the harvests on which he relied for sustenance, or the rains cause the green corn to 'rot ere its youth attains a beard.' A sudden blast engulfs him in the waters of the lake or bay from which he seeks his food, a false step or a broken twig precipitates him from the tree which he had climbed for its fruit; oaks falling in the storm, rocks toppling down from the precipices, are so many dangers which beset his life."[2]

According to the caption that heads the song *Excelsior,*[3] any human in search of his ultimate becomes a stranger to "the everyday comforts of life, the allurements of love, and the warnings of experience." Like a pathfinder, he "presses forward on" his "solitary path," keeping in mind the guiding motto, Excelsior. The word fires an aspiration after the highest attainments. The caption states, in conclusion, that the song is meant to describe "the progress of the Soul."

[2]William Cullen Bryant, in *Prose Writings,* 2 vols., ed. Parke Godwin (1884), reprint (New York: Russell & Russell 1964) I; 222.

For us, this statement is a significant key to the meaning of countless compositions where the protagonist has wandered far from home, never quite attaining the graillike goal before his eyes. In younger years, he might have tied a high-principled marker to a bundle of self-serving sentiments, labeling as substantial what would turn out to be contents of negligible moral weight. Now he finds his conscience unable to abide the emptiness that is a residue of ambition and egotism. Something beyond and greater than ego must be sought after.

Having in mind the content of songs like *Excelsior*, Henry Tuckerman, in *The Optimist,* considered the question of man's testing and the results it could achieve. He wrote: "It is when we are overcome, and the pride of intellect vanquished before the truth of nature, when, instead of coming to a logical division, we are led to bow in profound reverence before the mysteries of life, when we are led back to childhood, or up to God, by some powerful revelation of the sage or minstrel, it is then our natures grow. To this end is all art. Exquisite vocalism . . . [has] for [its] great object . . . to move the whole nature by the perfection and truthfulness of [its] appeal."[4]

Vocal art is dedicated to making lucid the world of experience that symbolizes the wilderness of the spirit. The "I" of most serious songs appears exhausted after conflict with one superior force after another, with still the mightiest force of all before him—death. Thus far, no triumph has been realized. Every sally has terminated in defeat. He asks from whence will succor come? A generally experienced truth is here given a twist. When we weep for the sorrow of others, we usually also weep for a sorrow we fear may become our own. The reverse is heard in song. The sufferer weeps for himself and, by so doing, weeps for all humanity.

IN THE WILDERNESS

From birth until departure, obedience to a divine spirit who guides thought and action had been a commandment enjoined by parents,

---

[3]*Excelsior,* w. Henry W. Longfellow, m. The Hutchinson Family (New York: Firth & Hall 1843).

[4]Henry T. Tuckerman, *The Optimist* (New York: Putnam 1852) 22.

ministers, and teachers. But on leaving arcadia, the young traveler found himself at liberty to reexamine his learned beliefs. No longer did passive acceptance suffice. The assistance of God, the Father, had to be ardently and actively sought, owing to overwhelming human needs. These needs arose as the end products of conflict.

The songs show the "I" struggling against nature, which arrays tempests at sea and blizzards in the mountains against him. He struggles against other men, who rob, starve, and imprison him. He struggles against himself, his *hubris* and tilt toward narcissism.[5] He strives to conquer, to prosper, to attain the top of ambition's hill. Frequently, it seems, he expects by gaining lasting fame to insure a kind of immortality for himself.[6]

After many years have receded into the past, what is he left with? He knows no kind hearts who care about him. In the words of one song: "O, 'mid the old friends I no more see/Is there a kind thought ever for me?/If there's but one hope, one wish, though vain,/If there's but one sigh, I'll not complain." In words of another: "Who henceforth will sing to me, when my forehead aches with pain?"[7]

He experiences complete aloneness when stripped of his beloved's love:

> Like a doomed shade I wander,
> To dark despair a prey,
> As streams thro' vales meander,
> Where sun ne'er sheds a ray;

[5]See the texts of songs like *Axes to Grind,* as sung by John W. Hutchinson (New York: Firth & Hall 1843); and *The Tempest,* w. James T. Field, m. Nathan Barker (Boston: March 1849). In most songs, struggle is something understood to have taken place in the past. It is mentioned only briefly and generally. The main interest is in the condition of the spirit as a consequence of a life of strife.

[6]For background on the universality of such attitudes, see Robert Bechtold Heilman, *Tragedy and Melodrama* (Seattle: University of Washington Press 1968) 40–59; Ernest Becker, *The Denial of Death* (New York: Free Press 1973) 3; Clemens E. Benda, *The Image of Love* (New York: Free Press 1961) 171–72; Carl Jung, "Approaching the Unconscious," in Jung *et al., Man and His Symbols* (New York: Dell 1968) 85.

[7]*Old Friends and Old Times,* w. Charles Swain, m. J.R. Thomas (Boston: Tolman 1856); *Brother, Speak in Whispers Light,* w. Captain Patten, U.S.A., m. Bernard Covert (Boston: A. & J. Ordway 1850).

> Each tree around seems bending
> To the breeze that bears my moan,
> While pining echo mocks my sigh,
> And cries, "Alone, alone."[8]

He begs for an end to his wretchedness. He longs for a "resting place from sorrow, sin, and death":

> Tell me, ye winds that round my pathway roar,
> Do ye not know some spot, where mortals weep no more,
> Some lone and pleasant dell, some valley in the west,
> Where free from toil and pain, the weary soul may rest?
> The loud winds dwindled to a whisper low
> And sighed for pity as it [sic] answered,
> "No! No!"
>
> Tell me, thou mighty deep, whose billows round me play,
> Know'st thou some favored spot, some island far away,
> Where weary man may find the bliss for which he sighs,
> Where sorrow never lives and friendship never dies?
> The loud waves rolling in perpetual flow
> Stopped for a while and sighed to answer,
> "No! No!"
>
> And thou, serenest Moon, that with such holy face
> Dost look upon the earth, asleep in night's embrace;
> Tell me all thy round, hast thou not found some spot
> Where we poor wretched men may find a happier lot?
> Behind a cloud the Moon withdrew in woe
> And in a voice sweet but sad responded,
> "No! No!"[9]

The portrait just drawn is of a human beset by anxiety, and with no way of handling it and decreasing its firm fix upon the spirit. A nullity adrift in a landscape essentially impervious to meaning, he realizes his vulnerability to the threats from outer forces. Worried that his inner world has ceased to hang together, he finds that faith in himself, like trust in others, is becoming an impossibility. Knowledge

---

[8]*Alone, Alone*, w. S.S. Steele, m. T. Comer (Boston: Prentiss & Clark 1847).
[9]*Where Can the Soul Find Rest?*, m. John C. Baker (Boston: Keith 1847).

of his own helplessness has replaced confidence. Infirmity of purpose has supplanted certainty. To him, all things appear bent toward crushing an insectile being of infinite contemptibleness. In short, after decades of striving he meditates the confusion of experience, the unpredictability of chance happenings, and the unfathomable deeps of the future—or, to put it differently, he confronts the life he has allowed himself no time to scrutinize, so busy has he been passing through it. The prize of meditation may be that some element of agreement may be unearthed, that sense may emerge from the muddle. If truly fortunate, he may contemplate a different and agreeable world, more genuine than the dangerous one surrounding him.

Stripped of illusion, he murmurs:

> Ah! sing again,
>> And let it be a measure sweet and low,
> Not one that giveth pain,
>> But such as we have oft heard long ago,
> When fortune ne'er denying,
>> Did give us home and friends that made it dear;
> And time so quickly flying,
>> Was bringing us new joys with ev'ry year.
> Sing of the past,
>> When all the joyous dreams of youth now gone
> Their brightest pictures cast
>> Around our hearts while bidding us speed on.[10]

But the past is a world he can only dream about and can never achieve again. He knows that "these scenes have fled" and that "those bright days are now forever flown." At the same time, look back he must, to a time when his person was valued, and his mind easeful. In order to survive, he has to remember that he had once led a decent life assessed at more than a penny's worth. Here is another explanation for the hundreds of songs that insistently call to memory "old friends and old times," the "old folks at home," and "the cot

---

[10] *Ah! Sing Again,* m. H. Avery (Boston: Ditson 1857).

[11] *Old Friends and Old Times* (see note 7); *Old Folks at Home,* w. and m. Stephen C. Foster (New York: Firth, Pond 1851); *The Cot Where I Was Born,* m. L. Heath, arr. George Hews (Boston: Ditson 1844).

where I was born,"[11] and for other songs that plaintively inquire, "Do they miss me at home?" and, are there still former friends in whose thoughts "we're not forgot?"[12]

A return to arcadian existence is impossible, because nothing has remained unchanged. Bluntly, an acquaintance tells Ben Bolt that the lovingly remembered "running brook has dried up," the schoolmaster is no more, that the mill where he once played "has decayed." The wanderer's childhood playmate, "sweet Alice," "has died." Mills and other arcadian edifices, if not decayed, have been "torn away/And a factory dark and high/Looms like a tower and puffs its smoke/Over the clear blue sky." Sorrow and, worse still, death have invaded the home of his parents. "Sad news from home" arrives; a father has died; a weeping mother desires "her lov'd ones by her side." Nevertheless, "far away" he must continue "to roam, far from . . . [his] native land."[13] During one conspicuously regressive moment, he blurts out:

> In a pretty little valley where I lived,
> In the midst of a wild wood;
> Oh! would that I were there again,
> Now again in my childhood!

Another wanderer reminds himself that his parents are dead, his brothers and sisters have scattered, and "our little humble dwelling now is alone/And the place seems another."[14]

An important image in the songs of experience is one of the protagonist afloat on a vast, empty, untamed sea. The sea, in popular works of the nineteenth century, is a frequently evoked symbol to depict life outside of arcadia. "And see this Atlantic," Emerson

---

[12]*Do They Miss Me at Home?*, m. S.M. Grannis (Boston: Ditson 1852); *'Tis Sweet To Be Remembered*, w. John S. Adams, m. George O. Farmer (Boston: Ditson 1849).

[13]See, respectively, *Ben Bolt*, m. Nelson Kneass (Louisville: Peters 1848); *Sweet Alice*, w. T.D. English, m. Nathan Barker (Boston: Reed 1850); *The Old Mill*, m. H.A. Whitney (Boston: Ditson 1854); *Sad News from Home*, w. and m. P.S. Gilmore (Boston: Reed 1854); *Be Kind To The Loved Ones at Home*, m. I.B. Woodbury (Boston: Ordway 1847); *Years Ago*, w. and m. Andrew J. McDowall (New York: Riley 1842).

[14]*The Grave of My Mother*, w. Henry O. Upton (Boston: Ditson 1857).

writes, "stretching its stormy chaos from pole to pole terrible by its storms, by its cold, by its ice-bergs, by its Gulf stream . . . the desert in which no caravan loiters, but all hurry as thro' the valley of the Shadow of Death."

Adding to this vision, Oliver Wendell Holmes says: "You can domesticate mountains, but the sea is *ferae naturae* . . . The sea remembers nothing. It is feline. It licks your feet,—its huge flanks purr very pleasantly for you; but it will crack your bones and eat you, for all that, and wipe the crimsoned foam from its jaws as if nothing had happened . . . the sea has a fascinating, treacherous intelligence . . . the sea drowns out humanity and time; it has no sympathy with either; for it belongs to eternity."[15]

We begin to realize that quite a few Americans had no intention of overromanticizing the sea, but instead considered it "desparately monotonous" and safer "looked at from shore, as mountains are from the plain."[16] Yet the vast, restless waters, whose horizons edged on the nameless, seemed an appropriate image of existence to them. Of course, songs did appear in which the "I" spurned the security of shorelines in order to praise the nervous thrills of seafaring. Such works, however, were comparatively few, and they alluded to youth's innocent dreams and anticipations. For the older protagonist in song, the sea always had a sterner aspect. And in all serious pieces, it represents the years of adulthood: "O, the sea to us shall a picture be,/Of our unknown future, love."[17]

Even when the sea is less directly the subject of a song, it is consistently imagined as an endless, inscrutable unfolding. For example, in one song, the pilgrim has abandoned his home to become "a stranger" roaming "o'er the wide waste of waters"; in another, he is "left on life's rough billow/With no earthly friend or guide"; in still

[15]Ralph Waldo Emerson, *The Journals and Miscellaneous Notebooks* (Cambridge, Mass.: Belknap Press 1969–1975) X, ed. Merton M. Sealts, Jr. (1973), 17; see also Oliver Wendell Holmes, *The Autocrat of the Breakfast-Table* (1858), reprinted in Vol. I of *Works,* (Boston: Houghton Mifflin 1891–1892) 270.

[16]James Russell Lowell, *Fireside Travels* (1864), in Vol. I of *The Complete Writings of James Russell Lowell,* (New York: AMS 1966) 121; see also Holmes, *Autocrat* 264-65.

[17] *Come Over the Hills to the Sea, Love,* w. "A.G.H.", m. F.W. Smith (Boston: Russell & Richardson 1857).

another, he surveys "the mighty deep" on which no island appears, no place "where weary man may find the bliss for which he sighs/ Where sorrow never lives, and friendship never dies."[18] A "troubled" immensity shrouded in mists, disturbed by "dark, cold" winds, and roiled by menacing "wild waves" is indifferent to pity and to propitiation.[19]

An affecting letter, written around 1860 by Emily Dickinson to Mrs. Samuel Bowles, who was grieving over her third stillborn child, underlines the commonality of the symbol: "Don't cry, dear Mary. Let us do that for you, because you are too tired now. We don't know how dark it is, but if you are at sea, perhaps when we say that we are there, you won't be afraid. The waves are very big, but every one that covers you, covers us, too."[20]

The ocean's waves eventually cover every human. Down, the body sinks, to disappear, to dissolve into the nothingness from before creation. The archetypal conception of watery depths as the primal womb from which life emerged and to which it must return lies behind the message of many compositions. Especially the return is described in vivid, and usually harrowing, language. Note the fearsome picture painted in Woodbury's *The Sailor Boy's Last Dream*. "Wild winds and mad waves" wreck the boy's ship:

> Like mountains the billows tremendously swell—
> In vain the lost wretch calls on mercy to save;
> Unseen hands of spirits are ringing his knell,
> And the death angel flaps his broad wing o'er the wave.
>
> Oh! sailor boy! wo [sic] to thy dream of delight!
> In darkness dissolves the gay frost work of bliss.
> Where now is the picture that fancy touched bright,
> Thy parents' fond pressure, and love's honeyed kiss?

[18]*Recollections of Home*, m. Asa B. Hutchinson, arr. E.L. White (Boston: Ditson 1846); *The Blind Orphan Boy*, m. T. Wood (Boston: Ditson 1858); *Where Can The Soul Find Rest?* (see note 9).

[19]*Marion Lee*, m. H.S. Thompson (Boston: Ditson 1858); *The Rock Beside the Sea*, m. Charlie C. Converse (Philadelphia: Lee & Walker 1857).

[20]Emily Dickinson, *Letters* 2, vols., ed Thomas H. Johnson (Cambridge, Mass.: Belknap Press 1965) II, 361.

Oh! sailor boy! sailor boy! never again
   Shall home, love or kindred thy wishes repay;
Unblessed and unhonored, down deep in the main
   Full many a fathom thy frame shall decay.

Days, months, years and ages shall circle away
   And still the vast waters above thee shall roll;
Earth loses thy pattern for ever and aye—
   Oh! sailor boy! sailor boy! peace to thy soul.[21]

GUIDANCE AND COMPANIONSHIP

Sigmund Freud, Erich Fromm, and other psychoanalysts maintain that human beings find necessary a "magic helper" to take their part against the world's threats. The transference to another of one's terror of life and apprehension of death is a way to tame inner fear.[22] In mid-nineteenth-century song, the magic helper is portrayed as a guide whose strength is love and whose ally is God.

The pilgrimaging everyman had left behind—with the pure love of his unsullied beloved and patient mother—the habits of innocence, and all that the heart values and the mind must grow to understand. During the ensuing years he may have almost lost touch with the good and gentle; but he has retained a system of beliefs that have helped ward off evil and caused him to reach out for a nobility never quite within his grasp. And as Goethe concludes, in *Faust:* "Who'ere aspires unwearedly/Is not beyond redeeming." The instrument for redemption is at hand.[23]

On occasion, the loving helpmate who guides the traveler and delivers him from danger's bondage is a deific star, as in *Star of the Evening.* "Follow me," it seems to call. He replies: "Shine on, oh

---

[21] *The Sailor Boy's Last Dream,* w. Dimond, m. I.B. Woodbury (Boston: Bradlee, 1846).

[22] Becker, *Denial of Death* 134, 145–48.

[23] See Henry Alonzo Myers, *Tragedy: A View of Life* (Ithaca, N.Y.: Cornell University Press, 1956) 12, for further discussion of this point. In addition, see Oscar and Mary F. Handlin, *Facing Life* (Boston: Little, Brown 1971) 83.

star of love divine,/And may our soul's affections twine/Around thee
as thou movest afar."[24] Assuredly, some sort of magical transference
is imbedded in this image. A star, especially the North Star, in its
predictable constancy has an important guardian relationship to the
helmsman of a ship. Thus, the metaphor of the steadfast star faith-
fully guiding man over turbulent waters is a redirection of the star's
virtues, from the real world of journeying sailing ships to the idealized one of the seafaring pilgrim.

In the song lyric that follows, the guide is a benevolent luminosity.
It directs the "I" unfailingly by means of a pure and "true" incandescence:

> The fresh'ning breeze now swells our sail,
>   A storm is on,
> The weary moon's dim lustre fails!
>   The stars are gone!
> Not so fades love's eternal light
>   When storm clouds weep:
> I know one heart's with me tonight
>   Upon the deep.[25]

At other times a praying mother's voice gives guidance. Her
words penetrate the gloom and warn of the evils along "life's devi-
ous way." Suddenly appreciating the need for her direction, the "I"
in one song says:

> Mother dear, O pray for me,
>   When all looks bright and fair
> That I may all my danger see,
>   For surely then 'tis near.[26]

It is mostly the beloved who supports him. Though distant from
her, he constantly sees her image in his mind's eye and feels her love
commanding his emotional wellspring. "Forever" shall her name
and memory "be a spell to lift my thoughts to heav'n," says the

---

[24] *Star of the Evening,* w. and melody James M. Sayles, arr. Henry Tucker (Boston: Ditson 1855).

[25] *My Bark Is Out Upon The Sea,* w. and melody George P. Morris, arr. Charles E.
Horn (Boston: Oakes 1840).

[26] *Mother Dear, O Pray for Me,* w. and m. I.B. Woodbury (Boston: Reed 1850).

journeyer in *The Sun Is in the West*. To the traveler in *The Beloved One*, she becomes the star of truth, never to be doubted, always to be followed:

> Thou art the star that guides me
> Along life's troubled sea,
> And whatever fate betides me
> This heart still turns to thee.

An almost identical statement finds its way into the song *When Other Friends Are Round Thee*.[27]

The helper need not stay alive. In fact, many songs either fail to make clear whether the guide still breathes, or they state outright that the guide is a spirit. In 1974 Lily Pincus wrote, in *Death and The Family*, on how the bereaved one keeps on searching for the one who has died, especially in dreams. She adds that there is an inner need to search, which comes to the fore especially at times of greatest strain, weakness, or illness.[28] Does not Stephen Foster state the same thing in *I See Her Still in My Dreams* and *The Voice of By Gone Days?* The desolate protagonist of the first song says that although the loved one "hath passed from the light/I see her still in my dreams." In the second song, Foster's bereaved man has suffered the loss of his "fair and gentle" loved one, who is now "beloved of angels bright." He feels "weary hearted" and seems about to collapse under the burden of his mental tensions. She, however, comes back "radiant as light" and soothes him. Her voice sounds in his "fancy" to revive hope and joy.[29]

The role of the dead guardian is made more explicit in *Yes! 'Tis True That Thy Kate Now Is Sleeping*: "For by day and by night she is near thee./Tho' she rests now in peace beneath the sod/. . . For a

---

[27] *The Sun Is In The West*, m. Lady Amateur [Mrs. C.E. Habicht], arr. Theodore T. Baker (Boston: Reed 1848); *The Beloved One*, m. George O. Farmer (Boston: Bradlee 1845); *When Other Friends Are Round Thee*, w. George P. Morris, m. C.R.W. (Baltimore: Benteen 1846).

[28] Lily Pincus, *Death and The Family* (New York: Pantheon 1974), 116.

[29] *I See Her Still In My Dreams*, w. and m. Stephen C. Foster (New York: Firth, Pond 1857); *The Voice of By Gone Days*, w. and m. Stephen C. Foster (New York: Firth, Pond 1850).

love that can not fade or perish,/Watcheth all thy pathway o'er."
The deceased Kate speaks directly to her despondent Dermot:

> For a love like mine declineth never
>   Tho' the spirit be freed from earthly clay,
> But unseen at thy side, Dermot, ever,
>   It lighteth thy path with its ray.[30]

When the British song *The Lament of the Irish Immigrant,* words by
Lady Dufferin, became popular in the early 1840s, an American
Answer was felt necessary and was quickly issued in order to counter
the message of unrelieved despair over the death of a wife and child.
The dead wife, of the *Answer,* is made to tell her husband:

> Though Erin's shores you leave, Willie,
>   An angel follows thee;
> Thy baby's spirit linked with mine
>   Shall watch thee o'er the sea;
> And when beneath the stranger's sod
>   Thy wearied form shall lie;
> Our triune shade will peaceful seek
>   Its home beyond the sky.[31]

A child alone is the magic helper in William Martin's *Come This
Way, My Father.* Making this song doubly interesting is the composer's unsubstantiated claim that the text is based on a true-life
incident. One day, while the child still lived, the father had gone
fishing, become enshrouded in dense fog, and grown desparate for
his life. At a crucial moment his boy, who was standing on a high
rock, called out to him: "Come this way, my father. I am waiting for
thee." Two weeks later, the boy died. But the father continued to
hear the voice calling out to him: "I am calling you, father. Oh! can
you not hear/The voice of your darling as you toss on life's sea?/For
on a bright shore I am waiting for thee/ . . . Come this way, father—
Oh, steer straight for me!"[32]

---

[30] *Yes! 'Tis True that Thy Kate Now Is Sleeping,* w. Rosa Hughes, m. Charles Jarvis
(Philadelphia: Gould 1853).

[31] *The Answer To The Lament of The Irish Immigrant,* w. John S. Murphy, m. T.
Bissell (Boston: Keith 1844).

[32] *Come This Way, My Father,* m. William Martin (Boston: Ditson 1855).

The 1840s and '50s were years when spiritualism invaded American minds and hotted up superstition. There became evident a widespread preoccupation with the belief that a human's spiritual entity lived on after death and could make itself known to the living. Famous spiritualists like the Fox sisters practiced and propagated the doctrine of intercourse with supernatural beings, whether through thought transference, clairvoyant revelation, transient possession, or direct contact with ghostly shapes. Popular songs swiftly recorded this national enchantment with spirits.

Several composers, around 1848, set Longfellow's poem *"Footsteps of Angels"*:

> When the hours of day are numbered,
>   And the voices of the night
> Wake the better soul that slumbered
>   To a holy, calm delight;
> Ere the evening lamps are lighted,
>   And, like phantoms grim and tall,
> Shadows from the fitful firelight
>   Dance upon the parlour wall;
> Then the forms of the departed
>   Enter at the open door;
> The beloved, the true-hearted,
>   Come to visit me once more.[33]

An almost corporeal phantom appears in the Turner-Beardslee *Spirit Voice of Bell Brandon.* The dead Bell materializes before the eyes of her mourning lover and tells him:

> List my love, I meet thee here,
>   While evening's lonely shadows fling
> Leaflets of mem'ry o'er thy cheer.
>   I come on cleaving spirit wing
> From afar beyond the cloud . . . .
>   At that sweet hour we loved so well,
> List my love, the footsteps light
>   Of thy angel birdling Bell.

---

[33]One of the most popular settings was made by William Dempster and published in Boston by Ditson in 1848.

> Her spirit hand's within thine own,
>   And rustling near her zeph'rous wings
> While through woodland haunts we roam,
>   To thee her love she ever sings.[34]

The description of an infant's apparition is perhaps overly graphic in *The Little Shroud:*

> His shroud was damp, his face was white,
>   He said, "I cannot sleep,
> Your tears have made my shroud so wet,
>   O, mother, do not weep!"[35]

These works, so directly connected with spiritualism, do give forth a consistent message relating them to compositions on magic helpers. The dead are called back by a shared, all-compelling love. They return to comfort and guide the earthbound, and to testify to the existence of a hereafter where immortal souls abide in peace and joy. The bereft mourner, held in duress by the grim world of experience, succeeds for a tranquil moment in beholding the object of his search.

A fortunate individual, according to nineteenth-century popular song, is one who can enjoy the aid of a living and closeby companion capable of the utmost faithfulness and love-giving. The valued companion had a steadfast nature that made the "I" feel secure, and a moral strength that bolstered the "I" when courage faltered. On the simplest level, the companion might be an animal, like Foster's old dog Tray, "ever faithful," "gentle," and "kind"; and "a friend" who stays by your side and will not ever abandon you: "His eyes are on me cast/I know that he feels what my breaking heart would say . . ./Grief cannot drive him away."[36]

On the most exalted level, the symbol of ideal companionship is a wife. Again and again, songs tell us how the pinnacle of love is the devotion between husband and wife. She epitomizes goodness and

---

[34]*Spirit Voice of Bell Brandon,* w. Dr. Carolus Francis Turner, m. John B. Beardslee (Boston: Ditson 1858).

[35]*The Little Shroud,* w. Miss L.E. Landon, m. I.N. Metcalf (Boston: Prentiss 1844).

[36]*Old Dog Tray,* w. and m. Stephen C. Foster (New York: Firth, Pond 1853).

stands unquestioningly by her husband through every difficulty.

The outer world of experience, Emerson once said, is a societal wilderness where nobody can realize "his natural dimensions" or expect "any sentiment, any truth, any human encouragement" but instead finds people who are "mutual corrupters and spectacles of meanness and atrophy to each other."[37] To counter the ravages of temptation, strife, and overall sordidness, man needs "to seek consolation and correction from one who is placed beyond their influence," states James Fenimore Cooper.[38]

Emerson, Cooper, and other contemporary writers convey man's awareness of contamination by society and the feelings of guilt caused by participation in its activities. Only the hermit and monk can stand undefiled, and even they are prey to inner misgivings. Hence the need for the symbol of woman, who, like the Virgin Mary, senses all suffering yet remains untainted. She can ease all feelings of guilt, asking nothing for herself. In her wifely incarnation, she has the home as sanctuary, as the focus of safety and healing in a dangerous and diseased environment.

A moving example of how man can feel placed beyond the influence of conflict and corruption is given by James Russell Lowell. He wrote to John Francis Heath on 15 December 1842 and described a typical evening with his wife Maria: "What strange goblins are gambolling, what gentle spirits are watching in the darkness beyond, I know not—save by force of imagination. One spirit, whiter and purer than the snow which covers the fields now, I know sits beside me and guards me. I feel the gentle and holy presence of her soul all around mine, like the deep, still blue around a star, or like the all-embracing hope that circled warmly the heart of young Leander as he struck out boldly through the narrow strait between life and death."[39]

An occasional song shows a man reluctant to marry his beloved, because then she will be subjected to the distress of having to share

---

[37]Emerson, *Journals* VIII, ed. William H. Gilman and J.E. Parsons (1970) 322.

[38]James Fenimore Cooper, *Notions of the Americans,* 2 vols. (1828), reprint (New York: Ungar 1963) I, 105–06).

[39]Lowell, *Letters, Vol. I,* in Vol. XIV of *Complete Writings,* 100.

his hard fortune.[40] But a work of this sort actually is designed to establish how selflessly a woman should be loved and is not designed to indicate a final decision of the "I" to remain celibate. When given the opportunity, he generally marries.

Alone, as he is in a majority of the songs, he has needed to imagine a distant or dead helper. Married, he has one who is palpable and ever present—surely a more satisfactory alternative. And the "I" does have a wife in a large minority of the songs that are centered on the years of experience. Interestingly, when she is present no spirit appears; nor is one needed.

Wait for the Wagon employs the wagon as the symbol for home. The newly wedded couple mounts the vehicle to begin a life's trip whose ultimate destination is the tomb and arrival in eternity:

> Together on life's journey, we'll travel 'till we stop,
>   And if we have no trouble, we'll reach the happy top.
> Then come with me, sweet Phyllis, my dear, my lovely bride,
>   We'll jump into the Wagon, and all take a ride.[41]

Although the text seems to indicate a farm as an interim goal—where she will "mind the dairy" and he will "guide the plough"—the refrain repeatedly reminds the listeners that they must all "wait for the wagon" and "all take a ride." The final "happy top," where a halt to life's journey will be made, must of necessity be heaven.

The usual symbol for home outside of arcadia is a boat trying to stay afloat on a treacherous sea. In *Maggie By My Side*, the "I" departs the secure shore and, with Maggie, makes a "home . . . on the waters wide." Winds howl, storms rage, and dark waves threaten their fragile craft; but her love, goodness, and faith help see them through. He fears nothing while she remains steadfastly beside him:

> Storms can appal me never, while her brow is clear,
>   Fair weather lingers ever, where her smiles appear.
> When sorrow's breakers 'round my heart shall hide,
>   Still may I find her sitting by my side.[42]

---

[40]See, for example, *I'd Offer Thee This Hand of Mine*, m. L.T. Chadwick (New York: Firth, Hall & Pond 1842).

[41]*Wait For the Wagon*, by G.P. Knauff (Baltimore: Benteen 1851).

[42]*Maggie By My Side*, w. and m. Stephen C. Foster (New York: Firth, Pond 1852).

Whatever afflictions the outside world introduces (phrased poetically: "Tho' the storm hath encompassed the sea"), husband and wife continue to delight in each other—an observation made in *Row Thy Boat Lightly*. The rowboat in this song, however, is no staunch oceangoing vessel. Eventually it founders, and husband and wife die: "Together they go/To the still depths of the caverns below."[43]

Earlier, in the discussion of *The Sailor Boy's Last Dream*, the ocean's depths were seen to serve as an archetypal metaphor for the primal womb. No "unblessed" dying occurs in *Row Thy Boat Lightly*, as it did in *The Sailor Boy's Last Dream*. The sailor boy had died on a strange vessel distant from home. In *Row Thy Boat Lightly*, the boat *is* home, and this alters the implication of the act of death. Water has taken on another dimension. It consecrates the expiring couple, since drowning can also symbolize purification; that is to say, a baptism by total immersion preparatory to spiritual rebirth. No special horror attends the couple's death. They are people who have lived full lives, insofar as any human can in this world. One might even add that their lives have ended in an appropriately Christian manner.

In general, and apart from the husband-wife relationship, the "I" sees himself isolated from society by a spiritual debilitation that has become life-threatening. Because he finds it impossible to become one with his surroundings, he needs to see through the veils of his depression to someone who acknowledges and values his existence. The first lesson, therefore, that his life in the world has taught him is the necessity for faith in some being who confirms his immeasurable importance, whether imaged as a guiding star, a mother's voice, the beloved's spirit, or the unsunderable union with a wife.

Furthermore, he has learned that no escape from suffering is possible on earth, even though in an occasional song, like *Come Away, Love* or *Bermuda's Fairy Isle*, he may dream wistfully of discovering a land where falseness and sorrow are unknown. Hawthorne had come to a similar conclusion when, in 1836, he jotted an idea for a story into his notebook. Two lovers wish to build a pleasure-house on

---

[43] *Row Thy Boat Lightly*, w. Miss H.F. Woodman, m. I.B. Woodbury (Boston: Prentiss & Clark 1847).

a certain spot but see there some miserable children, other people plotting a crime, and the dead body of a dear friend. "And instead of a pleasure-house, they build a tomb. The moral,—that there is no place on earth fit for the site of a pleasure-house, because there is no spot that may not have been saddened by human grief, stained by crime, or hallowed by death."[44]

Another lesson learned is the realization that pain can have meaning. The more he has been assailed by evil, the more he has come to prize and desire the good. To paraphrase Emerson, he may not have been pious, but he has become a lover of the pious.[45] Like the Prodigal Son, he found only deception where he expected pleasure. Now his spirit pauses on the threshold and begs the consolation of the Father.

While anxiety continues real enough, its resolution is close at hand. At least he now recognizes the clash between man's secular and spiritual goals, understands how the strife grew, and knows he must set about reordering his objectives.

JOURNEY'S END

How can we account for the fervor that attended the singing of songs on death and dying? I surmise it was partly owing to the disillusionment of the nineteenth-century multitudes with mundane existence, and to this music's unequaled power to reach the heart of their spiritual preoccupations. Numbered among these heavy-hearted Americans were those who had profited greatly in the competition for worldly goods: they, too, felt cut off from the traditions that had held their parents' generation together and to which they could not return. In the swiftly changing antebellum United States, there seemed to be in place no new national framework that could satisfy even rudimentary moral wants. Every personal spiritual con-

[44]*Come Away, Love,* by Mrs. Bailey (Baltimore: Willig, 1846); *Bermuda's Fairy Isle,* w. T.M.Y., m. Henry Williams (Boston: Tolman, 1854); Nathaniel Hawthorne, in Vol. XVII of *The Complete Works* (Boston: Houghton Mifflin 1884) 37–38.

[45]Emerson, *Journals* VII, ed. A.W. Plumstead and Harrison Hayford (1969), 460.

sideration fell a prey to the ceaseless contention over slavery, states' rights, the settlement of the western territories, industrialization, and foreign trade. Several years of economic depression and the scramble to keep ahead of competition for jobs and housing unhinged any feeling of security.

If the life about them afforded no satisfaction, what then? Mankind's time-honored answer was also theirs; fulfillment came only with death. It was important to Americans to have their songs of death show what the human spirit is like when it is aware of the possibility of its moral worth, to exemplify how the mettle in the mind of the faithful should manifest itself, and to indicate where the search for serenity must end.

Because we live in a twentieth century obsessed with youth and uncomfortable about thoughts of aging and dying, we find it difficult to understand why the mid-nineteenth century was a period when people had a close relationship with death. A century and a half ago, family members and friends in full health one day might die suddenly on the next. Cholera, for example, struck the cities of America in 1832, 1849, 1850, and 1854; yellow fever, in 1841, 1847, 1850, 1852, and 1855. The life expectancy of the average American was under forty years. During the 1840s and '50s, every fourth death in New York City was that of an infant or little child. About 46 percent of all deaths in Boston during the 1840s were of children under five. Young women often died during or soon after childbirth. Young men often died by accident. Fatal disease respected neither rich nor poor.[46] Note Emily Dickinson's realism, in a letter sent to Abiah Root, in 1845: "Mrs. Jones and Mrs. S. Mack have both of them a little *daughter*. Very promising *Children* I understand. I don't doubt if they live they will be ornaments to society."[47] Already at fifteen years of age, she was conversant with death.

[46]Lewis O. Saum, "Death in the Popular Mind of Pre–Civil War America," in David E. Stannard, ed., *Death in America*, (Philadelphia: University of Pennsylvania Press 1975), Russell 33; B. Nye, *Society and Culture in America, 1830–1860* (New York: Harper & Row 1974) 340; Carl Bode, *The Anatomy of American Popular Culture* (Berkeley: University of California Press 1959) 206; Wilma Clark, "Four Popular Poets: A Century of Taste," *New Dimensions in Popular Culture*, ed. Russell B. Nye (Bowling Green, Ohio: Bowling Green University Popular Press 1972) 193.

[47]Dickinson, *Letters* I, 17.

When contemporary writers like Donald Mitchell spoke of death, they drew from their own intimate experiences. Mitchell's earliest memories included the dying of a baby brother and sister, the serious childhood illnesses and the resultant physical disabilities of his brother Louis, the destruction of his mother's health when he was fifteen and her death two years later, the death of his brother Stephen shortly after that of his mother, and the death of his sister Elizabeth two years later.[48]

What made nineteenth-century Americans feel the brevity and unpredictable termination of life much more intensely than heretofore was the spreading conviction that neither fate, nor sin, nor free-will act of the victim could explain what happened. They knew that science and medicine were moving at a fast pace. Malnutrition and unsanitary living conditions, investigators were now saying, undermined health. Natural catastrophe could be anticipated in many instances; disease, averted or cured. But, unfortunately, most of the solutions were still in the future. Because too many people still died before their time, even as expectancy of remedy lay just over the horizon, a keen poignancy attended every death that onlookers believed might have been avoided.

Given such feelings, the public wished its popular songs to serve as a catharsis, delivering bereaved ones of their freight of tragic remembrances and directing them to sources for renewed strength. A song of death was meant to leave the listener humble in spirit and compassionate toward others. Ideally, it subdued the tendency to flee from the frightening unknown, encouraged sympathetic understanding of the processes of dying, and affirmed one's belief in life's continuity beyond the grave.

Such a song appraised grief itself realistically, albeit in nineteenth-century terms. It made no attempt to sweep grief into a cobwebby corner of the heart and smother it with a blanket of forgetfulness. Moreover, grief frequently became the culminating emotion that etched the unavoidable consequences of earthly life on the consciousness with the thrusts of a sharp stylus.

Popular songs were expected to be sensitive to the several phases

[48]Waldo H. Dunn, *The Life of Donald G. Mitchell* (New York: Scribner's Sons 1922) 50–51.

that the grief-stricken went through. They portrayed the mourner acting lost, bewildered, empty of certitude, and lacking energy to go on living. Stupification shortly gave way to attacks of anguish and longing for the departed one. This change is exemplified in Foster's *Gentle Annie* (1856):

> Thou wilt come no more, gentle Annie,
>   Like a flower thy spirit did depart;
> Thou are gone, alas! like the many
>   That have bloomed in the summer of my heart.
> Shall we never more behold thee;
>   Never hear thy winning voice again—
> When the Spring time comes, gentle Annie,
>   When the wild flowers are scattered o'er the plain?

He may also feel uneasy about having abandoned the now lifeless beloved, mother, or father. He may find himself blameworthy for not having been "kind to the loved ones at home"—to quote a Woodbury song that warns you that the living can unexpectedly become the dead, and with them dies good intentions.

Everything relatable to the dead grew precious. Hence the countless musical compositions lauding old Bibles, armchairs, locks of hair, and whatnot. When a surrogate presence proved unsatisfactory, the mourner reunited with the object of his pining through intense reveries or mightly materializations; thus the songs that begin: "I dream of . . . " or "I see her spirit . . . " The viewpoint taken is that grief is better faced and felt in its fullest intensity than avoided or repressed. Man can not escape pain but must learn to live with it.

In time the mourner recognizes the futility of his desire for earthly reunion. A solid understanding of the world has now become possible, if the mourner will only take the opportunity afforded—so the songs claim. The vehemence of sorrow has freed him from his material surroundings and opened the way toward a clairvoyant perception of life's scheme and, ultimately, toward a fresh, transcendent goal.

At the least, giving a musical expression to bereftness was psychotherapeutic. Bottled-up feelings were provided a tongue. Songs gathered the totality of pain, made it tangible, and helped expurgate it from the soul.

Another, no less important role for song was to confront an individual's anxieties about his own death, as well as the death of a loved one, with a network of beliefs that provided for a person's future welfare. We get a sense of how everyone's natural and comprehensive terror over lifelessness obliged humans to create a common symbology to cope with their fears by translating beliefs into readily understandable and convincing images. I am reminded of Ernest Becker's statement, in *The Denial of Death,* that man tries hard "to protect himself against the accidents of life and danger of death, trying to use the symbols of culture as a sure means of triumph over natural mystery, trying to pass himself off as anything but an animal."[49]

Assuredly, triumph over death's mystery is a first-line principle in popular works dealing with man's final hour. A person needs to expect an end to grief and a reunion with the dead, however much the evidence of the senses seems to negate the possibility. In the song *No More,* the protagonist cannot bear the loss of a loved one. He asks if they will meet again and hears the reply, "No more." He then speaks for the song's audience when he rejects this answer:

> Oh in that word there is a spell
>   Sinks to my bosom's inmost core,
> To live, yet hear that hated knell
>   Proclaim'd on earth, we meet no more.
> Then may we hope in Heaven to meet
>   Where all our sorrows will be o'er,
> To find at last a sure retreat
>   Where worldly wisdom guides no more?

Even more positive is the voice of the "I" in *Lorena.* He makes it clear he will never forget his beloved. Both are mortal; both must die. But:

> There is a Future! O, thank God,
>   Of life *this* is so small a part!
> 'Tis dust to dust beneath the sod;
>   But there, *up there,* 'tis heart to heart.[50]

[49]Becker, *Denial of Death* 32.
[50]*No More,* by a Young Lady of Georgia (Philadelphia: Osbourn 1836); *Lorena,* w. Rev. H.D.L. Webster, m. J.P. Webster (Chicago: Higgins 1857).

123

The listener hears how man is of the earth, but of heaven, too. When his body crumbles, his spirit soars. For him, for everyone he loves, there is a future superintended by an all-powerful deity who commands the seeming impossibilities attending postmortem life.

To summarize, the potency of song's death symbols is felt in three ways. First, the symbols transmute the dead from an earthly corpse into a happy spirit abiding in a divine realm; thus, despair is replaced with revived hope. Second, they allay whatever guilt the living person feels about the dead, by demonstrating the inevitability of all that has happened. Third, they give the earthbound survivor a confidence in his own immortality, assuring him that personality will endure and that spiritual existence will be guaranteed.[51]

In our twentieth century, hospitals conceal most of the dying— and funeral parlors, most of the newly dead—from the living. Prescribed hospital visiting hours limit the stay of adults; the desire to prolong innocence prohibits the attendance of children. Impersonal rooms, ominous tubes and monitors, business-bent nurses, and desensitizing tranquilizers cut off communication between visitor and patient. Unctuous funeral directors and blandly contrived arrangements dilute the confrontation with mortality.[52]

Most nineteenth-century Americans rejected placebos that drained meaning from the deathwatch. The culminating stage in man's earthly progress, the passage to eternity, was far too important to treat in emotionally neutralizing fashion. The deathbed was fraught with revelation. Therefore, family and friends gathered to keep vigil by the bedside, witness the moment of dying, and contemplate the resurgence of the deceased.

Songs scarcely minimized the distress of the onlookers. They did, however, impart a standardized expression to it, which insured immediate assimilability and universal comprehensiveness. Commonly encountered phrases describe the scene: *Cora Lee*'s "We stood in grief around the bed of dying Cora Lee"; *Lilly Dale*'s "Friends mute with grief stood around the death bed"; *Sad News from Home*'s "Friends

---

[51]For a commentary on the function of death symbols, see W. Lloyd Warner, *The Living and the Dead: A Study of the Symbolic Life of Americans* (New Haven, Conn.: Yale University Press 1959) 308.

[52]Pincus, *Death* 252.

gather there in gloom" and a wife weeps for a dying husband, with "her lov'd ones by her side." One bereft individual laments his sister's dying:

> I remember well my sorrow, as I stood beside her bed,
>> And my deep and heartfelt anguish, when they told me *she was dead.*
>
> And oh! that cup of bitterness—*let not my heart rebel . . .*[53]

and echoes Donald Mitchell's description of a brother's dying. He, a sister Nelly, and his mother watch and weep as "little Charlie's" life ebbs to nothing. The mother tells the doctor she is calm, even as "deep, smothered sobs" rack her body. Then comes the witnessing of death: "The doctor lifts you in his arms, that you may see—that pale head—those blue eyes all sunken—that flaxen hair gone—those white lips pinched and hard!—Never, never, will the boy forget his first terrible sight of Death!"[54]

Compare this final sentence with the similar one uttered in the song *The Parting Requiem:*

> We parted in silence our cheeks were wet,
>> With tears that were past controlling,
> And we vow'd that we'd never, no, never forget,
>> And the vows at the time were consoling.[55]

The composition gives a picture, first, of death at night just before rebirth into the light of heaven; second, of feelings so benumbing that all conversation soon ceases; and third, of love so profound that it bespeaks permanency.

Oliver Wendell Holmes would like us to believe that "almost always there is a preparation made by Nature for unearthing a soul." The dying are weary and want rest; or in pain and want relief; or narcotized and unaware of their surroundings; or looking forward to

---

[53] *Cora Lee,* w. and m. W. Irving Hartshorne (Boston: Ditson 1855); *Lilly Dale,* w. and m. H.S. Thompson (Boston: Ditson 1852); *Sad News from Home,* w. and m. P.S. Gilmore (Boston: Reed 1854); *He Doeth All Things Well,* w. F.M.E., m. I.B. Woodbury (Boston: Reed 1844).

[54] [Donald G. Mitchell], *Dream Life,* by Ik Marvel (New York: Scribner 1854) 70–71.

[55] *The Parting Requiem,* m. John C. Baker (Boston: Keith 1847).

eternity, so strong is their faith.[56] On the other hand, many songs tell us nothing of the sort. The dying, they say, are almost always in extreme terror before they make their peace with their fate. They mourn for themselves and, by so doing, blunt their intense apprehension of what is to come. Those departing this life beg to be encircled and comforted by those they know. "Come to me quickly," one of them pleads with "lov'd ones . . . in a distant land," for "trembling I stand on this mortal shore." Another feels a "chilly dampness" reaching into the body, like the underground coldness of the "drear old church yard." Still another is aghast at dying "alone in the night of the grave"; as the "beautiful world" he loves recedes from view, he panics and clutches his mother's hand, whispering: "The grave is deep and dark, mother/And heaven seems far away."[57]

The mother of the last song never loosens her grip until her son senses a new light illumining his exit, realizes "death is the gate of life," and dies feeling himself drawn "on high" to another existence.

Apparently, song lyrics like this last one confirm the conclusion of Jacques Choron, in *Modern Man and Mortality* (1964), who writes that uppermost in the mind is the fear of the act of dying, since this means possible suffering and a necessary confrontation with the knowledge of your own ending. Add the Christian apprehension that the departing soul may be waylaid by the forces of evil, and we can understand the dying one's desire for assistance of every kind in order to pass safely into the hereafter.[58] For this reason, the mother assists her dying boy by praying by the bedside and telling him to watch for "the child with the angel wing" who comes to bear him to the place "where the seraphs sweetly sing." For this same reason, the onlooker assists his dying friend with the comforting "pressure of

[56]Oliver Wendell Holmes, *The Professor at the Breakfast-Table* (1859), reprinted as Vol. II of *Works,* 276.

[57]*Come To Me Quickly,* w. and m. George Root (New York: Hall 1855); *The Dying Girl,* m. William H. Doane (Boston: Ditson 1858); *Bury Me In The Morn, Mother,* w. Mrs. S.J. Hale, m. G.A. Smith (Boston: Ditson 1857).

[58]Jacques Choron, *Modern Man and Mortality* (New York: Macmillan 1964) 77–78.

the hand" and the "good-bye" (meaning, God be with you) at "the look of the closing eye," so that the dead can go heavenward at peace with themselves.[59]

Even as they comforted the dying loved one, family members and friends watched closely for spontaneous signs of Christian resoluteness and acquiescence to God's will, since in these signs was hope for themselves. During their bedside attendance, they expected to have their minds stimulated by a knowledge of divine power and their hearts quickened by an intimation of divine concern.

Especially instructive was the change from earthly suffering to eternal peace that they viewed on the face of the heavenbound. In real life, the description of this change and other lessons garnered at the bedside became the subject matter of lengthy letters to distant correspondents anxious about the final hours of the deceased. After Henry Longfellow's wife Mary died, in December 1835, he sent to a friend a detailed description of her gradual vanquishment by illness and an assurance that both Mary and he had bowed in submission to God's decree. Another Mary, wife of William Foster, Stephen Foster's brother, died suddenly while away from home, in January 1838. A long letter from Mary's brother to her husband informed him that she was "calm and composed, her tranquil spirit patiently awaited its last moment of time on earth. The family were called up to witness her last moments at 4 o'clock A.M. . . . ."

A final example, a communication from Emily Dickinson to Abiah Root, sent in March 1846, describes her dying friend Sophia Holland: "She lay mild & beautiful as in health & her pale features lit up with an unearthly—smile. I looked as long as friends would permit."[60]

Death taught the living to cherish one another, to realize how

[59] *Child of The Angel Wing,* w. Mrs. R.S. Nichols, m. Charles Balmer (St. Louis: Balmer & Weber 1849); *Good Bye,* m. J.R. Thomas (New York: Waters 1853).

[60] Longfellow, *Letters,* 2 vols. (Cambridge, Mass.: Belknap Press 1966) I, 526–28; Evelyn Foster Morneweck, *Chronicles of Stephen Foster's Family,* 2 vols. (Pittsburgh: University of Pittsburgh Press 1944) I, 135; Dickinson, *Letters* I, 32. See also Saum, "Death" 34, 43–44; Pincus, *Death* 250.

everyone lives but a moment, and then dies. Why mark this ephemerality with delusory strife? As one song states:

> Be kind to each other!
>   The night's coming on,
> When friend and when brother,
>   Perchance may be gone!
> Then 'midst our dejection,
>   How sweet to have earned
> The blest recollection
>   Of kindness returned.
> When day hath departed,
>   And memory keeps
> Her watch broken-hearted
>   Where all she loved sleeps! . . .
>
> Let falsehood assail not,
>   Nor envy disprove—
> Let trifles prevail not—
>   Against those ye love!
> Nor change with tomorrow,
>   Should fortune take wing,
> But the deeper the sorrow,
>   The closer still cling![61]

Letter writers always encircled the deathbed with comforting onlookers. To die triumphantly meant the conquest of terror, the winning of the serenity that came with accepting God's determination, and (not least) the calming of the anxieties over death felt by all persons. A special wisdom might come from the lips of the dying, which would instruct the listeners in righteous behavior and the nature of the post-death life.

Phineas Taylor Barnum, the master showman, says that at fifteen years of age, he with his family watched his grandmother slowly fade away: "The day before she died she sent for her grandchildren to take final leave of them. I shall never forget the sensations I experienced when she took me by the hand and besought me to lead a

[61]*Be Kind to Each Other,* w. Charles Swain, m. C.E. Phillips (Boston: Bradle\ 1845).

religious life, and especially to remember that I could in no way so effectually prove my love to God as by loving my fellow-beings."[62]

A second example shows that wisdom may come by merely viewing the passage from life to death. After Stephen Foster's sister Charlotte died distant from home, in November 1829, Hill Rowan, one of several friends who had witnessed her death, wrote to Ann Eliza, another of Foster's sisters. Rowan states that Charlotte sang a little during her last hours. Then: "There were prayers for blessings upon you all—after this she soon became flighty and talked much, and until within twenty minutes of her death, and never, never have I seen anyone die so easy, no convulsions, not the writhing of a feature—There she lay serene, placid & quiescent—all the innocence of her soul complexion'd out in a countenance which seemed chastened by the tranquillity of a sweet sleep."[63]

Uncle Tom's Cabin, both the novel and its dramatized version, which was the great stage hit of the mid-nineteenth century, inspired several song writers to produce compositions based on its subject and characters. One of these works, *I Am Going There,* records the deathbed wisdom of little Eva. Calling her father, "she sweetly said, 'O father, my strength it is failing fast,/Do let me speak ere it all hath fled!'/Then she spoke to her friends—'forever love/All that is holy, and good, and fair.' " She prophesied to Uncle Tom: "We shall meet above,/Above—with the holy angels there." Then came the final, hushed moment for revelation:

> In a breathless silence her friends came round;
> While her large clear eyes so fix'd and fair,
> Look'd up to heaven—and a whispering sound
> Said gently and sweetly—"I'm going there."
>
> A glorious smile o'er her features played,
> Seldom seen in a changing world like this,
> Then the gentlest of earth—sweet Eva—strayed
> Forth to a world of endless bliss.[64]

[62]Phineas T. Barnum, *Struggles and Triumphs* (Buffalo: Courier 1875), 38.
[63]Morneweck, *Foster's Family* I, 73–74.
[64]*I Am Going There,* w. John S. Adams, adapted to a favorite melody (Boston: Ditson 1852).

The vision of the dying Cora Lee is more explicit than that of Eva. The bedside witnesses watch Cora Lee expire willingly, after she announces:

> Bright angels now are hov'ring near,
>   Their fairy forms I see;
> Oh! farewell all—They're calling now
>   For your poor Cora Lee.[65]

Song after song stresses the importance of the gathering of family and friends to comfort and learn from the dying. Lewis Saum, writing about death in antebellum America, states that "humble folk" lived in fear of the "spiritual and emotional loss incurred by an unattended death." He quotes a poem occasioned by the death of Ephraim Beeson, in the Iowa Territory, in 1843:

> But if no parents near him stand
>   To raise the drooping head,
> If no kind sister lend a hand
>   To smooth the sufferer's bed,
> Oh then let pitty [sic] more and more
>   Tears of affection shed,
> For him who on the stranger's shore
>   Now sleeps among the dead.[66]

Note the dismay expressed in *The Gold-Digger's Grave,* a song from the gold-rush days. A man has died alone in the wilderness. Strangers have dug a grave and "left him in the solitude." How terrible it is to know: "No bell peal'd forth its solemn toll,/To tell the transit of his soul;/No prayer was o'er him slowly said/By those who buried up the dead."[67]

Sadder than a death on land is one taking place at sea and away from loved ones. In *The Ocean Burial,* a wanderer is dying on board a ship sailing him back to his parents. He begs not to be immediately buried, but to be returned to his family and to a place where people

---

[65] *Cora Lee* (see note 53).

[66] Saum, "Death" 42.

[67] *The Gold-Digger's Grave,* w. Marshall S. Pike, m. N.P.B. Curtiss (Boston: Prentiss 1850).

will weep for and pray over him. He fears that his body will be dropped overboard into an ocean wilderness: "Where no light will break through the dark, cold wave/And no sunbeam rest upon my grave." He envisions himself lying on the ocean bed, his body entwined in the icy coils of a sea snake. His mother, he says, "hath twined these locks, and hath kissed this brow./In the hair she hath wreathed, shall the sea snake hiss?/And the brow she hath pressed, shall the cold wave kiss?"[68] This is his ultimate horror.

A loved one's land burial close to home was, of course, desired by those who would cherish the deceased's memory. A nearby interment meant the feelings that had united family and friends to the loved one during life could now center themselves on the departed's tomb. Moreover, a mourner could reexperience important truths while contemplating the grave site. Standing at the consecrated spot, a sensitive human absorbed a never-ending stillness in which time and motion became suspended. Longfellow once sent a letter to his mother, telling her he had recently experienced the death of a close friend. He felt drawn to the cemetery where his friend lay, attracted by the quiet sanctity of the place: "I stand within this sanctuary of the dead and reflect what silent dissolution is going on around me and how dust is gradually loosening itself from the form into which nature had moulded it, and mingling with dust again—I forget the world and all its cares. I feel the religion of the place—for here is set a limit to humanity—The afflicted have found consolation and the weary rest. What a lesson is here for pride—that it must soon lay down side by side with the humblest child of day! What a lesson for ambition—that a few feet of earth must ere long be the boundary of its possessions! What a lesson for passion—that the grave is so cold and senseless, and that friend and foe are at rest together."[69]

The grave site furnished a mourner like Longfellow with concrete images about every person's destiny. Before him were objects to which his mind's deepest imaginings and most secret misgivings could cling. True, they pointed to the inevitability of his earthly extinction and the doubtfulness of his own postmortal securement. But

---

[68] *The Ocean Burial*, m. George N. Allen (Boston: Ditson 1850).
[69] Longfellow, *Letters* I, 119–20.

at the same time, these objects were societally sanctioned accoutrements of all cemeteries. They symbolized a faith that could rekindle his hopes.

Songs exploited the emblems of death. They showed the tombstone standing impervious to decay, and with the dead one's name engraved into obdurate granite or marble. Below, the tomb held "a treasure . . . in its close embrace." From this tomb the soul would be resurrected into "a world of endless bliss."[70] Every dead human had a "spirit immortal" that "the tomb cannot bind."[71] A second symbol was the towering tree. Invariably, the burial takes place " 'neath the old Arbor tree . . . whose spreading boughs sweep the ground." A tree, particularly "the broad and waving willow," will guard the grave and, in the tree's eternal winter's slumbering and spring's awakening, will betoken eternal life. *The Old Mill* tells us that the miller is dead; but the willow has turned green again and will send his sad Lily "a sprig to remind" her "of him."[72] Life's continuity is on occasion symbolized by an evergreen or, very rarely, by an "old grape bower."[73]

To complete the scene, water flowing nearby was essential. The brook, like an individual's life, merged with other brooks to become rivers, which in turn merged to become an ocean. The soul also flows downstream after death to fuse with other souls. Therefore, Lilly Dale lies " 'neath the chestnut tree," while nearby a "stream ripples forth"; "darling little blue-eyed Nell" lies in a "shady dell" "where the placid little stream/Seems to murmur in a dream"; and the "dark Virginny bride," Nelly, lies "close by de margin ob de water,/Whar de love weeping willow grows."[74]

Often the dead are depicted as crossing over the water to "the far

[70] *I Am Going There* (see note 64).

[71] *The Grave of Bonaparte*, m. L. Heath (Boston: Ditson, 1843).

[72] *Bell Brandon*, w. T. Ellwood Garrett, m. Francis Woolcott (St. Louis: Balmer 1854); *The Willow Song*, w. J. Wesley Hanson, m. L.N. Metcalf (Boston: Prentiss & Clark 1847); *The Old Mill*, m. H.A. Whitney (Boston: Ditson 1854).

[73] See, for example, *Cara Lee*, m. T.H. Howe (Boston: Ditson 1854).

[74] *Lilly Dale* (see note 53); *Darling Little Blue Eyed Nell*, w. B.E. Woolf, m. Frederick Buckley (New York: Firth, Pond 1859); *Nelly Was a Lady*, w. and m. Stephen C. Foster (New York: Firth, Pond 1849).

more beautiful shore of the stream of life so fair." Especially fortunate are those whom God himself guides over the waters "to the bright blissful shore."[75]

Immortality is the final aim of humans unable to accept the idea of their own dissolution into nothingness. Emily Dickinson once wrote that she found it impossible to believe she would ever cease to live.[76] Whittier insisted his desire for immortality was neither "egoistic" nor "sensual," for "human intercourse" was "sweet" and God will not be so cruel as to not will "what is best for man."[77]

The songs show us nineteenth-century Americans growing older and worrying increasingly about death. They seem to have felt that a significant effect on their earthly situation and on their future destiny would take place, if only they believed absolutely that life had meaning beyond mere worldly survival. Somehow, immortality would be conferred as a gift on those who trusted in it. They had "met the world with all its change,/And sought its pleasures—felt its pain." Belief that their lives had purpose made them "young again, brothers . . . in love and truth." The fear of death collapsed before the persuasion that "old friends" awaited them "in realms above," where they would learn "the heart's the same—'tis love renewed."[78] We are reminded of Ernest Becker's assertion that the urge to immortality is not merely a product of death anxiety but a reaching out of one's entire being toward life, since God and immortality are "a logical fulfillment of the Agape side of man's nature."[79]

Surprisingly few songs describe the afterlife. It would seem that the usual American, like Emily Dickinson, saw "nothing but . . . angels bearing" the deceased into "the blue sky of which we don't know anything." Those one or two songs that do give a description usually see heaven through a child's eyes. Typical of the child's view

[75]*Aleen*, m. George Root (Boston: Russell & Tolman 1858); *The Indian's Lament*, by The Hutchinson Family, arr. Edward L. White (Boston: Marsh 1846).

[76]Dickinson, *Letters* I, 28.

[77]Norman Foerster, *Nature in American Literature* (New York: Russell & Russell 1958), 36.

[78]*Give Me Your Hand, Old Friend of Youth*, w. and m. John P. Ordway (Boston: Ordway 1858).

[79]Becker, *Denial of Death* 152–53.

is Woodbury's *We Are Happy Now, Dear Mother*, where a vague place of "glorious sunlight," flowers, mild "zephyrs," and beauty that "never pales" is mentioned. Again, Covert's *The Child's Dream* tells of a garden containing orange trees, singing birds, and "groves of light"—nothing more.[80] Apparently, to die a Christian was sufficient for the masses who enjoyed popular songs. To hope for immortality was joy enough; to ponder an existence that was beyond their experience and that was incapable of demonstration was profitless.

Innocents, however, were preeminantly suited to the relaying of whatever information on immortality was vouchsafed mankind. When a child's or young beloved's life was cut off, the innocent "died ere scarce a shade of care/Had touched her little heart./She knew not what it was to bear/Affliction's painful smart."[81] Some, though themselves undefiled, had grieved for the "wrong," "pain," and "sin" of the world. When they died, they remained "sweet," "gentle," and capable of "love so measureless"—therefore, worthy of joining the "blessed angels."[82] These guiltless ones died oftentimes with lives incomplete, potentialities unrealized. For them, postmortal continuation had to be postulated if existence was to make any sense at all. Although these innocents might return scant intelligence of the beyond, they were expected to intercede with all the strength of the pure on behalf of the living. Every human needed a personal friend in the heavenly court. So Eva as an angel will pray for her father's "peace and comfort"; and Bell Brandon will watch until "the toils of life are o'er," then "bear" her loved one "to the blest."[83]

Hawthorne's comment, in his *Notebook* of 1838, helps illustrate this last point: "L.H.—. She was unwilling to die, because she had no friends to meet her in the other world. Her little son F. being very ill, on his recovery she confessed a feeling of disappointment, having supposed that he would have gone before and welcomed her into

---

[80]Dickinson, *Letters* II, 362; *We Are Happy Now, Dear Mother,* m. I.B. Woodbury (New York: Waters 1853); *The Child's Dream,* m. Bernard Covert (Boston: Wade 1848).

[81]*Jenny Dale,* w. S.H. Hazeltine, m. J.C. Bowker (Boston: Ditson 1854).

[82]*Little Eva,* w. John G. Whittier, m. Manuel Emilio (Boston: Jewett 1852).

[83]*Eva To Her Papa,* w. and m. George C. Howard (New York: Waters 1853).

heaven!"[84] Or consider Donald Mitchell's comment, in *Dream Life*, on a brother's death: "You feel an access of goodness growing out of your boyish grief: you feel right-minded: it seems as if your little brother, in going to Heaven, had opened a pathway thither . . ."[85] As one song sets forth, it is the spirit voice of an innocent that can confidently call out to the dying: "Oh, steer straight for me!/Here safely in heaven, I'm waiting for thee." Oftentimes, songs like the one just quoted hint at a psychic need to rediscover a dear one whose death the mourner cannot fully accept. They exemplify a conclusion reached by Lily Pincus, after she had spent many hour monitoring the mental state of the bereaved. She found the more the initial pain of separation decreased, the more there commenced a "searching," which might "lead to finding a sense of the lost person's presence."[86]

Again and again the songs affirm that loved ones, particularly those who died lamblike, did become angel-spirits after death. Survivors could communicate with them, whether the spirit is one of a mother, sister, brother, or beloved—so the song *The Three Angel Visitants* shows.[87] At what time? Usually at night, when "stars are burning bright"—in the words of *Bell Brandon*. What is the conduit for communication? The answer, a shared love enduring even after death:

> Tho' they may lay beneath the ground
>   The form of Allee dear,
> I know his spirit hovers round
>   And mingles with us here.
> His home may be in heav'n above
>   Yet oft to us below
> He will return to breathe his love,
>   The Angels told me so.[88]

In writing: "The love which survives the tomb is one of the noblest attributes of the soul," Washington Irving sums up nineteenth-

[84]Hawthorne, *Works* in Vol. XVIII of 207.

[85][Mitchell], *Dream Life* 72.

[86]*Come This Way, My Father* (see note 32); Pincus, *Death* 116.

[87]*The Three Angel Visitants*, m. C.M. Cady (Chicago: Higgins 1857).

[88]*The Angels Told Me So*, w. Sidney Dyer, m. H.A. Pond (Boston: Ditson 1858).

century attitudes toward this motivating force in human affairs.[89] At this point it would seem helpful to recapitulate briefly, and add to, some of the statements made about love in Chapter 2. Certainly the love portrayed in popular works is remarkably proper. In their songs, Americans had never swerved from the view that love was a drawing toward and devotion for another person, who compelled esteem and wonder, evoked generous impulses, and aroused continuous charitableness for others. The selfish sexual appetites embodied in libidinous arousal found no admission into the concept. While they appreciated the pleasures of the flesh and the driving force of sexual excitation, they thought these were private feelings and not ones for voyeuristic viewing—at least, not in serious compositions.

The startingly coarse, frequently debased, eroticism of late-twentieth-century popular song was scarcely essayed. Rather, the affection put on public view was emotion formed spontaneously in the heart, then freely flowing outward without consideration of self-interest or sexual gratification. Unsatisfied with the statement of this love as an abstraction, the American public required popular works to shape it into a concrete object, whether in the form of a child, mother, or beloved. By so doing, its history could be traced from the joyful arcadian stage, to the chastening in the crucible of experience, to the final restatement as the fundamental emotion of every God-bent Christian. Death contributed the final loop to love's mandala. The ceaseless exertion to reintegrate the self ended with the completion of life's circle and the immortalization of love united to spirit.

Eventually, every human should welcome death as a friend who directed the soul to peace, to reunion with loved ones, and to entry into everyman's permanent home. To be "free from earth's sorrows," to be "safely at home" is the theme of song after song.[90] At last, the traveler could say of himself:

[89]Washington Irving, *The Sketch Book,* new ed., 2 vols. (London: Murray 1821) I, 240.

[90]See, for example, *Low in the Dust of the Valley He Sleeps,* w. and m. George Root (Boston: Russell & Tolman 1859); *Oh! Boys, Carry me 'Long,* w. and m. Stephen C. Foster (New York: Firth, Pond 1851); *Cara Lee* (see note 73); *Annie Darling,* w. and m. J.H. McNaughton (New York: Firth, Pond 1859).

Thy bark hath passed the rough sea's foam!
Now the long yearnings of the soul are stilled,
Home! Home! thy peace is won, thy heart is filled.[91]

We must conclude that Americans yearned to see purpose behind the vagaries of day-to-day coping, the pain of repeated tragedy, and the terror of helpless confrontations with one's own physical ripening and decay. Early popular songs show their society, however numerous and serious its failings, committed to faith in a basically moral, just, and loving direction of the cosmos. It affected mankind during and after the earthly state of existence. Consequently, life always had significance. Although the individual did experience inner suffering and disorder, he need never know utter hopelessness. At the end, there was the promise of heaven.

[91] *Thou Art Gone Home,* w. Mrs. Hemans, m. Eleazar T. Fitch (New York: Firth, Pond 1850).

CHAPTER 4

The Unillusioned Song

The rich emotional diet offered by serious song required lean, tart music to offset it. That music was the hardheaded comic song, which confronted reality without illusion, sentimentality, or gullibility. Its protagonist was not the dreamer contemplating a vision, but a jester coping ludicrously with the necessities of actual existence.

Such a jester could reach the many in the audience who had turned off the moralizers and emotionalists. He could introduce a host of ideas denied the speaker in serious song. And he could wield the weapon of laughter to ridicule duplicity in thought and action, abase the mighty and untouchable, and censure the camp followers of frivolous high society.

How absurd and nonsensical life is, shouts comic song's clown. The facts of life demonstrate only confusion to him, not order, foolishness not profundity, meaninglessness not intelligibility, and inharmony not congruity. In short, the clown extracts a fuller meaning out of the human experience by opposing the significant patterns of inner life with the chaotic everyday matters that seem to negate these patterns.[1]

This was one *raison d'être* for the whiteface comic and blackface minstrel songs that were created in the antebellum years, and that make up the bulk of the vocal compositions examined in this chapter.

[1]See Henry Alonzo Myers, *Tragedy: A View of Life* (Ithaca, N.Y.: Cornell University Press 1956) 113–14.

The composers of these pieces assumed that laughter could relieve the pressures resulting from the perversities in the world. At the least, they agreed with William Levison when he wrote: "As to my kreed . . . fust, I blebe in laffin, kase it eases de conshunce, aids digestion, and laxitudes de muzzle ob de face." Bayard Taylor is quoted by Austin as writing, in 1849, that Foster's comic minstrel songs had "quaint, mock-sentimental cadences, so well suited to the broad absurdity of the words—their reckless gaiety and irreverent familiarity with serious subjects—and their spirit of antagonism and perseverance—are true expressions of the more popular sides of the national character."[2]

The song writers also assumed that most Americans saw themselves as having in their makeup more than a touch of the fool buffeted by circumstance. It is not surprising, therefore, to discover the Ethiopian buffoon, in *Commence Ye Darkies All!*, pointing to his audience and insisting:

> White folks, I'm going to sing
> A song dat am quite new—
> Of myself, an' banjo string—
> An' you, an' you, an' you![3]

The audience that sponsored these unsentimental compositions was the broad mass of men and women caught up in the flux of the Jacksonian era. They considered themselves different from Europeans. They were responsive to any vivid depiction of what they perceived as the indigenous American character. This sort of depiction began to appear in plays, books, paintings, and songs.[4]

Inherent in the delineation were liberal infusions of regional droll-

[2]William Levison, *Black Diamonds* (1857), reprint (Upper Saddle River, N.J.: Literature House 1969) 89. Arthur Koestler, *The Act of Creation* (New York: Macmillan 1964) 57, writes about laughter as "an emotive discharge of tension." For the Taylor quote, see William W. Austin, *"Susanna," "Jeannie," and "The Old Folks at Home"* (New York: Macmillan 1975) 29.

[3]*Commence Ye Darkies All!*, w. and m. W.D. Corrister (New York: Firth, Pond 1849).

[4]Richard M. Dorson, *American Folklore* (Chicago: University of Chicago Press 1959), 48–49.

ery, local color, and vernacular speech. The tongue-in-cheek brag, idiosyncratic toggery, erratic behavior, and uncouth uniqueness of the American riverboatman, frontiersman, Yankee peddler, city tough, and black Southern slave and Northern freeman became standard constructs of popular entertainment. However exaggerated were the characteristics of these stock figures, they were recognized by Americans as their own. In a way, the portraiture was a thumbing of the nose at European and native elitist critics who proclaimed American civilization vile, vulgar, and unredeemable.

Most significantly, while the lyric of serious song permitted no aesthetic distance between the listener and the "I," assuming both were the same, the lyric of comic song, owing to its larger-than-life characterizations, allowed for and even required a separation between protagonist and audience. Yes, comic song did depict "you, an' you, an' you." But the image was as if seen through a telescope—looming grandly before the eye, yet viewed from a distance. Emerson once stated: "The most flagrant nonsense will not keep its nature if you come into the humorist's or fool's point of view, but, unhappily, we find it fast becoming sense and we must flee again into the distance if we would laugh."[5] So it was with comic song.

Another important reason for the distance is given by Oliver Wendell Holmes, in *The Autocrat of the Breakfast-Table*, where he writes: "Do you know that you feel a little superior to every man who makes you laugh, whether by making faces or verses? Are you aware that you have a pleasant sense of patronizing him, when you condescend so far as to let him turn somersets, literal or literary, for your royal delight?"[6] In short, no member of the audience could feel superior to, or patronizing toward, himself. He could, however, laugh at a surrogate who incarnated his and other Americans' failings, and at the insane consequences that these failings produced.

The funniness of the palpable absurdity or eccentricity was trans-

---

[5]Ralph Waldo Emerson, *The Journals and Miscellaneous Notebooks,* (Cambridge: Belknap Press, 1970), VIII, ed. William H. Gilman and J.E. Parsons (1970), 402.

[6]Oliver Wendell Holmes, *The Autocrat of the Breakfast-Table* (1858), reprinted Vol. I of *Works,* 14 vols. (Boston: Houghton Mifflin, 1891–1892) 91.

formed into farce by making it extravagant or idiotic. The ridiculousness of overweening vanity or inappropriate egotism was blown up into ludicrousness by making it so foolish that it provoked guffaws and contempt. The heroic Andrew Jackson fighting off the British at New Orleans is not comical. The blackface minstrel in tattered dress who, in a comic song, claims he ran in front of Jackson and eased the General's way through the foe is comical because he has been found out in an atrocious lie, and because his appearance, speech, and manner falls far short of heroic measure.

The language employed in these songs, particularly the minstrel songs, is equally as singular as the figures who mouth it. Speech is lusty and mannered, in grotesque imitation of the colorful Americans who originally gave it shape. In this context, quoting Emerson again is appropriate. He found the strong language of ordinary Americans "laconic and brisk" beside that of educated writers. "Cut these words and they would bleed," he states. "They are vascular and alive; they walk and run . . . It is a shower of bullets."[7]

Comic song's text is filled with slang, platitudes, mixed-up syntax, malapropisms, mispronunciations, outrageous metaphors and similes, and pompous phrases. And, of course, the minstrel lyric is fleshed with an artificial dialect supposedly derived from the speech of black Americans.

A typical example of antebellum slang is found in the sentence, "For Ise de grit, de go, de cheese," from *The Dandy Broadway Swell*[8] — the *grit* meaning a person with an unconquerable spirit; the *go,* a person on the move; and the *cheese,* a person of tip-top quality. For gross punning, see the text of *Away Down East,*[9] where a weeping mother, mourning her drowned son, "is ever on the look out to see her rising son;/But she may strain her eyes in vain./Her son has set in regions wet away down east."

[7]Emerson, *Journals,* VII, ed. A.W. Plumstead and Harrison Hayford (1969), 374. For a discussion of comic dialogue, see L.J. Potts, *Comedy* (London: Hutchinson University Library 1949) 76.

[8]*The Dandy Broadway Swell,* as sung by the Christy Minstrels (New York: Holt 1848).

[9]*Away Down East,* w. Arthur Morrell, m. Hutchinson Family, arr. E.L. White (Boston: Ditson 1846).

Stephen Foster and other composers of minstrel songs often re-sorted to wild contradictions, like "the sun so hot I frose to death" and "De Shanghai's tall but his appetite is small/He'll only swallow ebry thing that he can overhaul,/Four bags of wheat just as certain as your born/A bushel of potatoes and a tub full of corn."[10]

Or they indulged in fantastically preposterous figures of speech, as in the following two stanzas, the first from *Pop Goes De Weasel*, the second from *Kiss Me Quick and Go:*[11]

> When de night walks in black as sheep,
>   And de hen and her eggs am fast asleep,
> Den into her nest with a sarpent's creep,
>   "Pop goes de Weasel."

> One Sunday night we sat together
>   Sighing side by side,
> Just like two wilted leaves of cabbage
>   In the sunshine fried.

Or they featured absurd words, some new-minted by the lyric writer, some borrowed from one of the regional vocabularies. The second stanza of *Belle ob Baltimore* begins as follows:

> My Belle is tall and slender
>   And sings so berry clear
> You'd tink she was an owlingale,
>   If once her woice you hear.

and the fifth stanza of *The Fine Old Colored Gentleman* begins:

> When dis nigga stood uprigh an
>   Wasn't slantindicular . . .[12]

---

[10]*Oh! Susanna*, w. and m. Stephen C. Foster (New York: Holt 1848); *Don't Bet Your Money On De Shanghai*, w. and m. Stephen C. Foster (New York: Firth, Pond 1861).

[11]*Pop Goes De Weasel*, arr. Charles Twiggs (New York: Gordon 1853); *Kiss Me Quick and Go*, w. S.S. Steele, m. Fred. Buckley (New York: Firth, Pond 1856).

[12]*Belle Ob Baltimore*, w. and m. J.G. Evans (Boston: Ordway 1848); *The Fine Old Colored Gentleman*, w. Dan D. Emmett, arr. Rice (Boston: Keith 1843). For further information on the derivation of words like *slantindicular*, see Constance Rourke, *American Humor* (Garden City, N.Y.: Doubleday 1953) 58.

Or they stress the obvious. *The Fine Old Colored Gentleman* contains these lines to explain why the gentleman is named Sambo: "The reason why da call dat was because it was his name." And later, after the gentleman dies: "De verdict ob de jury was, he died for want ob breath." Note, also, the silly advice in the following, from *De Boatmen's Dance:*

> De oyster boat should keep to de shore,
> De fishin smack should venture more,
> De schoomer sails before de wind,
> De steamboat leaves a streak behind.[13]

Finally, scarcely a comic song is found that does not resort to some form of nonsensical exaggeration:

> Angelina am so tall
> She nebber sees de ground,
> She hab to take a wellumscope
> To look down on de town.

and:

> De days out west dey are so long
> De clocks run down at noon;
> And twice a month dey always hab
> A glorious full new moon.

and:

> I wish I may be burnt If I don't lub Rose,
> Make hase, Rose, I almoe froze.[14]

During the 1830s and the two decades or more that followed, lyrics like the ones quoted were the epitome of humorous speech. Admittedly, minstrel compositions often mirror the racial prejudices of the time and project an offensive travesty of black life. This unsavory aspect of mid-nineteenth-century song has been thoroughly ex-

---

[13]*De Boatmen's Dance,* melody Dan D. Emmett (Boston: Keith 1843).

[14]*Angelina Baker,* w. and m. Stephen C. Foster (Baltimore: Benteen 1850); *The Negro Traveller,* w. and melody Samuel Beeman, arr. Frank Spencer (New York: Firth, Pond 1848); *The Coal Black Rose,* w. White Snyder (Philadelphia: Author 1829), respectively.

amined in several recent books.[15] The purpose of this book is not to fare over roads previously traveled by others. Rather, it is to examine the comic songs for their commentaries on nineteenth-century American society in general.

SATIRIC BURLESQUE

Comic songs at their best did help men and women overcome disenchantment with their less than ideal world and with the fraudulent and lack-witted aspects of their society. Americans could contemplate oppression and bungling, then shake off the enervation that threatened to ensue, by means of cathartic laughter. After seeing the imperfections in themselves and other, they found it essential to siphon away their feelings of unease, alarm, and culpableness. Relief came through the merriment afforded by compositions that wisecracked sagely about human foibles.

Over and over again, these songs contrast the orderly stages of man's subjective life and its spiritual subtance with man's daily encounters with an insensitive world of one damned thing after another. There is a variance, they demonstrate, between what ought to be and what actually is. By opposing the sublime and somber expressions of serious songs with the impudent cockalorum of comedy, they restore balance to the human spirit.

Mark in what follows, how a commonplace symbol in serious song—the dream of floating on life's stream—is knocked on the head. The listener is jolted back to a ruthless here and now:

> My sister Rose de oder night did dream,
>   Dat she was floating up and down de stream,
>   And when she woke she began to cry,
>   And de white cat pecked out de black cat's eye.[16]

---

[15]See, for example, Robert C. Toll's *Blacking Up: The Minstrel Show in Nineteenth-Century America* (New York: Oxford University Press 1974) and Sam Dennison's *Scandalize My Name: Black Imagery in American Popular Music* (New York: Garland 1982).

[16]*Jim Along Josey*, as sung by John N. Smith (New York: Firth & Hall 1840).

In the same way, the arcadian symbols of innocent childhood and unassuming womankind are given a sarcastic twist:

> And children dey are born so smart
> Dat nobody dar can teach 'em.
>
> . . . . .
>
> De women dar hab forms so fair
> Dat ornaments don't grace 'em.[17]

These are representative examples of the opposite thinking that crops up constantly in unillusioned lyrics. Faithful friends turn into untrustworthy acquaintances; loyal beloveds become treacherous and fickle girlfriends; and kind strangers are really out for themselves. Commitment to another is replaced by watching out for *number one;* enduring love, by easily displaced liking; pure motivation, by self-serving drives; grand and meaningful actions, by picayune and ridiculous feats; simple morality, by the empty dictates of fashion; and the attempt to walk in God's ways, by the dedication to taking pleasure where one can.

Irreverent parody was a favorite weapon in the attack against pretense and high-flown feeling. The bereft wanderer of ethereal song would think over his suffering and long for the innocence he lost and the death that will give him relief. The destitute wanderer in hard-bitten song indulges in no such exquisite thoughts. They are luxuries he cannot afford. His complaints are down to earth:

> I've been to California and I haven't got a dime,
>   I've lost my health, my strength, my hope, and I have lost
>   my time,
> I've only got a spade and pick and if I felt quite brave,
>   I'd use the two of them 'ere things to scoop me out a grave.
> This digging hard for gold may be politic and bold,
>   But you could not make *me* think so; but *you* may if you are
>   told.
> Oh! I've been to California and I'm minus all the gold,
>   For instead of riches plenty I have only got a cold.[18]

---

[17] *The Negro Traveller* (see note 14).
[18] *California As It Is,* written by Thaddeus W. Meighan (New York: Hall 1849).

Even the awesome natural sights of America undergo deflation. The much romanticized spectacle of Niagara Falls, for example, is unglorified in a composition that purports to praise one of the wonders of the world:

> Rumbling tumbling tearing away,
>   Wallowing bellowing wet with spray,
>   Like Aunt Deborah's washing day,
>   This trip to Niagra Falls.[19]

The sanctimonious hypocrites, outwardly high-minded, inwardly false, and the narrow moralists out of touch with reality are pilloried in naughty ditties like *The Tee-Tó-Tal Society*, which backhandedly extols the salutary effects of imbibing only water:

> I wander about doing good, our society pays all my charges,
>   Preaching two hours at least to coal heavers working on
>   barges.
> But they say, "If you carried our coals, of beer you'll soon see
>   the propriety."[20]

The coal heavers show no reverence for work, as do the people of serious song. Nor, in *The Glendy Burk*,[21] do boatmen "bless" their watchful captain, who "keep his eye on de crew," drives it "too hard," and causes its members to desert. One deserter tries laboring on a farm and finds he must "work all night in de wind and storm" and "all day in de rain." When he tried to "mow in de hay field," he injures his head "wid de flail"—quite a different picture from that of the contented farmer of arcadia.

Many performers, through their peculiar dress, and many song lyrics, through their allusion to specific comic symbols derived from the world of the snobby rich, stimulated the laughter of Americans. These were men and women who had little regard for "social forms and fashions" that debilitated "the spirit and health of humanity." With pleasure, audiences watched and listened as performer after

---

[19]*Niagra Falls,* w. and m. Mr. Winchell (Boston: Prentiss 1847).

[20]*The Tee-Tó-Tal Society,* as sung by Mr. Chapman, arr. George De Luce (New York: Atwill 1840).

[21]*The Glendy Burk,* w. and m. Stephen C. Foster (New York: Firth, Pond 1860).

performer pilloried the "vice and follies" of the would-be trendsetters.[22]

The strutting dandy of foppish appearance is taken mercilessly and mirthfully to task in songs like *Dandy Broadway Swell* and *My Long Tail Blue:*

> If you want to win the Ladies' hearts,
>   I'll tell you what to do;
> Go to a tip top Tailor's shop,
>   And by a long tail blue.[23]

If that doesn't succeed with the ladies, one song advises, "Don't ever give up in despair/For . . . no matter what may be your age/ . . . you will suit all the girls to a hair,/If you've only got a moustache."[24]

The silliness of modish women is likewise mocked. When the scenting of letter paper (and even of sheet music) that young women purchased was all the rage, there appeared *The Belle ob Baltimore:*

> I wrote my lub a letter,
>   And scented it so sweet
> De musk, de clobes, and peppermint
>   Stuck out about a feet!

It was decreed that a genteel upbringing required some accomplishment on the piano or guitar. *Commence, Ye Darkies All!* confirmed this stylish necessity:

> "O for a piano or guitar!"
>   I hear a fair one cry;
> But when I hear dese instruments,
>   I tink I'd like to die!

Even the most serious theme of dying and death was viewed from a comic perspective. Why? Let Oliver Wendell Holmes suggest a reason. In *The Autocrat of the Breakfast-Table*, he writes: "The ludicrous

---

[22]The quotations are from [Donald G. Mitchell], *The Lorgnette*, 10th ed., (New York: Scribner 1853) II, 90. Koestler, *Creation*, 61, discusses laughter as a response to stimuli.

[23]*My Long Tail Blue* (New York: Atwill, c. 1834).

[24]*If You've Only Got a Moustache* (New York: Waters 1864).

has its place in the universe; it is not a human invention, but one of the Divine ideas. . . . How curious it is that we always consider solemnity and the absence of all gay surprises and encounter of wits as essential to the idea of the future life of those whom we thus deprive of half their faculties and then call *blessed!* There are not a few who . . . seem to be preparing themselves for that smileless eternity to which they look forward, by banishing all gayety from their hearts and all joyousness from their countenances."[25]

Comic songs rarely examine the future life. Nor are they interested in preparing a person for eternity. They seem to declare that a person dead is dead and nothing else; a body is to be interred expeditiously, even routinely:

> When I'm dead and laid on the counter,
>   The people all making a show,
> Just sprinkle plain whiskey and water,
>   On the corpse of Old Rosin the beau.
>
> Then pick me out six trusty fellows,
>   And let them all stand in a row,
> And dig a big hole in the circle,
>   And in it toss Old Rosin the beau.
>
> Then let those six trusty fellows,
>   Oh, let them all stand in a row,
> And rake down that great big round bottle
>   And drink to Old Rosin the beau.[26]

Note, in the song that follows, the irreverent and exaggerated mourning over a human surrogate—in this instance, a cigar; a last cigar being smoked on board a ship crossing the Atlantic:

> I watched the ashes as it came
>   Fast drawing toward the end;
> I watched it as a friend would watch
>   Beside a dying friend.

. . . . .

[25] Holmes, *Autocrat,* 92.
[26] *Old Rosin the Beau* (Boston: Ditson c. 1844).

> I've seen the land of all I love
> Fade in the distance dim:
> I've watched above the blighted heart,
> Where once proud hope hath been;
> But I've never known a sorrow
> That could with that compare,
> When off the blue Canaries,
> I smoked my last Cigar.[27]

The sentiments are those of serious song; the impact is anything but serious.

Without question, the most ubiquitous theme of comic song involves love, courtship, and marriage. Only here, every precept of serious song is turned topsy-turvy. The violations of staid society's commandments are many in *The Unfortunate Man*, whose protagonist complains that a girl he thought loved him has taken up with a handsomer man, that he has been caught running off with another man's wife, that an old maid is suing him for breach of promise, and that he needs to beautify his facial features since there is a real question whether any "damsel would pity my case and think more of my heart than she does of my face."[28]

In song after song, young women are ready to accept a beau and marry for reasons other than love. Get a stylish haircut, grow a moustache, and dress in the latest fashion, and someone will take you on. As the song *My Long Tale Blue* advises:

> Now all you chaps that wants a wife,
> And don't know what to do;
> Just look at me, and I'll show you how
> To swing your long-tail blue.

In *Billy Grimes,* a young man learns that he is considered "a dirty, ugly drover," until he inherits $10,000. After learning of Billy's new wealth, the greedy mother tells her daughter that Billy is "a clever lad and no doubt loves you dearly!" In *The Female Auctioneer,* a woman unable to find a man to marry her has hit on a novel solution

---

[27]*My Last Cigar,* w. by a student of Harvard University, m. J.M. Hubbard (Boston: Ditson 1848).
   [28]*The Unfortunate Man,* w. and m. Ossian E. Dodge (Boston: Ditson 1852).

to her problem—she will auction herself off to the highest bidder.[29]

To love is neither a profound nor a life-or-death activity. A lover may repeatedly say: "I'd gin my life to bin in dar," when he sees his beloved at the window. Yet, when he discovers another man with her, he shows his resiliency by leaving her and remarking laconically and unemotionally: "I wish dat nigger hadn't been dar." No broken heart for him![30] Besides, if he truly had wanted her, he simply would have barged into the house and kicked out his rival.

The fickle lover, male and female, is a constant figure, and "gay deceiver" a stock phrase, in comic songs. Moreover, in some instances, the knowledge that a suitor is also pursuing a second person is no deterrent to a bit of hugging and kissing on the part of the jilted one.[31]

Marriage is not the sacred, inviolable union of two people that is pictured in serious song. Husbands and wives frequently quarrel in comic songs. When men get drunk, their knowing wives get even with them. If a spouse dies, one finds another marriage partner quickly enough.[32]

Whether impermanent or lasting, the love of suitor and wooed, of husband and wife, is clearly seen as physically expressed. There are no taboos against bodily contact, no fear of what such affection entails. One young woman rejects her grandmother's prudish counsels:

[29]*Billy Grimes,* w. Richard Coe, m. W.H. Oakley (New York: Firth, Pond 1852); *The Female Auctioneer,* composed by the Orphean Family (Boston: Ditson 1850).

[30]*I Seen Her at the Window,* w. and m. J.P. Carter (New York: Holt 1848).

[31]Reference to a gay deceiver, for example, occurs in *Dixie's Land,* w. and m. Dan D. Emmett (New York: Firth, Pond 1860); and in *Belle ob Baltimore* (see note 12). *Bobbin' Around,* w. and m. W.J. Florence (New York: Jollie 1855) has a woman petting with a man who she knows loves "another gal." *Joe Hardy,* w. and melody James Pierpont, arr. Edward Leroy (Boston: Ditson 1853) equates loves with the most superficial sentimentality.

[32]See, respectively, *Mr. Burns and His Wife,* w. and m. Gentleman of Maryland (Baltimore: Cole 1824); *My Wife Is a Most Knowing Woman* (New York: Waters 1863); *Miss Lucey Long* (New York: Millet c. 1842); *Young Clem Brown,* w. Marshall S. Pike, m. L.V.H. Crosby (Boston: Ordway 1846); *Alabama Joe,* written by R.W. Smith (Boston: Prentiss 1840).

151

> Thinks I to myself there's some mistake,
>> What a fuss these old folks make;
> If the boys and girls had all been so fraid,
>> Then Grandma herself would have died an old maid.[33]

Another young woman allows her lover to grasp her firmly and kiss her boldly, all the while protesting she will call her mother if he continues. But when he gets up to leave, she says:

> I felt more grief than I can tell
>> When with a kiss he rose to leave me.
> "Oh, John!" said I, "and must thou go!"[34]

Russell Nye, in *The Unembarrassed Muse,* asserts that the minstrel show and its songs were never sexually suggestive; their humorous allusions never vulgar.[35] Nevertheless, on occasion, some hint at sexuality may be presumed. For example, the male, in *Coal Black Rose,* tells Rose to "make hase," because he is "almos tiff as poker tanden here," and she replies: "Cum in . . . de fire is burnin, de hoe-cake a bakin." The reference to male stiffness and a female with a fire burning in her oven are commonplace symbols in sexual innuendo.

To give a second example, how really innocent is the song *The Old Grey Goose,* if it portrays Dinah loosing her shoe and her male companion pointing to great big holes in her stockings through which her heels stick out? Dinah replies: "I want em to stick out." And the song closes on the observation: "Look right ober yander. Don't you see de Ole Grey Goose smiling at de Gander?" Is the meaning of the word goose a double one?

A third song, *Gwine to de Mill,* makes constant reference to a grist mill, certainly a hoary sexual symbol. Possibly there is a hidden interpretation to the stanza:

> O, Jule got lazy an she came to me
>> To cure an ache in her misery.
> I gin her a hickory mesmerizing,
>> An de way I cured her was surprising.

---

[33]*My Grandmother's Advice,* w. and m. by "M," arr. Edward Kanski (New York: Waters 1857).

[34]*Be Quiet, Do!,* w. from the *Albion* (New York: Dubois 1841).

[35]Russell Blaine Nye, *The Unembarrassed Muse* (New York: Dial 1970) 164–65.

Banjo Isam and Jule Glover enter the grist mill together.[36]

It is admittedly true that comic songs are not overtly suggestive. On the other hand, it must be conjectured that compositions like those just quoted show some recognition of carnal pleasure. Assuredly, the more obvious reference to sexual matters in some of the other comic literature of the time is, at the minimum, palely reflected in comic song. Benjamin Shillaber, in *Life and Sayings of Mrs. Partington* (1854), to give one instance, relates the following: " 'Your plants are most flagrantly odious,' said Mrs. Partington. . . . 'How beautiful they are!' she continued. 'Do you profligate your plants by slips?' " Then, the "editor" comments that in this world many "slips" are made by men and women. Reflecting on this, he adds: "Dear old lady! Your humble chronicler remembers that many of the young and beautiful are profligated by slips."[37]

Jule Glover and Mrs. Partington come from the same comic milieu. It can be supposed they share a naughty-but-nice approach to sexual matters.

THE LITTLE MAN AS SURVIVOR

Whether as philosophic purveyor of preposterous truths, as flawed expert on habits of the *beau monde,* or as indomitable scrapper, however great the odds, the protagonist of comic song is a distorted image of the ordinary citizen. He strives to achieve the status of wise man, but, like the ordinary citizen, he is flawed. Despite his pretensions, as often as not he appears as an ill-educated, narrow-thinking, and uncouth bumbler. On the other hand, there is something irrepressible about him. Nothing keeps him down for long. In song after song, when bravery may not pay off, he turns into a sly, quick-witted clown. When tested through circumstances, he tries to resolve his difficulties by means of common sense and past experience, never through learning and detached thinking. As might be expected, such

[36] *The Old Grey Goose* (Philadelphia: Fiot 1844); *Gwine to De Mill,* w. and m. Jay R. Jenkins (Boston: Bradlee 1846).

[37] Benjamin P. Shillaber, *Life and Sayings of Mrs. Partington* (1854), reprint (Upper Saddle River, N.J.: Literature House 1969) 57–58.

a character has faith in what he can perceive through his senses and has allegiance to whatever he hopes will maintain him.

In a vexatious existence, where right action may bring self-destruction, it is diverting to see a rascal completely free of moralistic impediments, ready to best his opponents through adroit resourcefulness and craft.

The protagonist of comic song finds his disbelief in societal values growing as he watches the chicanery practised everywhere:

> Goosy, goosy gander, from Bank to Bank I wander,
>   From City, Globe and Exchange to Gen'ral Int'rest
>   Chamber.
> There sit the Cashiers, the specie they refuse,
>   While all the Bank Directors are clapping on the screws.
>
> Goosy, goosy gander, all around I wander,
>   Sawdust and Humbug, in the Doctor's chamber.
> There sits the victim looking rather thin,
>   While old Father Longface pulls the rhino in.[38]

Nor is there any escape. *Ching A Ring Chaw*[39] makes out a case for fleeing elsewhere, to a place where everybody has wealth and belongs to the *bon ton*. But a kind of bitter laughter comes when the common man recognizes that this is a never-never land—another chimera, promised and impossible to make real. He laughs because he immediately perceives the enormous gap between his present difficulties and his perception of what life ought to be. He laughs because laughter represents an open defiance of circumstances that seem unalterable and a psychological conquest of otherwise insoluble problems.[40]

What must the little man fashion himself into to stay alive? One song states: "Like a sassy monkey up a sour apple tree . . . big pig or little pig must root, hog, or die." Another song states, like the

[38] *The Times,* m. John Smith (Boston: Parker & Ditson 1839).
[39] *Ching A Ring Chaw* (Baltimore: Willig c. 1833).
[40] James Feibleman has valuable things to say about laughter as a means of surmounting difficulties, in his book *In Praise of Comedy* (1939), reissued (New York: Russell & Russell 1962) 191.

blue-tail fly, who has a mighty sting that belies his tininess. Be cautious of altruism, a third song warns—love everyone, but love yourself the best. Be shrewd, a fourth song advises; be up to people's tricks and turn their roguery into profit for yourself. Feeling defeated is a mistake; your adversary is not that formidable. He is like "de Shanghai" rooster and "can't fight a bit." So, "don't bet your money on de Shanghai! Take de little chicken in de middle of de ring."[41]

When songs glorify the pugnacious clown, they do so to personify the invincible individual, who seems to be making the statement: "I *am* important. I *am* unconquerable. Knock me down and, one way or another, I'll haul myself up and carry on." Without question this is what Susanne Langer had in mind when she describes the buffoon as a symbol of "the indomitable living creature fending for itself, tumbling and stumbling . . . from one situation into another, getting into scrape after scrape and getting out again, with or without a thrashing. He is personified *élan vitae* . . . His whole improvised existence has the rhythm of primitive, savage, if not animalian life, coping with a world that is forever taking new uncalculated turns, frustrating but exciting. He is neither a good man nor a bad one, but is genuinely amoral,—now triumphant, now worsted and rueful, but in his ruefulness and dismay he is funny, because his energy is really unimpaired and each failure prepares the situation for a new fantastic move."[42]

Pugnaciousness verges on brag and bluster in songs like *Jim Brown:*

> I caution all de New York niggers not to stop my way,
>> For if he play de fool wid me dey in de gutter lay;
> For when I was at New Orleans and only three feet high,
>> I run before ole General Jack, and make de red coats fly.[43]

[41]These songs are, respectively, *Root, Hog, or Die,* arr. George W.H. Griffin (New York: Waters 1856); *Jim Crack Corn* (Baltimore: Benteen 1846); *Little More Cider,* written and arr. Austin Hart (Boston: Ditson 1853); *Dat Nigga's In Lub Wid Dinah,* w. Cool White, m. J.R. Myers (Boston: Keith 1844); and *Don't Bet Your Money On De Shanghai* (see note 10).

[42]Susanne K. Langer, *Feeling and Form* (New York: Scribner's Sons 1953) 342.

[43]*Jim Brown* (New York: Hewitt 1835).

and *I'm One of the Boys:*

> Now if any of you get in a row,
>   And you cannot get out,
> You mustn't go to law, for that's a way
>   Too far and round about.
> If any loafer insults you,
>   Or in any way annoys,
> Just find out the number of our Engine
>   And call on "one of the *Boys.*"[44]

The fighter in these songs is inseparable from the swaggerer. Jim Brown boasts that he is a "roarer" able to "whip my weight in wildcats," and an alligator eater. When he hits anybody, nothing is left " 'sept a little grease spot." Gumbo Chaff, in the song of the same name, asserts he is so strong that he lifts huge bales of cotton with such ease that even strangers know "it was de debil or old Gumbo Chaff" doing the lifting. The Dandy Broadway Swell not only warns off all rivals but casually tells the girls to "take care . . . an mind your sefs,/For if I roll dis eye,/You'll gib a shake, a sigh an groan,/An den flop down an die." And Dandy Jim is insufferable when he claims he is the handsomest and fightingest person in South Carolina. So breathtaking is his appearance that Dinah, his love, writes him letters that say only "Dandy Jim," and the parson looks at him in church and abandons his sermon to take as his text, "Dandy Jim from Caroline." Even when old age arrives, he is someone to reckon with:

> Old age came on, his teeth dropt out, it made no odds to him,
>   He eat as many taters and he drank as many gin;
> He swallowed two small railroads wid a spoonful of ice cream,
>   And a locomotive bulgine while dey blowin off de steam.[45]

The aggressive swaggerer achieves national status in *Crow Out Shanghai,* when the British battling at Sebastopol are told: "The only thing that's wanting now to set the matter right,/Is for 'Sam' to take

---

[44] *I'm One of the Boys,* w. T.G. Booth, m. John Quill (Boston: Keith 1845).
[45] *Jim Crow* (New York: Riley c. 1830); *Gumbo Chaff* (New York: Firth & Hall c. 1836); *The Dandy Broadway Swell* (see note 8); *Dandy Jim from Carolina* (New York: Firth & Hall, 1843); *The Fine Old Colored Gentleman* (see note 12).

the thing in hand and show them how to fight!'' Similarly, in *Jordan Is a Hard Road to Travel,* Louis Napoleon of France is warned that, though "all Europe begins to tremble" at his power, "the Yankees don't care for if with us he wants to fight/He'll wish he'd staid on de oder side ob Jordan."[46]

We should be careful how we belittle these examples of bombast. In their day, they had important therapeutic functions to perform. Through them, the member of the audience who felt disturbed about the world he lived in, who felt guilty over his own misdoings, or who felt undervalued or rejected by others had his destructive energies siphoned off into harmless musical channels.

The overstatement in these songs is also in the nature of a hilarious hoodwink. The protagonist plays a part and can at any moment shed his costume and personality and show the audience who he really is. Why doesn't he do so? Because the audience is already in on the secret.

We are reminded of an elaborate hoax carried out by Abraham Lincoln. As Walter Blair describes it, Lincoln, who looked like an awkward hayseed, could "play the part of the bumpkin to perfection. In the spring of 1849, two Hoosiers—Thomas H. Nelson and Judge Abram Hammond of Terre Haute—found this out when they took an all-day trip by stage coach from their home town to Indianapolis.'' They saw a lank individual stretched out, asleep in the coach, and awakened him. Because he looked so poorly dressed and countrified, they teased him for laughs. Lincoln, in turn, played the stupid, naive yokel. Always guarding his cheap hat as if it were priceless, he listened humbly to their lies and deceptions, acting as if honored by their attention and dazzled by their tall tale about a comet in the skies. They were delighted at having taken him in. But later that day, in Indianapolis, they discovered he was Abe Lincoln and a member of Congress. "Nelson and Hammond sneaked out by a back door so that they would miss seeing the man who, by acting

---

[46]*Crow Out Shanghai!,* w. and m. W. Percival (New York: Dressler & Clayton 1855); *Jordan Is a Hard Road to Travel,* m. Dan D. Emmett (Cincinnati: Truax 1853).

the fool so well, had taken them in.''[47]

Comic songs, too, revel in whimsical hyperbole and double-distilled trickery. These are psychological masks, the way the minstrel singer's blackface and eccentric costume are physical masks—mummeries to assist in the search for truth.

The uncouth comic songs conclusively demonstrated the barbarity of American democratic culture to British critics of the gentle class. These songs, also, obliterated Rousseau's vision of the unspoiled, natural man, and they cut to the bone of American experience. The indifferent shooting of a man "trough de libber," in *Long Time Ago,* is the height of inhumanity. Old Dan Tucker behaves like natural man gone bad. The message in *Oh, Susanna* is that anything in creation may be at sixes and sevens. Yet, recalling Abe Lincoln's playing the part of brutish rube, we must beware of the put-on, and pause and wonder whether in the next instant the song will clothe itself in mufti and appear quite sane, after all. In this respect, it is highly significant, as was said in an earlier chapter, that the covers of published minstrel songs often show the singers first in blackface regalia and grotesque postures; and second, in ordinary dress and dignified poses.

On a few occasions, the truth is so close to the surface, the laughter leaves an unpleasant aftertaste. The words in *Jim Crow,* in at least two of its stanzas, are so astringent with satire that the listener's chuckle catches in the throat:

> Now my brudder niggers,
> I do not think it right,
> Dat you should laugh at dem
> What happen to be white.
>
> Kase it dar misfortune,
> An dey'd spend ebery dollar,
> If dey only could be,
> Gentlemen ob colour.

[47]Walter Blair, *Horse Sense in American Humor* (New York: Russell & Russell 1962) 128–30.

It almost break my heart,
To see dem envy me,
An from my soul I wish dem,
Full so black as we.[48]

Through its laughter, the audience perceives all is not right in this less than perfect world. Existence is flawed by fuzzy thinking, selfishness, ignorance, and surface morality. Everybody contributes to the woes of society: *they, you,* and *I.* All of us are villains and victims. Look to what we do, not just to what we say, is the message. If we fall short of our ideals, we and others must suffer. But however much we suffer, whether owing to ourselves or others, we must never throw in our chips and act the part of cowards. By refusing to accept defeat and taking the attitude that you have only begun to fight, you might—just possibly might—win, or at worst come out of crisis with a whole skin.

[48]See note 45.

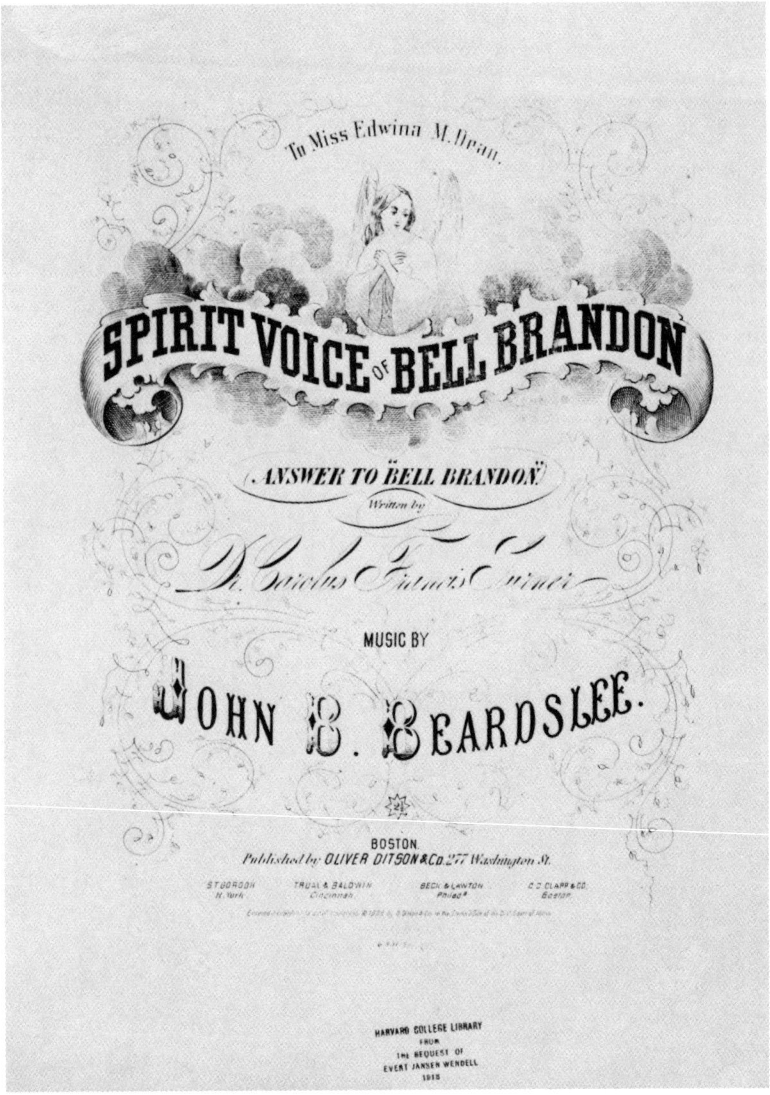

Plate 4. *Spirit Voice of Bell Brandon.* The guardian spirit of the dead loved one who watches over you and succors you when you are in need.

CHAPTER 5

Music

It is far more troublesome to characterize the meaning of musical sounds than that of words. Not least among the difficulties is the need to capture in language that which is essentially nonverbal (even antiverbal) and, therefore, fundamentally unamenable to translation. One resource for the investigator of nineteenth-century popular song is the commentary of contemporary Americans on music's significance for them. As established in my book *Sweet Songs for Gentle Americans,* the preponderance of these nineteenth-century observations referred to the music of serious popular song.

To set the dominant tenor of the discussion that follows, I start with a reference to John Moore, New England newspaperman, amateur musician, and editor of several collections of vocal and instrumental music. After eighteen years of effort, he published his *Complete Encyclopaedia of Music* (1854), which is recognized as a landmark in American writing on music. In it, under the heading "Ballad," he sets forth his and, he claims, his contemporaries' views on the significance of the music put to a serious-song text. He starts by observing the tremendous influence of "song singing" on the American "multitude," and finds this activity salutary. The music, he says, can animate the depressed, inspire and give courage to the timid, and increase feelings of devotion. This music "is predominantly the language of the heart," which "is excited to emotion through tones falling on the ear."

Moore continues by stating that while music may take some coloration from words, it is more "associated with the employments and happiness of heaven," not "with the wailings and convulsions of reprobate spirits." The latter association "would be doing violence, as all feel, to our conceptions of its true character." In short, according to Moore, music seeks to dwell in the eternal, not in the world of passing emotions and finite yearnings alone, which is the domain of words. Thus, it "deals with abstract beauty, and so lifts man to the source of all beauty—from finite to infinite, and from the world of matter to the world of spirits and to God." Nowhere does he mention the composer's conscious attempt to reflect the implications of the text.[1]

One thread that runs through the observations of contemporary writers is the view that such music can bring the listener into a stable and serene state, that it can revive him psychologically through some sort of emotional evocation that transcends the meaning of words. Assuredly this is what William Cullen Bryant had in mind in his remarks on song, in an address delivered in 1856: "The effect of music is to soothe, to tranquillize; a series of sweet sounds, skillfully modulated, occupies the attention agreeably and without fatigue; it refreshes us like rest."[2]

The music lover is revived because he has been excited to feel joy, to regulate distress, and to become a stronger person bolstered by the moral imperatives in his life. Thus, William S. Porter, in his *Musical Cyclopedia,* claims: "Most persons have experienced that, when they have been delighted with a new air which rivets their attention, it will haunt them for days, and that without any effort of their own. If the ears of children are early cultivated, and pleasing airs with good moral words are early impressed on their minds, they will never be effaced. Their songs will be their companions through life, giving them consolation in times of affliction and trial, furnishing them with rational amusement for leisure hours, when otherwise

[1]John W. Moore, *Complete Encyclopaedia of Music* (Boston: Ditson 1854), s.v. "Ballad."

[2]William Cullen Bryant, *Prose Writings,* 2 vols. (1884), reprint (New York: Russell & Russell 1964) II, 203. See Nicholas E. Tawa, also *Sweet Songs for Gentle Americans: The Parlor Song in America, 1790–1860* (Bowling Green, Ohio: Bowling Green University Popular Press 1980) 36–38.

they might be led astray; and, in circumstances of temptation, they will appear unbidden, and, by a silent warning which will not excite opposition, effectually deter from temptation and danger."[3]

Of the greatest importance to nineteenth-century writers on music is song's perceived ability to represent the spiritual and immortal nature of humans, by summoning to the mind and feelings perfect examples of beauty transcending the merely physical. Certainly this was John Moore's conclusion. To cite another source, Christopher Cranch writes: "Music is an attempt to paint on the black canvas of the present . . . the soul's ideal reminiscences of the scenery of its native clime."[4] From this perspective, music embodies what the psyche longs to express but cannot through other means. It stands for what is permanent, as opposed to the transient values of everyday existence.[5]

Music as therapeutic agent, as aid to moral perception, and as representative of the ideally beautiful—these are the three principal ideas that contemporary writers attached to the sounds of serious song.

THE SOUND OF POPULAR SONG

What is the relation of the music to the lyric in serious song? The music to nineteenth-century popular song makes no attempt to interpret the words of the lyric, whether dramatically, emotionally, or realistically. As William Porter asserts, in his *Cyclopedia*, composers err if they attempt "to express words and not ideas." They should seek to capture what is otherwise ineffable and beyond words.[6]

[3]William S. Porter, *The Musical Cyclopedia* (Boston: Loring 1834) s.v. "Ear." A lengthy discussion of song's moral influence will be found in Moore, *Encyclopaedia*, s.v. "Ballad."

[4]Quoted in E. Douglas Branch, *The Sentimental Years, 1836–1860* (1962), reprint (New York: Hill & Wang 1965) 184.

[5]See John Hospers, *Meaning and Truth in the Arts* (Hamdon, Conn.: Archon 1964) 235; Susanne K. Langer, *Philosophy in a New Key* (New York: Penguin 1948) 34–35.

[6]Porter, *Cyclopedia* s.v. "Expression."

Rarely does an American song from the period under investigation ever explore the emotional implications of the words, and the one or two that do, like Elam Ives's *The Galley Slave*,[7] proceed awkwardly, with the self-consciousness of the composer obvious. Furthermore, they number among the less popular compositions of the time.

Someone versed in the music of this period might point to a song like Bradbury's *The Lament of the Blind Orphan Girl* as having music that was popular and sensitive to the emotional colorations of the text. However, save for four measures, the entire song is set to a lovely waltz tune in a major modality. The aforementioned four measures resort to a perfunctory G-minor pensiveness, on the words "O, when shall I see them; I'm blind; O, I'm blind."[8] It should be added, also, that the song is atypical, not only because of its momentary turn to the minor mode, but also because of its triple time. Most American popular songs of this period are in duple time and major mode throughout.

Equally rare are songs whose music literally interprets a word here and there. On occasion a simplistic realism is discovered, as in the sudden drop of the melody on the phrase "caverns below," in Woodbury's *Row Thy Boat Lightly*.[9] This song was widely admired for the overall appeal of the tune, certainly not for this solitary pictorialism.

After studying hundreds of songs written by Americans between the years 1828 and 1860, I concluded that music is not the servant of the lyric. Rather, it takes command of the words, giving them a new direction and implication. It embraces the poem's subject and places it within a universal order. The words are rendered up to the musical sound and modify their own rhythm, pitch, and tempo in favor of those imposed by the melody. "When words and music come together in song, music swallows the words. . . . Song is not a com-

[7] *The Galley Slave*, m. Elam Ives, Junior (Philadelphia: Kretshmar & Nunns c. 1835).

[8] *The Lament of the Blind Orphan Girl*, w. Allenroc, m. William B. Bradbury (New York: Atwill 1847).

[9] *Row Thy Boat Lightly*, w. Miss H.F. Woodman, m. I.B. Woodbury (Boston: Prentiss & Clark 1847).

promise between poetry and music," writes Susanne Langer. "Song is music."[10] And Edgar Allan Poe, speaking for his earlier generation, is thinking along similar lines when he describes poems set to music as unique, being both separate "from ordinary literature" and independent of the "ordinary proprieties."[11]

If we look at a typical song, for example Charlie Converse's *The Rock Beside the Sea,*[12] we find the verse in regular iambic meter, here   . The melody, however, enriches the short-long stresses via subtler inflections: . The composer's musical concept seems to have little to do with interpreting the emotional tensions contained in the text. A woman cries out in torment for her absent lover, fearing the sea may have claimed him. Yet, the melodic phrases unfold serenely, in relaxed descending lines, in the major mode. Nor does the underlying harmony indicate anything but a placid world. Save for one ordinary dominant-seventh, dissonance is absent and the progressions are commonplace ones, involving the three most frequently employed triads in music—I, V, and IV (Example 5-1).

It must not be thought that because the text and music seem to have different implications, the song embodies an aesthetic and emotional dichotomy. Lyric and music are each other's complements and are meant to fuse into a unity not predictable from the parts. The listener's mind inseparably links the words with the melody, imbuing the text with some of the fancies of the nonverbal imaginative world implicit in the melody, and the melody with the ideas and central meaning contained in the words. As with any well-written song, this work takes on a greater fullness of meaning than if its parts had never been joined.

As Victor Zuckerkandl writes, in *Man the Musician:* "Singing man reaches back deeper into himself, reaches out farther, and thus also gets farther out, penetrates deeper into things, than speaking

---

[10]Susanne K. Langer, *Feeling and Form* (New York: Scribner's Sons 1953) 152–53.

[11]Edgar Allan Poe, in *The Complete Works,* (New York: AMS 1965), X 41. The comment appeared in the *Southern Literary Messenger* (April 1849).

[12]*The Rock Beside the Sea,* m. Charlie C. Converse (Philadelphia: Lee & Walker 1857).

Example 5–1. Charlie C. Converse, *The Rock Beside the Sea* (Philadelphia: Lee & Walker 1857), mm. 37–44.

man. . . . The tone the singer adds to the word does not cancel out the word, but rather gives it the sharpest edge, makes it vibrate with the highest frequency, so that it penetrates things to a greater depth. . . . Singing man reaches a new depth of the world, and by the same token a deeper level of himself."[13]

[13]Victor Zuckerkandl, *Man the Musician,* trans. Norbert Guterman (Princeton: Princeton University Press 1973) 50.

166

One word occurs again and again in contemporary descriptions of the serious song's melody, and that word is *sweet*. In the song *Going Home* is the line "Dear old home! Sweet music in that strain"; *The Willow Song* refers to "silver music" that is "sweet and clear"; and *There's Music in a Mother's Voice* describes that music as "more sweet than breezes sighing."[14] Emerson speaks of song's melody as a "sweet yet perfect empire," and Emily Dickinson praises a popular song she is learning, *Maiden Weep No More*, for being a "sweet little song."[15] And finally, William Cullen Bryant, in 1856, observed that Americans loved the singing voice, enjoyed the joining of intelligible words to melody, and had an acute "perception of the beauty of sweet sounds artfully modulated."[16]

The designation of melodies as sweet—however varying the meanings of the lyrics in different songs—underlines the universality of serious song's sound as contrasted to the greater particularity of its words. *Sweet* suggests that the music is normally pleasing, agreeable, gentle, and undisquieting. To explore further its connotations, it is sound that charms because it is temperate. Owing to this quality, it permits the listener to react sympathetically and wholeheartedly to the subject of the text.

To make certain that the melody sounds sweet, the popular composer has it move mostly stepwise or through small and easy skips. The extremes of range are avoided, so that the tune is not sung with breathiness or with a screech. Half and full stops in the melody occur usually in the lower part of the range, giving the effect of calm and repose. The melody is balanced through judicious phrase repetition, regular phrase length, and gravitation of the notes toward either the tonic of the dominant tone. The usual pace of the music is dignified and moderately slow.

[14]*Going Home,* w. and m. John Ordway (Boston: Ordway 1855); *The Willow Song,* w. J. Wesley Hanson, m. L.N. Metcalf (Boston: Prentiss 1847); *There's Music In A Mother's Voice,* m. I.B. Woodbury (Boston: Ditson 1847).

[15]Ralph Waldo Emerson, *The Journals and Miscellaneous Notebooks,* (Cambridge, Mass.: Belknap Press, VIII, ed. A.W. Plumstead and Harrison Hayford (1969), 249; Emily Dickinson, *Letters,* 2 vols., ed. Thomas H. Johnson (Cambridge, Mass.: Belknap Press 1965) I, 18.

[16]Bryant, *Prose,* II, 206–07.

Another attribute of the melody, in the best popular songs, according to contemporary writers, is a beautiful simplicity, which enables the sound to stimulate the imagination of ordinary people and to call up human feelings submerged by the brutalizing necessities of everyday coping.[17] To keep the melody simple, ornaments, runs, turns, and trills are few and are introduced only circumspectly. This lessens the difficulties for the singer, focuses the listener's ear on the expressive core of the music, and imbues the sound with a pure, unassuming sincerity.

It was the conviction of contemporary song composers that melodic simplicity coupled with melodic sweetness "soothes the spirit in sorrow," produces enchantment and "joy profound," and even approximates the "pure celestial song" of "angels' voices."[18] Here is a strong echo of Moore's reference of the "world of spirits and to God."

The writings on song stress the supreme importance of melody that is sufficient unto itself, requiring no "accompaniment or any other collatoral assistance." When an instrumental accompaniment is added, it must be unobtrusive; the harmonies produced must be limited to the most common chords, with the "almost entire exclusion of discords." Otherwise, there is a danger of diminishing "the pleasing effect to the untutored ear."[19]

Chromaticism and the minor mode are normally absent from this sort of melody. Why? Owing to the way that the former rasps on people's nerves, "like the filing of one's teeth," according to one writer. Owing to the way that the latter produces an impression so "saccharine" the music cannot "bear frequent repetition," according to another writer.[20] Whether these are the explanations that the

[17]Moore, *Encyclopedia* s.v. "Melody" and "Simplicity"; Porter, *Cyclopedia* s.v. "Melody"; Bryant, *Prose* II, 207.

[18]The quotations are taken from George F. Root's *There's Music in the Air* (Boston: Russell & Tolman 1857), a song whose lyric attempts to explain what music's effect is. In the lyric of another song, *When the Moon on the Lake Is Beaming*, w. and m. Stephen C. Massett (New York: Dubois 1842), is a reference to melody as "sweet" and "simple" and having "a kinship to love."

[19]*American Musical Review* (1 November 1850) 133; *The Musical World and Times* (4 September 1852) 13; (5 November, 1853) 69–70.

[20]*American Musical Review* (1 November 1850) 133; *The Singer's Companion* (New York: Stringer & Townsend 1854) 19.

majority of music lovers would have given is uncertain. Besides being difficult to sing, possibly the confusion of added accidentals—sharps, flats, and naturals—is avoided in order not to hamper understanding. This, however, cannot be proven. As for the exclusion of the minor mode, nowhere is it really discussed.

Example 5–1 illustrates the several points just made. Note how each phrase descends stepwise and ends either in its lower or middle range. Phrase two skips upward a minor third; phrase four, up a minor sixth and down a diminished fifth. Since all three skips conform to the underlying harmony, no problems of execution arise. Note also the absence of chromatics, the bare-bones accompaniment, the abstention from ornamentation in the melody and in the piano music, and the strict adherence to the major mode. It is indeed sweet and simple music, thus conforming to the aesthetic precepts of the time.

The music of comic and, especially, minstrel song, while equally simple, cannot be designated as sweet. Much of it is in a faster, more rhythmic duple time and has a close kinship to the jig and reel. Melody is more athletic, more likely to leap about, at times behaving in an eccentric manner. According to an unidentified writer in the *Musical World and Times* (1853), such music "captures the popular heart" with its "freshness" and "great vitality"—overcoming the scruples of "the most staid and sober-minded persons."

The melody is aggressive, from earthside and not heavenly. It stems from the uncouth clog dances and stomps of rivermen, sailors, backwoodsmen, and black plantation workers. It shows more than a little resemblance to Irish and Scottish dance tunes.[21] It darts for-

---

[21]Robert P. Nevin, "Stephen C. Foster and Negro Minstrelsy," *The Atlantic Monthly* (November 1867) 611, writes that the song derive from the music "in vogue among Hard-Shell Baptists in Tennessee and at Methodist camp-meetings in Kentucky," and also from the "backwoods melodies such as had been invented for native ballads by 'settlement' masters and brought into general circulation by stage-drivers, wagoners, cattle-drovers, and other such itinerants of earlier days." The characteristics of minstrel song are taken up in William W. Austin, *"Susanna," "Jeannie," and "The Old Folks at Home"* (New York: Macmillan 1975) 80; Charles Hamm, *Yesterdays* (New York: Norton 1979) 124–26, 137–38; Hans Nathan, *Dan Emmett and the Rise of Negro Minstrelsy* (Norman: University of Oklahoma Press 1962) 159–88.

ward and suddenly stops, in the short jagged phrases of the here and now. Often the tune lands on one tone and repeats it two or more times. Or it brings the listener up abruptly with an unexpected syncopation. Sentimental sighs and soft cadences dying on the ear are anathematic to this kind of tune. Instead, explosive snorts and swift cutoffs of sound characterize the procedure in some songs, while a jaunty, devil-may-care, finger-snapping lilt characterizes that in other songs.

Hans Nathan writes that "the minstrel tunes of the forties are no longer mere echoes of the Old World," but have "a character all their own." They can be charming like children's song but have the rhythmic persistence of ethnically primitive music. They have a "deadpan" jolliness about them that is part of the American-humor tradition.[22]

Example 5–2, *Brack Eyed Susianna* (Philadelphia: Fiot 1846), composer unidentified, illustrates the average run of music found in comic song. Note the choppiness of the tune. Leaps and repeated tones abound. Stepwise progressions are few. The phrases lurch forward in two one-measure segments and a two-measure close, ending on a syncopation. The flow of the tune is further interrupted by holds, indicated at the end of each phrase. These pauses introduce an element of eccentricity into an otherwise straightforward though vulgar dance. The music is simple. It is assuredly not sweet.

The nineteenth-century comic song and serious song existed side by side and were frequently mingled in the same concert. Without question, each was a check and balance on the other, circumscribing its excesses and keeping it honest.

MUSIC AS FEELING

The nineteenth-century music lovers believed completely in music's ability to convey feeling and mood. They came to performances prepared to respond emotionally to the stimulation of sound wrapped around verbal symbols. What is more, they fervently desired to feel deeply and strongly.

[22]Nathan, *Emmett* 181–82.

Example 5-2. *Brack Eyed Susianna* (Philadelphia: Fiot 1846), mm. 9–17.

At the same time, these Americans generally were agreed that "the same music was capable of expressing different and even opposite emotions."[23] Yet this was a strength, not a weakness, for vagueness to them was one of music's charms, "a sweet mystery" that

[23] Porter, *Cyclopedia* s.v. "Expression."

171

releases the imagination and leads the person to an ideal world and a finer "spiritual life."[24]

Edgar Allan Poe held that the emotional effect of music was beyond verbal analysis: "the sentimental pleasure derivable from music is nearly in the ratio of its indefinitiveness. Give to music any undue *decision*—imbue it with any *determinate* tone—and you deprive it, at once, of its ethereal, its ideal, and, I sincerely believe, of its intrinsic and essential character."[25]

Because of its indefiniteness and, paradoxically, its perceived emotional and aesthetic beauty, music helped the listener probe into himself, and added vast extra significances to the listener's perception of the words. In 1838, Emerson told Elizabeth Hoar that music "has a privilege of speaking truth which all Philistia is unable to challenge. Music is the poor man's Parnassus. With the very first note of the flute or horn or the first strain of a song, we leave the world of common sense and launch at once into the eternal sea of ideas and emotions."[26]

The words as symbols directed the attention to particular psychic areas of the listener's personality, which the music then explored. While the lyrics usually contained "the theme of more natural human love and sorrow," music's peculiarity was the "investing of one thought or subject with a finished expression of all that it can suggest."[27] Moreover, when a lyric was "expressed . . . in a single and pleasing tune," the result was *"pure and original Music,* not merely *soothing to the ear,* but *affecting to the heart,* not an *imitation of nature,* but the *voice of nature herself.* "[28]

To plump out a bit more the significance of music to these Americans, another quotation from Emerson is reproduced here. We should keep in mind that Emerson is not referring to the genres of

---

[24]Henry T. Tuckerman, *The Optimist* (New York: Putnam 1852) 60–61.

[25]Poe, in *Works,* (New York: Redfield 1856) X, 41–42. See also Poe, *Letters,* vols., ed. J.W. Ostrom (Cambridge, Mass.: Harvard University Press 1948) I, 257f.

[26]Emerson, *Journals,* VII, ed. A.W. Plumstead and Harrison Hayford (1969), 217–18.

[27]*The Musical Times* (27 December 1851) 118.

[28]"Reflections," by a Lady, Boston Euterpeiad (13 October 1821) 115.

symphony and art song, which he little appreciated, but to the plain American tunes he heard about him: "So is music an asylum. It takes us out of the actual and whispers to us dim secrets that startle our wonder as to who we are, and for what, whence, and whereto. All the great interrogatories, like questioning angels, float in its waves of sound."[29]

Summarizing what has been stated concerning music's significance, it was thought that music by itself could express feeling, though not definite states of feeling. However, the words of the lyric served to direct attention to more specific emotions and mood, giving focus to the feeling contained in the music. Music always went beyond the subject stated in the text. Owing to its imprecision, it stimulated the imagination and suggested far more than the verbal message. Most importantly, music introduced the perceptive listener to the world of universal experience and mankind's shared truths.

To the skeptic who wondered whether music could express anything beyond the sound itself, a writer like Poe, Porter, or Emerson might reply that in the world of symbols, anything can represent anything. The question of whether music can in itself truly capture a feeling or idea is irrelevant. If an audience is agreed on what symbols mean—the accoutrements of sweet and simple melody, for example—then to all intents and purposes musical symbols not only can and do encompass feeling, but they can also go beyond feeling to the sphere of eternal values.

Some recent studies by psychologists and psychiatrists give support to this nineteenth-century viewpoint. Willard Gaylin, clinical professor of psychiatry at the Columbia University Medical School, for example, has written that music can give "a literal feeling" of being lifted out of one's seat, of being taken out of the world of survival and self-gratification into that of spiritual experience. The listener feels moved, transported, and brought into an exalted emotional state. It is, nevertheless, a private experience, not easily described: "Although the feeling is very specific in its quality, it is not so in its context. It is difficult to communicate about being moved across diverse experience." The feeling is not specifically linked to

---

[29]Emerson, *Journals,* V, 121.

an individual's particular emotions, like fear or guilt. These experiences, however, permit the listener "to abstract from them, to supply a general context in which the most elemental feelings—the 'vital signs,' such as fear, pride, and so on—are likely to occur for all."[30]

Hans and Shulamith Kreitler, in *Psychology of the Arts,* write that despite philosophical theorizing to the contrary, empirical studies repeatedly show that emotional, associational, imaginal, and ideational elements recur consistently in the responses of listeners to music. Furthermore, they add, the effects that seem most related to the enjoyment of music are those of emotion and mood, with general responses, such as restfulness, longing, reverence, and devotion, being more characteristic of listeners' reactions than definite emotions like anger, fear, and jealousy.[31] When one experiences anything from beyond one's self, including musical sound, there is no such thing as only "pure" sensation, states Zuckerkandl. "Sensations that are not in some way colored by feeling have no existence in reality."[32]

Gaylin, the Kreitlers, and Zuckerkandl make observations concerning music and its relation to feeling that parallel the prevalent views of antebellum American writers. What these writers of 140 years ago would have said, too, is that while the musically ill-educated Americans of their time might not form a correct estimate of a composer's musical expertness and ingenuity, they could understand a song in terms of what they felt. This comprehension of music was neither less discerning nor less solid than that of musically sophisticated listeners, who resorted to objective intellectualization. "With ordinary listeners," William Porter writes, in 1834, song "is more generally felt and understood than any other" form of artistry, and it does excite "the emotions of the mind" and awaken "the finer feelings."[33]

The lyrics of popular songs point up these conclusions. Melody "releases the springs of feeling" and recalls past happiness, according to the lyric of *Come Sing Again That Song.* "Sweet melody" stimu-

[30]Willard Gaylin, *Feelings* (New York: Harper & Row 1979) 198–200.
[31]Hans and Shulamith Kreitler, *Psychology of the Arts* (Durham, N.C.: Duke University Press 1972) 280–81.
[32]Zuckerkandl, *Man the Musician* 58.
[33]Porter, *Cyclopedia* s.v. "Ballad," "Expression."

lates the senses and brings "joy and gladness," asserts *The Bird of Beauty.* "Sweetest sounds to love are wed," states *Silver Moonlight Winds.*[34]

Henry Tuckerman, in 1852, said that music calls forth sentiments that appeal "to the very depths of our nature" and address "the memory with singular power. How often it breaks up at once the deep of the affections, and conjures back all that is beautiful and dear in the domain of the past."[35]

Another claim for music is its ability to journey into the unknowable. In *Lily Ray,* a young man longs for his dead beloved, and "When liquid melody falls on my ear/Then I impulsively deem that thou art near." In *Come This Way, My Father,* the mysterious voice of the unseen child, which guided the father to safety, "sounded like music," across the waters.[36]

As is obvious, it is mainly the music of serious song that has just received attention. Comic song is not lovesome, nor is it a door opening onto the long vistas of eternity. It does, nevertheless, complement the feelings elicited by serious song. The listener is made to feel more viscerally, more kinetically, those emotions that go with the joy of knowing yourself to be buoyantly and vigorously alive. It is melody that accompanies the striking of "de toe and heel," the beating "on de old jawbone," and the energetic strumming of the banjo. The performer aims, not to make people sad and weepy, but "to give . . . all a little bit of fun." Quoting a few verses from *Jim Brown* (New York: Hewitt 1835) helps indicate the ambiance of comic song:

> I larnt to beat de cymbals, and I larnt to beat de drum,
>   And all de fancy tunes dis nigger he could cum;
> I went to de Tremont, to see what was dare.
>   Wid dis ole nigger, dey nothing to compare.

[34]*Come Sing Again That Song,* by Stephen C. Massett (New York: Waters 1853); *Bird of Beauty,* w. Ella of Woodlawn, m. M.B. Scott (Boston: Ditson 1856); *Silver Moonlight Winds,* w. and m. John P. Ordway (Boston: Ordway 1858).

[35]Tuckerman, *Optimist,* 64.

[36]*Lily Ray,* w. and m. Stephen C. Foster (New York: Firth, Pond 1850); *Come This Way, My Father,* m. William Martin (Boston: Ditson 1855).

De way I larnt to play de carry ob de sword,
  I practis on de Banjo sugar in de goard;
De niggers all dance when Jim begin to play,
  Dey dance from de mornin, to de closin ob de day.
I plays upon de fiddle, and I plays de claronet,
  I plays upon de cymbals till I make de nigger swet.

. . . .

Now I've sung you all I could, and told you all de cause,
  And if you think de song is good I want your applause;
And now I've sung you all I could, pray don't cry encore,
  Bekase you kill yourself a laffing if I sing any more.

This is hardly the sedate environment of serious song—"dey
nothing to compare." Its sound is the rough beat of cymbals, drums,
and banjos; the skirl of fiddles; and a rhythm so infectious it causes
people to wish to dance and sweat. The only crying allowed is the
"cry encore." While listening to comic song, the audience are
warned, they may kill themselves "a laffing."

In another comic song, *Commence Ye Darkies All!*, by Corrister (New
York: Firth, Pond, 1849), the singers says: "I'm goin' to sing a song
dat am quite new." How is this song performed?

Touch light de banjo string,
  An' rattle de ole jaw bone;
Oh, merrily sound de tamborine,
  An' make dat fiddle hum!
An' make dat fiddle hum, ole dad!
  De way dem bones will shake,
Am a caution to all living niggs,
  An' a death to rattle snakes!
Den commence, ye darkies all,
  As loud as you can bawl!

Delicacy and sensitivity have gone out the window. What remains is extroverted, shouting music. The melody and its accompaniment express the quintessence of common man's rude yet eager
enjoyment of life. The music that is produced sounds as irrepressible
as the grotesque character who sings and dances it.

176

EXCELLENCE IN POPULAR MUSIC

What are the musical qualities that denominated a mid-nineteenth-century popular song as particularly meritorious? Here, the postulates that underlie the critical evaluation of art music, intended for the musically sophisticated segment of society, can hardly form the basis for judgment. Such music serves vastly different aesthetic, social, and psychological functions. Moreover, to apply the premises subscribed to by a musical elite would damn popular music out of hand—a regrettable practice that has prevailed for over a century and a half now.

A more informative pursuit would be to inquire about the several characteristics possessed in common by compositions that achieved the highest popularity. Assuredly, the marked esteem of the American populace is of the essence here, in determining what popular songs are most worthy of examination. To say that there exist songs that are of great merit but that had scarcely any following is not only to betray an intellect still dominated by inapplicable criteria, at least for the purposes of this study, but also to keep shut the door to the popular mind.

Our initial conclusion, without doubt, is that to be worthy of widespread attention, the music must be tuneful and pared to its essentials. A song having knotty sounds with no easily discernible melody fails the test of first-rateness. Thus, John Moore's statement that "the reason of the popularity of Mr. Foster's songs lies in their easy, flowing melody, the adherence to plain chords in the accompaniments, and the avoidance of intricacy in the harmony, or embarrassing accidentals in the melody. He was 'the finder of many melodies,' and his compositions, if not his name, are familiar everywhere. He was, in his time, the ballad-writer of America."[37]

The successful (and, therefore, laudable) song can command and retain attention because its melody is given a clear, symmetrical shape. The several parts belong together, without artificial joining or superfluous notes. Once heard, the tune is impossible to forget. John Sullivan Dwight, a Boston elitist enamoured of German art music,

---

[37] *Encyclopaedia*, "Appendix" (added to 1880 ed.) s.v. "Foster, Stephen C."

abhorred Foster's songs. Yet in his *Dwight's Journal of Music* (19 November 1853), he was forced to admit that tunes like that of *Old Folks at Home* "persecute and haunt the morbidly sensitive nerves of deeply musical persons, so that they too hum and whistle them involuntarily, hating them even while they hum them."

It is instructive to take a close look at Foster's melody to *Old Folks at Home*, since it unquestionably is one of the most popular melodies in America's cultural history. The phrase patterns (see Example 5-3) are carefully balanced:

A   A¹   (strain 1)
A   A¹   (strain 2)
B   A¹   (strain 3)

The only significant difference between phrases A and A¹ is that the former closes on the tone e', and the latter on the tones e'-d'. Phrase B adds variety, achieves a cautious climax, and freshens up the final return of Phrase A¹. Note how the melody either moves from the tone f-sharp' to the tone d' (indicated by an *X*), or leaps up to d'' and skips down to b' (indicated by a *Y*). The bare beauty of the music appears enhanced by the repetition, and the repetition commits the notes quickly to memory.

Musical superiority does not depend on a genuinely different sound. Originality in itself is unimportant. So long as a tune sounds vital and makes the listener feel something, however inarticulate he may be about the feeling, it has worth. Scores of popular songs have melodies resembling that of *Old Folks at Home*.[38] It rarely occurred to anybody to worry about the originality of any of them. One who did, the popular-song composer George F. Root, decided that originality was scarcely to be found anywhere in music. Anyway, it did not matter one way of the other, either to the composer of popular songs or to the public.[39]

More important than originality was that the song's vocal line be expertly composed. Awkwardness here went unforgiven. Any melody with an inelegant phrase, an incongruous chromaticism, a hard

[38]See Tawa, *Sweet Songs* 162.
[39]See the New York *Musical Review* (10 January 1857) 6.

Example 5–3. Melody of Stephen C. Foster's *Old Folks at Home*
(New York: Firth, Pond 1851)

jump, or an arduous tessitura did not easily find its way into the
public's affection. The only exceptions were in the melodies of comic
song, where certain inelegances were acceptable. For example,
Hamm describes the tune of *Jim Crow* as "quite clumsy, sounding
almost like a patchwork of several different melodies." The melody
itself, he concludes, did not catch on with the public.[40]

Any melody that forewent a preponderantly syllabic setting of the
text (one note to a syllable) or that obscured the sense of the words
had to struggle for acceptance. Any melody that emphasized the
virtuosity of the singer at the expense of the sentiment was found
ridiculous.

[40]Hamm, *Yesterdays* 122–23.

179

In 1828, Francis Courtney Wemyss, a British actor touring America, attended a New York concert of Madame Fearon, "the best English singer who ever visited the United States." To his dismay, the American audience disliked the florid songs she performed, deciding they lacked feeling. In anger, Wemyss reacted with the following sarcasm: "The young ladies who are taught to beat a tune upon the piano for the amusement of papa and mama could not appreciate the difficulty of her 'cadenza,' or the study required to form a perfect singer: nay, they had the bad taste to laugh at some of the most beautiful and difficult passages, which she executed with such precision and brilliancy. The taste for opera . . . had no existence. . . . The prima donna of the Neapolitan theatre was doomed to return home, mortified with her reception, with no very exalted opinion of the American taste for music."[41] Wemyss failed to understand that, judged by the premises of popular music, Madame Fearon's art was decidedly wanting in excellence.

A favorite melody invariably is found to be adapted to the peculiarities, needs, and expectations of its mass audience. Whether the successful composers went about their task consciously or unconsciously, they wrote music that was precisely adjusted to satisfy mid-nineteenth-century expectations, so that listeners readily understood and took satisfaction from its sound. This suitability constitutes a major part of a popular song's excellence. Already mentioned were the virtues of brevity, simplicity, freshness, facility, symmetrical structure, and smooth fit of sound to text. These matters seen to, then "music" becomes "a powerful assistant to sentimental expression (I speak of vocal music) which, by the power of its charms, enforces our attention to some particular subject, adapted to some natural passion of mankind. Under such considerations, we are strongly impressed with the ideas of love, fear, pity, or some other natural affection. But to produce the effects of nature, the means must not be unnatural."[42]

By evoking strong feeling, the popular song reached the height of acceptability. The ultimate test of a song's excellence was the num-

---

[41] Francis Courtney Wemyss, *Theatrical Biography* (Glasgow 1848) 142.
[42] Boston *Euterpeiad* (27 April 1822) 19.

ber of people it pleased, whether at a given moment in time or over the years. In this regard, Foster's melodies have proven to be without peer. They were dominant in the American musical culture of the 1850s, met with approval among the peoples of many foreign countries within the next two decades, and continue to have a following 140 years after their first publication.

In *Dwight's Journal of Music,* 21 March 1857, an article by an unidentified writer begins: "Who wrote the Negro songs? The principal writer is Stephen C. Foster." The writer goes on to praise Foster's music and says it is now sung "wherever men sing. In the cotton fields of the South, among the mines of California and Australia, in the sea-coast cities of China, in Paris, in the London prison, everywhere in fact, his melodies are heard. 'Uncle Ned' was the first. This was published in 1845, and reached a sale unknown till then in the music publishing business. Of 'The Old Folks at Home', 100,000 copies have been sold in this country, and as many more in England. 'My Old Kentucky Home' and 'Old Dog Tray,' each had a sale of about 70,000. All his other songs have had a great run. All his compositions are simple, but they are natural, and find their way to the popular heart."

Individual melodies written by other American composers have also met this criterion of excellence, melodies like those of *Dixie's Land, Aura Lee,* and *Flow Gently, Sweet Afton,* to name three.

This study has examined the ways that popular songs had meaning in their own time. It closes by briefly suggesting that they can continue to have meaning in the late twentieth century, especially after "objective" art music has had such a long run. I would like to believe that more than nostalgia causes some of them still to be heard in song recitals and on recordings. On occasion, an early song rearranged to suit later tastes has again become a popular "hit." A few of these songs, mainly minstrel-types deriving their melody from folk sources, have found their way into compositions by twentieth-century composers. Aaron Copland, for example, in *Old American Songs,* gives us fresh settings of two minstrel songs—*De Boatman's Dance* and *Ching A Ring Chaw*—and one sentimental ballad—*Long Time Ago.* Charles Ives, in his Second Symphony, employs *Camptown Races* and *Long Time Ago;* in his Second String Quartet, *Dixie.* William Austin, in *"Susanna," "Jeanie,"* and *"The Old Folks at Home,"* discusses the several references to the songs of Stephen Foster in Ives's music especially, but also in Copland's and Thea Musgrave's music. Mention is also made of occurrences in music by Gershwin, Poulenc, and Lucas Foss.[43]

It is hoped that my discussion of these songs and their significance for the nineteenth-century public that sponsored them will encourage more twentieth-century Americans to hear and enjoy them.

---

[43]Austin, *"Susanna"* 317–37.

Bibliography

Ahlstrom, Sydney E. *A Religious History of the American People.* (New Haven, Conn.: Yale University Press 1972)

Alcott, William A. *The Young Wife.* (Boston: Light 1837)

Alexander, Samuel. *Beauty and Other Forms of Value.* (New York: Crowell 1968)

Alison, Archibald. *Essays On the Nature and Principles of Taste* (Edinburgh, 1811), reprint. (Boston: Cummings & Hilbard 1812)

The American National Song Book. (Boston: Mussey 1842)

Austin, William W. *"Susanna," "Jeanie," and "The Old Folks at Home."* (New York: Macmillan 1975)

Barnum, Phineas T. *Struggles and Triumphs.* (Buffalo: Courier 1875)

Bartlett, Irving H. *Daniel Webster.* (New York: Norton 1978)

Becker, Ernest. *The Denial of Death.* (New York: Free Press 1973)

———. *Escape From Evil.* (New York: Free Press 1975)

Benda, Clemens E. *The Image of Love.* (New York: Free Press 1961)

Bernard, Kenneth A. *Lincoln and the Music of the Civil War.* (Caldwell, Idaho: Caxton 1966)

Berthoff, Rowland. *An Unsettled People: Social Order and Disorder in American History.* (New York: Harper & Row 1971)

Blair, Walter. *Horse Sense in American Humor.* (New York: Russell & Russell 1962)

Boas, George, ed. *Romanticism in America.* (New York: Russell & Russell 1961)

Boas, Ralph P. *The Social Background of American Literature.* (Boston: Little, Brown 1940)

183

Bode, Carl, ed. *American Life in The 1840s.* (Garden City, N.Y.: Doubleday 1967)

Bode, Carl. *The Anatomy of American Popular Culture, 1840–1861.* (Berkeley: University of California Press 1959)

_____. *Antebellum Culture.* (Carbondale: Southern Illinois Press 1970)

Boorstin, Daniel J. *The Americans: The National Experience.* (New York: Random House 1965)

Branch, E. Douglas. *The Sentimental Years, 1836–1860* (1962), reprint. (New York: Hill & Wang 1965)

Brink, Carol. *Harps in the Wind: The Story of the Singing Hutchinsons.* (New York: Macmillan 1947)

Brinton, Crane. *A History of Western Morals.* (New York: Harcourt, Brace, & World 1959)

Brooks, Van Wyck. *The Flowering of New England.* (New York: Dutton 1952)

Brooks, Van Wyck. *The Times of Melville and Whitman.* (New York: Dutton 1947)

Brown, Calvin S. *Music and Literature.* (Athens: University of Georgia Press 1948)

Brown, Ina Corinne. *Understanding Other Cultures.* (Englewood Cliffs, N.J.: Prentice-Hall 1963)

Brown, Norman O. *Life Against Death.* (Middletown, Conn.: Wesleyan University Press 1959)

Browne, Junius Henri. *The Great Metropolis: A Mirror of New York.* (Hartford: American 1869)

Bruzelius, Nils. "Feeling Lonely," reprint of a report from the 1978 meeting of the American Psychological Association. Boston *Sunday Globe* (3 September 1978) 1, 13

Bryant, William Cullen. *Prose Writings,* 2 vols., ed. Parke Godwin (1884), reprint. (New York: Russell & Russell 1964)

Buckley, Jerome Hamilton. *The Victorian Temper.* (New York: Vintage 1951)

Cassier, Ernst. *An Essay on Man.* (New Haven, Conn.: Yale University Press 1962)

Cawelti, John G. "Myth, Symbol, and Formula," *Journal of Popular Culture* VIII (Summer 1974) 1–9

Charvat, William. *The Origins of American Critical Thought, 1810–1835.* (New York: Russell & Russell 1968)

Chase, Gilbert. *America's Music,* rev. ed. (New York: McGraw-Hill 1966)

Chase, Richard. *The American Novel and Its Traditions.* (Garden City, N.Y.: Doubleday 1957)

———. *Quest for Myth.* (Baton Rouge: Louisiana State University Press 1949)

Chevalier, Michel. *Society, Manners, and Politics in the United States,* ed. John William Ward. (Ithaca, N.Y.: Cornell University Press 1969)

Choron, Jacques. *Modern Man and Mortality.* (New York: Macmillan 1964)

Chudacoff, Howard P. *The Evolution of Urban Society.* (Englewood Cliffs, N.J.: Prentice-Hall 1975)

Claghorn, Charles Eugene. *The Mocking Bird: The Life and Diary of Its Author, Septimus Winner.* (Philadelphia: Magee 1937)

Conrad, Jack. *The Many Worlds of Man.* (New York: Crowell 1964)

Cooke, Deryck. *The Language of Music.* (London: Oxford University Press 1959)

Cooper, James Fenimore. *The American Democrat* (1838), reprint. (New York: Funk & Wagnalls 1969)

———. *Notions of the Americans,* 2 vols. (1828), reprint (New York: Ungar (1963)

Copeland, Robert Marshall. *The Life and Works of Isaac Baker Woodbury, 1819–1858.* (Ph.D. dissertation, University of Cincinnati 1974)

Corrigan, Robert W., ed. *Comedy, Meaning, and Form.* (San Francisco: Chandler 1965)

Crawford, Richard. *American Studies and American Musicology,* I.S.A.M. Monograph: No. 4. (Brooklyn: Institute for Studies in American Music, Brooklyn College 1975)

Critchley, MacDonald; Henson, R.A., eds. *Music and the Brain* (London: Heinemann 1977)

Culture for the Millions?, ed. Norman Jacobs. (Princeton, N.J.: D. Van Nostrand 1961)

Cunliffe, Marcus. *The Literature of the United States,* rev. ed. (Baltimore: Penguin 1964)

Curtis, George W. *The Potiphar Papers.* (New York: Putnam 1853)

Curtis, George W. *Prue and I.* (New York: Harper & Brothers 1856)

D'Arcy, M. C. *The Mind and Heart of Love.* (New York: Holt 1947)

Davidge, William. *Footlight Flashes.* (New York: American News 1866)

Davis, Fred. "Nostalgia, Identity, and the Current Nostalgia Wave," *Journal of Popular Culture* XI (Fall 1977) 414–24

Dennison, Sam. *Scandalize My Name: Black Imagery in American Popular Music.* (New York: Garland 1982)

Dickinson, Emily. *Letters,* 2 vols., ed. Thomas H. Johnson. (Cambridge, Mass.: Belknap Press 1965)

DiMaggio, Paul. "Market Structure, The Creative Process, and Popular Culture," *Journal of Popular Culture* XI (Fall 1977) 436–52.

Ditzion, Sidney Herbert. *Marriage, Morals, and Sex in America.* (New York: Bookman Associates 1953)

Dorson, Richard M. *American Folklore.* (Chicago: University of Chicago Press 1959)

Douglas, Ann. *The Feminization of American Culture.* (New York: Knopf 1977)

Dulles, Foster Rhea. *A History of Recreation,* 2nd ed. (New York: Appleton-Century-Crofts 1965)

Duncan, Hugh Dalziel. *Symbols in Society.* (New York: Oxford University Press 1968)

Dunlap, George Arthur. *The City in the American Novel, 1789–1900.* (Philadelphia: University of Pennsylvania Press 1934)

Dunn, Waldo H. *The Life of Donald G. Mitchell.* (New York: Scribner's Sons 1922)

Ellis, Havelock. *More Essays of Love and Virtue.* (Garden City, N.Y.: Doubleday, Doran 1931)

Emerson, Ralph Waldo. *Essays and Poems.* (New York: Harcourt, Brace 1921)

Emerson, Ralph Waldo. *The Journals and Miscellaneous Notebooks,* 17 vols. (Cambridge: Belknap Press 1960–1982), Vol. V, ed. Merton M. Sealts, Jr. (1965), Vol. VII, ed. A.W. Plumstead and Harrison Hayford (1969), Vol. VIII, ed. William H. Gilman and J.E. Parsons (1970), Vol. IX, ed. Ralph H. Onth and Alfred R. Ferguson (1971), Vol. X, ed. Merton H. Sealts, Jr. (1973), Vol. XI, ed. A.W. Plumstead and William H. Gilman (1975)

Ewen, David. *All the Years of American Popular Music.* (Englewood Cliffs, N.J.: Prentice-Hall 1977)

_____. *American Popular Songs from The Revolutionary War to The Present.* (New York: Random House 1966)

_____. *History of Popular Song.* (New York: Barnes & Noble 1961)

Feibleman, James. *In Praise of Comedy* (1939), reissued. (New York: Russell & Russell 1962)

Feidelson, Charles. *Symbolism and American Literature.* (Chicago: University of Chicago Press 1953)

Faner, Robert D. *Walt Whitman and Opera.* (Carbondale: Southern Illinois University Press 1972)

Ferguson, Donald N. *Music As Metaphor* (1960), reprint. (Westport, Conn.: Greenwood 1973)

Fiedler, Leslie A. *Love and Death in the American Novel,* rev. ed. (New York: Stein & Day 1966)

Fine, Gary Alan. "Popular Culture and Social Interaction," *Journal of Popular Culture* XI (Fall 1977) 453–66

Firth, Raymond. *Symbols, Public and Private.* (Ithaca, N.Y.: Cornell University Press 1973)

Fishwick, Marshall. *The Hero, American Style.* (New York: McKay 1969)

Foerster, Norman. *Nature in American Literature.* (New York: Russell & Russell 1958)

Folsom, Joseph Kirk. *The Family and Democratic Society.* (New York: Wiley & Son 1943)

Fromm, Erich. *The Art of Loving.* (New York: Harper & Bros. 1956)

Gabriel, Ralph H. *American Values.* (Westport, Conn.: Greenwood, 1974)

Gaylin, Willard. *Feelings.* (New York: Harper & Row 1979)

Goldschmidt, Walter. *Man's Way.* (New York: Holt, Rinehart & Winston 1959)

Goodman, Nelson. *Languages of Art: An Approach to a Theory of Symbols.* (Indianapolis: Bobbs-Merrill 1968)

Gottschalk, Louis Moreau. *Notes of a Pianist* (1881), ed. Jeanne Behrend. (New York: Knopf 1964)

Greven, Philip. *The Protestant Temperament.* (New York: Knopf 1977)

Griswald, Rufus Willmot. *The Poets and Poetry of America.* (Philadelphia: Carey & Hart 1842)

187

Grund, Francis J. *Aristocracy in America* (1839), reprint. (New York: Harper & Row 1959)

Hamm, Charles. *Yesterdays.* (New York: Norton 1979)

Handlin, Oscar; Handlin, Mary F. *Facing Life.* (Boston: Little, Brown, 1971)

Hareven, Tamara, ed. *Anonymous Americans.* (Englewood Cliffs, N.J.: Prentice-Hall 1971)

Hastings, Thomas. *Dissertation on Musical Taste* (New York: Mason Brothers 1853)

Hawthorne, Nathaniel. *The Complete Works,* 24 vols., ed. G.P. Lathrop (Boston: Houghton Mifflin 1884)

Heilman, Robert Bechtold. *Tragedy and Melodrama.* (Seattle: University of Washington Press 1968)

Hewitt, John H. *Shadows On the Wall.* (Baltimore: Turnbull Bros. 1877)

Hirsch, David H. *Reality and Idea in the Early American Novel.* (The Hague: Mouton 1971)

Hitchcock, H. Wiley. *Music in the United States: A Historical Introduction.* (Englewood Cliffs, N.J.: Prentice-Hall 1969)

Hodge, Francis. *Yankee Theatre: The Image of America on the Stage, 1825–1850.* (Austin: University of Texas Press 1964)

Hoffman, Daniel. *Form and Fable in America Fiction.* (New York: Oxford University Press 1965)

Holmes, Oliver Wendell. *The Autocrat of the Breakfast-Table* (1858), reprinted as Vol. I of *Works,* 14 vols. (Boston: Houghton Mifflin 1891–1892)

Holmes, Oliver Wendell. *The Professor at the Breakfast-Table* (1859), reprinted as Vol. II of *Works,* 14 vols. (Boston: Houghton Mifflin 1891–1892)

Hospers, John. *Meaning and Truth in the Arts.* (Hamden, Conn.: Archon Books 1964)

Howard, John Tasker. *Our American Music,* 4th ed. (New York: Crowell 1965)

––––––. *Stephen Foster: America's Troubadour.* (New York: Crowell 1953)

Hunt, Morton M. *The Natural History of Love.* (New York: Knopf 1959)

Hutchinson, John Wallace. *Story of the Hutchinsons,* 2 vols. (Boston: Lee & Shepard 1896)

Ireland, Joseph N. *Records of the New York Stage, from 1750 to 1860,* 2 vols. (New York: Morrell 1866–1867)

Irving, Washington. *The Sketch Book,* new ed., 2 vols. (London: Murray 1821)

Jackson, George Stuyvesant. *Early Songs of Uncle Sam.* (Boston: Bruce Humphries 1933)

Jones, Howard Mumford. *The Theory of American Literature.* (Ithaca, N.Y.: Cornell University Press 1965)

Jung, Carl G. *Analytical Psychology.* (New York: Random House 1968)

Jung, Carl G.; Henderson, Joseph L.; von Franz, M.L.; Jaffé, Aniela; Jacobi, Jolande. *Man and His Symbols.* (New York: Dell 1968)

Kallen, Horace M. *Culture and Democracy in the United States.* (New York: Boni & Liveright 1924)

Kellett, E.E. *Fashion in Literature.* (London: Routledge & Sons 1931)

Klapp, Orrin E. *Heroes, Villains, and Fools.* (Englewood Cliffs, N.J.: Prentice-Hall 1962)

Koestler, Arthur. *The Act of Creation.* (New York: Macmillan 1964)

Kouwenhoven, John A. *The Arts in Modern American Civilization.* (New York: Norton 1967)

Kreitler, Hans; Kreitler, Shulamith. *Psychology of the Arts.* (Durham, N.C.: Duke University Press 1972)

Lacour-Gayet, Robert. *Everyday Life in the United States Before the Civil War, 1830–1860,* trans. Mary Ilford. (New York: Ungar 1969)

Langer, Susanne K. *Feeling and Form.* (New York: Scribner's Sons 1953)

————. *Philosophy in a New Key.* (New York: Penguin 1948)

————, ed. *Reflections on Art* (Baltimore: Johns Hopkins University Press 1958)

Lee, Harold Newton. *Perception and Aesthetic Values.* (New York: Prentice-Hall 1938)

Lenhart, Charmenz S. *Musical Influence on American Poetry.* (Athens: University of Georgia Press 1956)

Levison, William. *Black Diamonds* (1857), reprint (Upper Saddle River, N.J.: Literature House 1969)

Lewis, R.W.B. *The American Adam: Innocence, Tragedy and Tradition in the Nineteenth Century.* (Chicago: University of Chicago Press 1955)

Lippmann, Walter. *Public Opinion*. (New York: Harcourt, Brace 1922)

[Long, Zadoc]. *From the Journal of Zadoc Long, 1800–1873*, ed. Peirce Long. (Caldwell, Idaho: Claxton 1943)

Longfellow, Henry Wadsworth. *Letters*, 2 vols. (Cambridge: Belknap Press 1966)

Lowell, James Russell. *The Bigelow Papers* (1848), as Vol. IX of The Writings of James Russell Lowell (Boston: Houghton Mifflin 1894)

————. *Fireside Travels* (1864), as Vol. I of The Complete Writings of James Russell Lowell (New York: AMS 1966)

————. *Letters, Vol. I*, ed. Charles Eliot Norton, as Vol. XIV of *The Complete Writings of James Russell Lowell*. (New York: AMS, 1966)

Lundin, Robert W. *An Objective Psychology of Music*. (New York: Ronald 1953)

Mannin, Ethel. *Loneliness*. (London: Hutchinson 1966)

Maretzek, Max. *Crotchets and Quavers*, (1855), reprinted as Part I of *Revelations of an Opera Manager in Nineteenth-Century America*. (New York: Dover 1968)

Martineau, Harriet. *Society in America*, 3 vols. (London: Saunders & Otley 1837)

Martinson, Floyd. *Marriage and the American Ideal*. (New York: Dodd, Mead 1960)

Marx, Leo. *The Machine in the Garden*. (New York: Oxford University Press 1964)

Matthiessen, F.O. *American Renaissance*. (New York: Oxford University Press 1941)

May, Rollo. *Love and Will*. (New York: Norton 1969)

————. *The Meaning of Anxiety*. (New York: Norton 1950)

McIntosh, Maria J. *Woman in America*. (New York: Appleton 1850)

Mellers, Wilfried. *Music in a New Found Land*. (New York: Knopf 1965)

Meyer, Leonard B. *Emotion and Meaning in Music*. (Chicago: University of Chicago Press 1956)

Milne, Gordon. *George William Curtis and the Genteel Tradition*. Bloomington: Indiana University Press 1956.

[Mitchell, Donald G.]. *Dream Life,* by Ik Marvel. (New York: Scribner 1854)

———. *The Lorgnette,* 2 vols. 2nd ed., (New York: Stringer & Townsend 1850) I

———. *The Lorgnette,* 10th ed., 2 vols. (New York: Scribner 1853) II

Montagu, Ashley, ed. *The Meaning of Love.* (New York: Julian 1953)

Moody, Richard. *America Takes the Stage: Romanticism in American Drama and Theatre, 1750–1900.* (Bloomington: Indiana University Press 1955)

Moore, John W. *Complete Encyclopaedia of Music.* (Boston: Ditson 1854), reprinted in 1880 with an added Appendix

Morison, Samuel Eliot. *The Oxford History of the American People.* (New York: Oxford University Press 1965)

Morneweck, Evelyn Foster. *Chronicles of Stephen Foster's Family,* 2 vols. (Pittsburgh: University of Pittsburgh Press, for the Foster Hall Collection 1944)

Morris, George P. *Poems,* with a Memoir of the Author by H.B. Wallace. (New York: Scribner 1860)

Mumford, Lewis. *The Conduct of Life.* (New York: Harcourt Brace Jovanovich 1970)

Myers, Henry Alonzo. *Are Men Equal?* (Ithaca, N.Y.: Cornell University Press 1955)

———. *Tragedy: A View of Life.* (Ithaca, N.Y.: Cornell University Press 1956)

Nathan, Hans. *Dan Emmett and the Rise of Early Negro Minstrelsy.* (Norman: University of Oklahoma Press 1962)

Nevin, Robert P. "Stephen C. Foster and Negro Minstrelsy," *The Atlantic Monthly* XX (November 1867) 608–616.

Nye, Russell B., ed., *New Dimensions in Popular Culture.* (Bowling Green, Ohio: Bowling Green University Popular Press 1972)

Nye, Russell B. *Society and Culture in America, 1830–1860.* (New York: Harper & Row 1974)

———. *The Unembarrassed Muse.* (New York: Dial 1970)

Oswalt, Wendell H. *Understanding Our Culture.* (New York: Holt, Rinehart & Winston 1970)

Parkes, Henry Bamford. *The American Experience.* (New York: Vintage 1959)

[Parton, Mrs. Sara Payson]. *Folly As It Flies,* by Fanny Fern. (New York: Carleton 1868)

Pattee, Fred Lewis. *The Feminine Fifties.* (Port Washington, N.Y.: Kennikat Press 1966)

Petter, Henri. *The Early American Novel.* (Columbus: Ohio State University Press 1971

Pincus, Lily. *Death and the Family.* (New York: Pantheon 1974)

Poe, Edgar Allan. *The Complete Works,* 17 vols. ed. James A. Harrison. (New York: AMS 1965) Vols. VIII, IX, X

_____. *Essays—Fanciful, Humorous and Serious.* (New York: MacLellan 1908)

_____. *Letters,* ed. J.W. Ostrom. (Cambridge, Mass.: Harvard University Press 1948)

_____. *Works,* 4 vols. (New York: Redfield 1856–1857) Vols. III, IV

Porter, William S. *The Musical Cyclopedia.* (Boston: Loring 1834)

Potts, L.J. *Comedy.* (London: Hutchinson University Library, 1949)

Reed, John Q. *Benjamin Penhallow Shillaber.* (New York: Twayne 1972)

Regin, Deric. *Culture and the Crowd.* (Philadelphia: Chilton 1968)

Rich, Arthur Lowndes. *Lowell Mason.* (Chapel Hill: University of North Carolina Press, 1946)

Root, George F. *The Story of a Musical Life.* (Cincinnati: Church 1891)

Roth, Martin. *Comedy and America.* (Port Washington, N.Y.: Kennikat 1976)

Rougemont, Denis de. *Love in the Western World,* rev. ed., trans. Montgomery Belgion. (New York: Harper & Row 1956)

Rourke, Constance. *American Humor.* (Garden City, N.Y.: Doubleday 1953)

_____. *The Roots of American Culture and Other Essays.* (New York: Harcourt, Brace 1942)

Russell, Henry. *Cheer! Boys, Cheer!* (London: Macqueen, 1895)

_____ . *The Sailor's Song Book.* (Boston: Kidder & Wright 1842)

Sanger, William W. *The History of Prostitution.* (New York: Harper 1858)

Schettler, Clarence. *Public Opinion in American Society.* (New York: Harper & Bros., 1960)

Schlesinger, Jr., Arthur M. *The Age of Jackson.* (Boston: Little, Brown 1945)

Schneiders, Alexander A. *The Anarchy of Feeling.* (New York: Sheed & Ward 1963)

Schroeder, Fred E.H. "The Discovery of Popular Culture Before Printing," *Journal of Popular Culture* XI (Winter 1977) 629–38

———. *Outlaw Aesthetics.* (Bowling Green, Ohio: Bowling Green University Popular Press 1977)

Scott, Wilbur S. *Five Approaches of Literary Criticism.* (New York: Macmillan 1962)

Sewall, Richard B. *The Vision of Tragedy.* (New Haven, Conn.: Yale University Press 1959)

Sharp, Frank Chapman. *The Aesthetic Element in Morality.* (New York: Macmillan 1893)

Shillaber, Benjamin P. *Life and Sayings of Mrs. Partington* (1854), reprint. (Upper Saddle River, N.J.: Literature House 1969)

Sigourney, Mrs. L.H. *Letters to My Pupils.* (New York: Carter & Bros. 1851)

The Singer's Companion. (New York: Stringer & Townsend 1854)

Smith, Henry Nash. *Virgin Land: The American West As Symbol and Myth.* (Cambridge, Mass.: Harvard University Press 1950)

Smith, Page. *Daughters of the Promised Land.* (Boston: Little, Brown 1970)

Spaeth, Sigmund. *A History of Popular Music in America.* (New York: Random House 1948)

Stannard, David E., ed. *Death in America.* (Philadelphia: University of Pennsylvania Press 1975)

Stephens, H. Marion. *Home Scenes and Home Sounds.* (Boston: Fetridge 1854)

Stewart, Randall. *American Literature and Christian Doctrine.* (Baton Rouge: Louisiana State University Press 1958)

Tandy, Jennette. *Crackerbox Philosophers in American Humor and Satire* (1925), reprint. (Port Washington, N.Y.: Kennikat, 1964)

Tawa, Nicholas E. *Sweet Songs for Gentle Americans: The Parlor Song in America, 1790–1860.* (Bowling Green, Ohio: Bowling Green University Popular Press 1980)

Thompson, William T. *Major Jones's Scenes in Georgia* (1844), reprint. (Upper Saddle River, N.J.: Literature House 1969)

Tocqueville, Alexis de. *Democracy in America,* 2 vols., the Henry Reeve Text, rev. Francis Brow, ed. Phillips Bradley. (New York: Knopf 1945)

Toll, Robert C. *Blacking Up: The Minstrel Show in Nineteenth-Century America.* (New York: Oxford University Press, 1974)

Tomisch, John. *A Genteel Endeavor: American Culture and Politics in the Gilded Age.* (Stanford, Calif.: Stanford University Press, 1971)

Tuckerman, Henry T. *America and Her Commentators* (1864), reprint. (New York: Antiquarian Press 1961)

_____. *The Optimist.* (New York: Putnam 1852)

Upton, William Treat. *Art-Song in America.* (Boston: Ditson 1930)

Walters, Ronald G. *Sexual Advice to Victorian America.* (Englewood, Cliffs, N.J.: Prentice-Hall, 1974)

Ware, Norman. *The Industrial Worker, 1840–1860* (1924), reprint. (New York: Quadrangle, 1974)

Warner, W. Lloyd. *The Living and the Dead: A Study of the Symbolic Life of Americans.* (New Haven, Conn.: Yale University Press 1959)

Wells, Henry W. *The American Way of Poetry.* (New York: Columbia University Press, 1943)

Welter, Rush. *Popular Education and Democratic Thought in America.* (New York: Columbia University Press 1962)

Wemyss, Francis Courtney. *Theatrical Biography.* (Glasgow 1848)

White, Morton; White, Lucia. *The Intellectual Versus the City.* (Cambridge: Harvard University Press 1962)

Williams, Jr., Robin M. *American Society,* 2nd rev. ed. (New York: Knopf 1960)

Wilson, Edward O. *On Human Nature.* (Cambridge, Mass.: Harvard University Press, 1978)

Wish, Harvey. Society and Thought in America, 2 vols., Vol. I, *Society and Thought in Early America.* (New York: Longmans, Green 1950)

Wishy, Bernard. *The Child and the Republic.* (Philadelphia: University of Pennsylvania Press 1968)

Wood, William B. *Personal Recollections of the Stage.* (Philadelphia 1855)

Woolson, Abba Goold. *Woman in American Society.* (Boston: Roberts Bros. 1873)

[Wright, Frances.] *Views of Society and Manners in America.* (London: Longman, Hurst, Rees, Arme & Brown 1821)

Wright, Louis B. *Culture on the Moving Frontier.* (Bloomington: Indiana University Press 1955)

Wunderlich, Charles Edward. *A History and Bibliography of Early American Musical Periodicals, 1782–1852.* (Ph.D. dissertation, University of Michigan 1962)

Yerbury, Grace D. *Song in America (from Early Times to About 1850).* (Metuchen, N.J.: Scarecrow 1971)

Zanden, James W. Vander. *Social Psychology.* (New York: Random House 1977)

Zuckerkandl, Victor. *Music and the Eternal World,* trans. Willard R. Trask. (Princeton, N.J.: Princeton University Press 1956)

———. *Man the Musician,* trans. Norbert Guterman. (Princeton, N.J.: Princeton University Press 1973)

Index